BLOOMSBURY ADVANCES IN TR

CU00938462

Quality in Professional Translation

Assessment and Improvement

JOANNA DRUGAN

BLOOMSBURY
LONDON · NEW DELHI · NEW YORK · SYDNEY

Bloomsbury Academic

An imprint of Bloomsbury Publishing Plc

50 Bedford Square	175 Fifth Avenue
London	New York
WC1B 3DP	NY 10010
UK	USA

www.bloomsbury.com

First published 2013

British Library Cataloguing-in-Publication Data
A catalogue record for this book is available from the British Library.

ISBN: HB: 978-1-4411-7664-6
PB: 978-1-4411-4954-1
ePub: 978-1-4411-9451-0
ePDF: 978-1-4411-6210-6

Library of Congress Cataloging-in-Publication Data
Drugan, Joanna.
Quality in Professional Translation : Assessment and Improvement / Joanna Drugan.
pages cm. – (Bloomsbury Advances in Translation)
Includes bibliographical references and index.
ISBN 978-1-4411-7664-6 (hardcover) – ISBN 978-1-4411-4954-1 (pbk.) –
ISBN (invalid) 978-1-4411-9451-0 (ebook (epub)) – ISBN (invalid) 978-1-4411-6210-6 (ebook
(pdf)) 1. Translating services. 2. Translating and interpreting. 3. Translating services–
Evaluation. 4. Translating and interpreting–Evaluation. I. Title.
P306.94.D78 2013
418'.02023–dc23
2012041378

Typeset by Newgen Imaging Systems Pvt Ltd, Chennai, India
Printed and bound in India

CONTENTS

SERIES EDITOR'S PREFACE

The aim of this new series is to provide an outlet for advanced research in the broad interdisciplinary field of translation studies. Consisting of monographs and edited themed collections of the latest works, it should be of particular interest to academics and postgraduate students researching in translation studies and related fields, and also to advanced students studying translation and interpreting modules.

Translation studies has enjoyed huge international growth over recent decades in tandem with the expansion in both the practice of translation globally and in related academic programmes. The understanding of the concept of translation itself has broadened to include not only interlingual but also various forms of intralingual translation. Specialized branches or sub-disciplines have developed for the study of interpretation, audiovisual translation and sign language, among others. Translation studies has also come to embrace a wide range of types of intercultural encounter and transfer, interfacing with disciplines as varied as applied linguistics, comparative literature, computational linguistics, creative writing, cultural studies, gender studies, philosophy, postcolonial studies, sociology, etc. Each provides a different and valid perspective on translation, and each has its place in this series.

This is an exciting time for translation studies, and the new Advances in Translation series promises to be an important new plank in the development of the discipline. As General Editor, I look forward to overseeing the publication of this important new work that will provide insights into all aspects of the field.

Jeremy Munday
General Editor
University of Leeds, UK

PREFACE

Translation quality has long been the focus of academic and industry attention but there are still no 'generally accepted objective criteria for evaluating the quality of translations' (Williams, 2009: 3). Yet every day, translation quality is evaluated. Clients expect quality guarantees. Agencies and organizations require that translators work to agreed standards. Professional translators have to demonstrate their work is superior to that of inexperienced bilinguals or machine translation (MT). Editors and revisers must justify judgements. By describing how translation quality is managed in the real world, this book offers a new, practical way of considering the issue.

For a sector whose entire raison d'être is communication, there is a surprising lack of awareness across the piece as to how other parts of the industry operate. This is explained in part by its nature and scale. Large, diverse and geographically dispersed, it encompasses the individual freelance working from a spare bedroom and multinational bodies employing thousands of specialists to work on translation and a host of related activities. Research for this book thus involved visiting the full range of language service providers (LSPs), from the smallest to the largest. Interviewees invariably wanted to know how peers, rivals, suppliers and clients were addressing the issues and challenges we discussed.

The first aim of this book is to provide a broad account of approaches to measuring and improving quality. Theorists' and professional assumptions about quality are identified and explained. Approaches to quality observed during research visits are outlined in order to identify patterns and group common methodologies together. Although the range of approaches is wide, I argue that they belong to two underlying ways of thinking: top-down and bottom-up. The second aim of the book is to examine these underlying assumptions critically and consider how fitting they are, given significant changes in the industry.

Who will benefit from this book? Translators will gain a broader understanding of what employers expect (and reward). Translation companies and organizations can learn how peers manage this sensitive area. Clients will discover what quality levels they can expect and common pitfalls they might avoid. Students and academics are given an insight into how the profession manages quality.

Writing about translation quality is dangerous: typos and other mistakes are inevitable, but doubly frustrating and embarrassing when discussing quality in others' work. Apologies in advance.

ACKNOWLEDGEMENTS

This overview of today's translation industry involved the participation of hundreds of translators, localizers, revisers, editors, managers, unit heads, tools developers, software engineers, terminologists, trainers, helpdesk and agency staff. Thanks to all, particularly Emma Wagner and Tim Martin of the European Commission, who arranged the first fruitful research placement. Translator communities and organizations provided concrete examples and informed feedback, including members of the ITI, CIoL, LinkedIn and Facebook groups and ProZ.com. The insider view supplied by Aslib, Common Sense Advisory, LISA, Localization World and TAUS helped in making sure the picture presented here was accurate and up-to-date. For their backing and patience, sincere thanks to Colleen Coalter, Gurdeep Mattu, Jeremy Munday and Laura Murray at Bloomsbury.

I am grateful to Leeds University alumni and students for stimulating discussion and feedback. Generous colleagues took on extra responsibilities to give me time to write, especially Terry Bradford, Svetlana Carsten, Debbie Elliot, Serge Sharoff and Daming Wu. Most of all, Bob Clark, Andy Rothwell and Mark Shuttleworth first encouraged my interest in the field and were superb role models with their boundless enthusiasm and inspired workarounds, all the more important in the dark days before Unicode when we carried our IBM Translation Manager files on floppy disks.

GLOSSARY OF ACRONYMS

ARTRAQ	Argumentation-Centred Translation Quality Approach
ATA	American Translators Association
CAT	Computer-Assisted Translation
CEN	European Committee for Standardization
CIoL	Chartered Institute of Linguists (United Kingdom)
CMS	Content Management System
CPD	Continuing Professional Development
CSA	Common Sense Advisory
DGT	European Commission Directorate-General for Translation
EBMT	Example-Based Machine Translation
FOSS	Free and Open Source Software
FTP	File Transfer Protocol
GIGO	Garbage In, Garbage Out
HMT	Hybrid Machine Translation
IATE	Inter-Active Terminology for Europe
ICR	In-Country Review
ISO	International Organization for Standardization
ITI	Institute of Translation and Interpreting (United Kingdom)
L10n	Localization
LISA	Localization Industry Standards Association
LSP	Language Service Provider
MLV	Multiple Language Vendor
MMOs, MMOGs	Massively Multiplayer Online Games
MOC	Massive Online Collaboration
MT	Machine Translation
NDA	Non-Disclosure Agreements
OS	Open Source
PM	Project Manager, Project Management
QA	Quality Assurance
QC	Quality Control
QE	Quality Evaluation
RBMT	Rule-Based Machine Translation

RFQ	Request For Quotation
ROI	Return On Investment
SaaS	Software as a Service
SEO	Search Engine Optimization
SICAL	Système canadien d'appréciation de la qualité linguistique; Canadian Language Quality Measurement System
SL	Source Language
SLV	Single Language Vendor
SMT	Statistical Machine Translation
ST	Source Text
TAPs	Think-Aloud Protocols
TAUS	Translation Automation User Society
TB	TermBase
TBX	TermBase eXchange format
TEP	Translate-Edit-Proofread
TL	Target Language
TM	Translation Memory
TMS	Terminology Management System
TMX	Translation Memory eXchange format
TQA	Translation Quality Assessment
TT	Target Text
VLTM	Wordfast's Very Large Translation Memory
WYSIWYG	What You See Is What You Get
XLIFF	XML Localization Interchange File Format

Introduction

Concern for quality has been evident as long as translation has taken place, but the industry's focus on quality has intensified recently. This introduction considers why this is so and why there is little material on the professional context, as distinct from academic theories. Research methods and chapter content are outlined.

The context in which translations are produced has changed in significant ways since the 1990s. First, demand for translations and the capacity of the tools which help produce them have soared since the advent of the Internet and globalization. These two developments are linked. Increasing translation demand could not be met without electronic tools which have been created or drastically refined recently. Nor would the tools have developed as they did without the surge in demand caused by the increasing production of information, and expectation that it be available in users' languages quickly and at low or no cost. These linked developments are changing the industry immeasurably and have helped build an unprecedented awareness of translation among new users who would previously have had little such awareness – even themselves joining in crowdsourcing[1] initiatives such as the translation of Facebook. All this has meant increasing attention to different levels of translation quality.

Another factor in the recent focus on quality is the general drive to establish industry-wide standards. Like many other industries, translation is increasingly bound by internationally agreed standards for service provision, through bodies like the CEN (European Committee for Standardization) and ISO (International Organization for Standardization). Establishing objective quality criteria has traditionally been seen as contentious, if not impossible, in translation studies; but in the real world, such criteria have indeed been defined and are increasingly applied to LSPs' work.

There is a sense across the industry that it is hard to know what is happening elsewhere. There are good reasons for this beyond the pace of change alone. LSPs can be wary of discussing problems and potential solutions because of concerns about confidentiality, competition or client objections. They are also focused on core activities of translating and winning new business so have neither time nor resources to research beyond their immediate rivals.

Large-scale providers like Lionbridge may know what direct competitors are concentrating on, and individual translators network with one another, but the big and the small often operate in mutual ignorance. Gouadec has argued that the sector's diversity makes it appropriate to refer to 'translation professions' (2007: xiv), concluding somewhat pessimistically that 'those who know the least about the profession are often the translators themselves' (ibid.).

There is a lack of information on real-world contexts in translation studies, and hence in translator training. Various factors account for this gap. Researchers have found gaining access to the industry challenging.[2] Funding bodies have been slow to support applied studies. Private sources (e.g. Google) support research of direct benefit to the funder, but not surveys of the entire industry. Most academics are not users of standard industry technical tools, and are hence ill-equipped to study their use. Time presents further challenges: industry pace of change is swift, so research findings quickly lose relevance. Researchers cannot easily spend sustained periods observing long-term, large-scale multilingual translation projects.

Such research has nonetheless long been recognized as necessary. Holmes' 1970s 'map' of the new discipline of translation studies[3] identified the need for *descriptive translation studies*, that is, the branch which 'constantly maintains the closest contact with the empirical phenomena under study' (2000: 184). Holmes identifies three sub-fields for descriptive empirical studies: 'product-oriented', 'function-oriented' and 'process-oriented' (ibid.: 184–5). His map has since been criticized and expanded,[4] but its call for studies of translation processes remains significant, particularly since those processes are now vastly more complex, and no longer locked inside the 'little black box' of the translator's 'mind' (ibid.: 185).

This book is based on such empirical research. It examines how quality is managed by those commissioning, producing and reviewing translations then describes and groups these approaches, rather than starting from abstract theoretical models. It aims to be the 'kind of study, with respect to translation or anything, that goes out into the world to see what is happening' (Pym, 2010b: 1). Pym holds that this approach is 'against an alternative kind of study that sees the world through the authoritative insights of others, mostly as recycled certitudes of theory'. This either/or position can perhaps be mitigated: starting from empirical study of the profession, insights from translation theorists can help interpret findings, then categorize and critique approaches observed 'in the world'. Williams and Chesterman further argue that 'while technology has become an integral part of the translation profession, there has been little, if any, research into many aspects of the technology itself' (2002: 14). They identify significant gaps in research including workflows, the translation process and 'mechanisms of quality control' (ibid.: 15), all of which are taken up here. They pinpoint appropriate research methods to explore these gaps which were indeed adopted, to whit 'a combination of observation, interviews and questionnaires' (ibid.: 23–4). How this was done is outlined next.

Conclusions presented here are based first on hundreds of interviews and questionnaires, completed during research visits to a representative range of LSPs, clients and support services since 2004. All those involved in managing or measuring translation quality in the industry were included: translators, of course, but also CEOs, clients, developers of national standards for translation quality, editors, end-users, heads of unit/section, project managers (PMs), revisers, sales and marketing staff, software engineers, terminologists, tools developers, trainers, webmasters and dedicated quality managers employed by some of the larger LSPs. The bedrock of the industry is the freelance translator. It was important to study a wide sample of these individuals, often neglected in research. Moving up the supply chain, the study includes over 100 agencies, companies and organizations offering one or multiple language pairs (SLVs – single language vendors and MLVs – multiple language vendors). In-house translators in the public and private sectors also contributed, from companies with only a few members of staff up to sizeable translation divisions and international organizations.

Research also entailed the use of work shadowing, that is 'accompany[ing] (a worker) in their daily activities for experience of or insight into a job' (*Concise OED*, 2009: 1320). This meant spending time observing individuals performing a variety of roles, often returning at intervals at different points in the workflow, particularly when they were concentrating on tasks related to translation quality. Think-aloud protocols (TAPs) were sometimes used to elucidate the reasons behind subjects' decisions (e.g. specific translation or revision choices),[5] along with prompting, questioning and retrospective interviews. Where possible, I attended training courses and inductions provided for new members of staff to learn how employers expected them to translate, use tools and meet quality expectations.

It was important to examine practice in translation sectors with an enhanced reputation for quality (financial, legal, medical, pharmaceutical, software and other technical domains). The research covered dozens of language pairs and locales, again targeting those with a reputation for quality (e.g. Nordic languages), and those facing special challenges for translation quality (e.g. Chinese)[6]. Emerging providers of 'community' translation are included, including *pro bono*, crowdsourced and voluntary translation. Professionals have expressed concern regarding quality levels among such providers, stressing their lack of training and experience.

One advantage of such a broad picture of the industry is that overall patterns emerge. Notably, approaches fall into two broad philosophical camps, described here as top-down and bottom-up. In summarizing the benefits and drawbacks of translation quality models for each, I aim to address an important issue identified by Chesterman and Wagner in their discussion of the gap between theory and translation practice. That is, theory usually only 'describe[s] and explain[s] the practice; but practitioners seem also to look to the theory for guidance' (2000: vii). It is hoped that practitioners will find a true reflection of their experience, placed in the context of the broader industry, and critical evaluation of different approaches.

The following outline of content is to help readers select the sections of most interest or use. Chapter One, *Today's translation profession*, summarizes industry changes since the 1990s, focusing on their relevance for quality. Chapter Two, *Translation quality: Importance and definitions*, contrasts academic approaches to quality with professional ones, arguing that more applied models are needed for industry purposes. It examines industry assumptions about quality and outlines why these issues are significant. Chapter Three, *Tools, workflow and quality*, evaluates the impact of electronic tools and new approaches to workflow on how translations are produced, and on quality. Real-world translation quality models are then described and critically assessed in two groups: traditional *Top-down models* (Chapter Four) and established and emerging *Bottom-up models* (Chapter Five). The conclusion presents some *Lessons from industry* and identifies further challenges facing the profession, implications for translator training, quality-related ethical issues and suggestions for future research. Throughout, real-world examples illustrate particular claims or scenarios. These are anonymized to respect confidentiality agreements but general information regarding size, sector and so on is included where this does not identify the company or individual concerned, so readers can assess how relevant a case is for their own situation.

CHAPTER ONE

Today's translation profession

1.0 Introduction: A revolution in communication

In 1991, only 2 per cent of those living in developing countries had any telephone access at all, fixed or mobile. A decade later, 31 per cent of the same population had such access.[1] By 2007, the International Telecommunication Union estimated that 45 per cent of people in developing countries had a mobile.[2] The story of phone access encapsulates how the world has changed dramatically in a very short period. A highly technical product, with no place in the lives of most people in recent memory, has become commonplace. User demand has soared in existing markets and in new ones with little prior experience of easy communication. The phones themselves are significantly more complex and powerful; new features and frequent upgrades are expected; yet their cost has plummeted: early 'bricks' cost several thousand US dollars. They are used in unanticipated ways (e.g. spawning new industries such as money transfer by phone and roadside charging stalls, transforming lives in regions with no banking infrastructure and restricted access to electricity). Such changes can naturally reinforce disadvantage or discrimination as well as improving lives. Even if far more inhabitants of developing countries have mobiles, overall figures disguise the patchy nature of access across different regions and groups due to corruption, war, monopolies, import tariffs, state control, poverty and gender inequalities. The story looks very different to an urban Egyptian male and a rural Zimbabwean female.

There are strong parallels between what has happened in telecoms and translation in recent decades. Accessing translation is now commonplace, not the preserve of specialist sectors or relatively wealthy clients. Use of online MT engines and multilingual websites means more people than ever before are aware of translation. The corollary is increasing awareness of the *lack* of translated material (e.g. when users click on links and find their language is not supported). Demand has thus soared for translation as for phones: much of the traffic on MT user groups consists of calls for the service to be provided in hitherto neglected yet widely spoken languages.[3]

Just as phones have become more complex and powerful, translation tasks are now more technically complicated and the impact of translation more extensive, with huge increases in content. Rapid spikes in demand for a service would normally lead to prices going up, yet client pressure, new ways of working and translation technologies have instead led to downward pressure on rates. Translations are therefore being commissioned, produced and used in new ways, with resulting uncertainty and shockwaves across the industry. As Vashee sympathetically notes, the 'poor translator' is caught in major shifts, yet has little influence on their development.[4]

The story of mobile phone access illuminates how translation has changed because of parallel developments in the two industries, but the telecoms revolution has also had a direct *impact* on translation. Global demand for such fast-changing products and services means that the need for translation has rocketed. Translation is now required throughout the phone production cycle. In the past, companies producing fixed-line telephones rarely sold their products in multiple regions or languages and users kept the same model for decades. Today, R&D, engineering, manufacturing, staff training, sales and marketing, user information and after-sales support all involve translation, across more languages and for new users who face particular challenges (e.g. low literacy levels or the need to understand material not in their native tongue). Translation jobs could traditionally be considered complete ('signed off') when returned to the client, but telecoms products and services are continuously updated, necessitating new kinds of rolling translation service and collaborative working. Time-to-market and simship[5] pressures in competitive commercial sectors like telecoms mean that translation deadlines have been forced down. Outsourcing to low-cost countries, usually China and India, has had an impact on translation like other industries.

This changed – and still-changing – paradigm has implications for translation quality. This chapter looks in more depth at how economic, social and technological changes are transforming the translation industry, and why it has increasingly focused on quality.

1.0.1 Translation: Industry or profession?

Industry: a particular branch of economic or commercial activity.

Profession: a paid occupation, especially one involving training and a formal qualification.

(CONCISE OED, 11TH EDN, 2009)

The terms translation industry and profession are used interchangeably in this book; this requires explanation. Even discounting the view of translation as an art or craft, there is debate over which term to use. A prominent topic of discussion since the 1950s, one established definition of a profession is that of a 'vocation whose practice is founded upon an understanding of the theoretical structure of some department of learning or science, and upon the abilities accompanying such understanding' (Cogan, 1953: 33). Some translators demonstrated a marked preference for the term profession. Others favoured industry, perhaps recognizing skilled translators who learned 'on the job' rather than studying for qualifications. Most, however, accepted both terms.

Translation clearly fulfils certain criteria of dictionary definitions for industry and profession. Both terms are used in most written accounts. Chriss (2006) switches without ado between the two, for instance, though his work is specifically directed at *Translation as a Profession*. Where the term profession is preferred, it can indicate regret regarding recent developments in translation, seen as a shift from a high-quality 'artisanal' tradition to one of mass production. Gouadec deems that 'translation now bears all the hallmarks of an industrial activity' (2007: 297) and later analyses the effects of this 'industrialization' (2009: 217–32), comparing translators' current fate to the earlier ruinous mechanization of French lace-making. Like Chriss, Gouadec refers to both industry and profession, but where Chriss uses them interchangeably, Gouadec often implies criticism, differentiating between two distinct approaches to translation.

Those who favour the term profession often allude to translation quality issues. They typically want to regulate the sector, believing that increasing profession*alization* is needed to improve quality. While entry to professions such as law, medicine or engineering is controlled, translation is unregulated in most countries, notwithstanding the explosion in training programmes (Caminade and Pym, 1995; Drugan and Rothwell, 2011), intermittent attempts to establish certification (sworn translators, chartered linguists), and calls for 'kitemarks' or periodic re-examination (Picken, 1994: 197).[6] Daunting accounts of professional translators' qualities are provided to indicate who might qualify. For example, in addition to the merely desirable 'good grounding in marketing, management and accountancy', Gouadec's professional paragon demonstrates:

> absolute linguistic proficiency, [. . .] perfect knowledge of the relevant cultural, technical, legal, commercial backgrounds, [. . .] full understanding of the subject matter involved, a gift for writing, an insatiable thirst for knowledge, [. . .] the stamina, thoroughness and sense of initiative needed to find any information (or informant) that

might be required to fully understand that subject matter, [. . .] the ability to relate both effectively and smoothly – both professionally and personally – with numerous partners. (2007: xiii)

Some who favour the term profession are crusading to raise the sector's status, visibility or remuneration levels. Venuti's 'call to action' on the translator's invisibility increased awareness of these issues (1995/2008: 265–77). Robinson uses the term faithfully, stating his aim as 'raising the status of the profession' (1997: 39). Cronin recognizes that 'the professional and the political are inextricably linked', calling for a 'more engaged, activist notion' of translators' responsibilities, both to defend professional interests and '[get] societies and cultures to realize how important translation is to comparative self-understanding and future development' (2003: 134). A few dislike either term, with Pym arguing (2006: 8) that, in the era of localization, 'there is no such thing as a "translation industry", in the singular'. What, though, do we then refer to? Pym himself notes that acronyms like GILT (Globalization, Internationalization, Localization, Translation) have failed to catch on. Despite its limits, he reverts to the convenient shorthand of 'industry' (singular) then to the 'translation and interpreting professions' a few lines later.

Both terms are used in the present book. They help distinguish between student translation, translation studies/theory and the kind of translation under discussion here: (usually) paid, for a client, to a deadline, with an intended end use and some sort of translation specification. As noted, most industry discussions use both terms. Finally, recent developments, particularly increasing integration of the 'gifted amateur or keen bilingual subject specialist', may herald dramatic change for the industry, even the 'closure of the cycle which began when translation became an "independent" profession' (García, 2009a: 199). Some of these developments are considered in relation to translation quality in this book, so it is helpful to be able to distinguish between the profession and newer approaches.

1.1 Changes affecting the translation industry

Strong growth has been accompanied by other significant changes: a huge increase in demand (volume) into a wider range of languages (reach), and a corresponding increase in awareness of translation. Translation is needed more quickly and to different kinds of deadline. Source content is more complex. The tools used to translate are more efficient, reliable and accessible, and cheaper than in the 1990s. These economic, societal and technological changes affecting translation in recent decades, and their implications for translation quality, are now examined in more depth.

1.1.1 *Market growth*

> In the course of the 50 years between 1950 and 2004, international
> trade enjoyed average annual growth of 4%, whereas the translation
> industry grew by a minimum of 5% each year. Clearly, the development
> in international trade generated a need for translation and will continue
> to ensure the almost parallel growth of the translation sector. (Boucau,
> 2006: 3)

Industry growth figures are difficult to establish and compare, given
the sector's diversity, global spread, shifting exchange rates, varying
conceptions of what should be measured and the fact that leading
companies are privately held and not obliged to share data on performance.
All surveys in the past two decades have nonetheless identified growth
outstripping that of trade in general. Specialist industry research provider,
Common Sense Advisory (CSA), made the staggering estimate that, from
US $9 billion in 2006, the market for 'outsourced language services' grew
by one-third in a single year, reaching US $12 billion by 2007, and further
predicted a compound annual growth rate of 14.6 per cent between
2008 and 2012 (Beninatto and De Palma, 2008: 1). The largest recent
European study estimated annual compound growth rate at 10 per cent
minimum from 2009–15, giving a European language industry valued at
a 'conservative' 16.5 billion € by 2015, with the 'real value' likely to be
above 20 billion € (Rinsche and Portera-Zanotti, 2009: ii). These large-
scale studies concur that economic downturns do not stop growth:

> The language industry seems to be less affected by the financial crisis
> than other industry sectors. Where turnovers from multilingual business
> activities have been negatively impacted, this has been mainly in the case
> of individuals and micro-companies dependant on a small number of
> clients, a quick recovery and continued steady growth of the market is
> forecasted. (ibid.)

The first survey following the global downturn supports this analysis,
claiming a 2009 growth rate of 13.15 per cent for translation and
interpreting and estimating the global market at US $26 billion in 2010
(Kelly and Stewart, 2010: 3).

Why should the translation market have grown more than international
trade in recent decades and continue to flourish even in troubled times?
In short, globalization.[7] The recent penetration of free- or mixed-market
economies across the globe has driven more translation, particularly since
the opening of huge new markets in Eastern Europe and China from the
early 1990s. The scale of this change is striking: '10–15 per cent of the

world's population were part of a market system at the beginning of the twentieth century, 40 per cent in 1970 and approximately 90 per cent at the century's end' (Mulgan, 1998: 54–5, cited in Cronin, 2003: 47). Huge new demand, particularly in the BRIC countries (Brazil, Russia, India, China), means that even in recession, companies need more translation, as they seek to drive sales beyond traditional declining markets. 'Producing a localized version of a product means that new markets are opened up for an existing or potential product. While a domestic market may be stagnant or in decline, international markets may be buoyant and may also support a higher price level' (Cronin, 2003: 14). Newer market economies also need translation to reach outwards. Translation has thus benefited not only from lowered trade barriers but also from factors such as the increasing ease of marketing to new regions online, and growing disposable incomes to access translated products and services.

Another feature of globalization explaining translation market growth in the last two decades is the 'Internet Age' – the digital and ICT revolutions (Lallana and Uy, 2003: 4–7). 'The Internet Age has led to insatiable demand for translation services that cannot be met with existing proprietary business models and the capacity of around 300,000 professional translators worldwide'.[8] Key features of these revolutions (personal computers, mobiles, the Internet) have meant both new products (software, games, apps) and growing need for internationalization,[9] localization and translation. Sprung points out that, as early as 1998, Microsoft gained over 60 per cent of revenues outside the United States of America and earned more than US $5 billion from translated products (2000b: ix). Wider availability of complex products has meant an increase in technical documentation, which is estimated to comprise 90 per cent of total translation output (Kingscott, cited in Byrne, 2006: 2). Translation volumes have also grown due to the way international business is conducted (e.g. securities and exchange traders must stay informed of developments in global markets so require translated information quickly round the clock).

Even this is only a partial picture. The market reflects growth in demand, but there is further demand that currently goes unmet. Increased demand for translation can be considered under two headings: volume (the amount required) and reach (range of languages/locales).

1.1.2 *Growth in demand – volume*

Globalization has led to increasing volumes of translation. A rise in migratory flows of people and growing number of international organizations[10] in recent decades has influenced demand. Increasing international cooperation (e.g. on peacekeeping, immigration, drug or people trafficking) is information-heavy and depends on translation. In particular, the growth of international organizations has created demand for translation, because 'it is discursively that most organizations of this nature have an effect on the world' (Cronin, 2003: 110):

> The vast majority of international organizations are heavily dependent on information both to inform *and* to give effect to their decisions. Any decisions which are taken that lead to the signing of international agreements and/or to the incorporation of appropriate measures into national law require the preliminary information-intensive activities of meetings, conferences, discussion documents, reports, media handling and so on. In addition, information in the form of data on the operations and decisions of the organizations must be provided to members, and as these supra-national entities function in a multilingual world of increasing complexity, they must perforce manage projects and activities across many different languages and cultures.

International organizations stimulate demand in other ways. For example, the flow of data is not only from organizations to members; those members also send huge volumes of data inwards, to be translated for discussion, comparison and dissemination, often into multiple languages. A case in point is the EU, where the Commission's Directorate-General for Translation (DGT) has for some time been the biggest single provider of human translation in the world (Brace, 2000: 219). By 2004, continual increases in content sent for translation led to a mounting backlog and the DGT adopted a 'Demand Management Strategy' (Drugan, 2007a: 136), limiting the number of source pages accepted for translation.

Increasingly, there is a legal obligation to translate certain materials (e.g. since 2010, EU citizens facing criminal proceedings in another member state are entitled to translation into their mother tongue[11]). Around the world, laws, directives and regulations 'require the provision of comprehensive, accurate and effective technical documentation in a variety of languages' (Byrne, 2006: 2). The legal imperative has driven growth in translation volume for materials such as contracts, copyright, patents and trademarks, required in ever more languages in the globalized context. In many countries, legal rights for migrants and minority language communities to use their own language in some domains (e.g. healthcare, justice) have driven growth. Since 2000, for instance, US institutions must provide services in users' mother tongues to qualify for federal aid; the American Translators Association (ATA) believes that this has had a significant effect on demand.[12] Finally, recognition of co-existing language communities have imposed translation obligations in some regions. For example, Section 21 of the Welsh Language Act 1993[13] enshrined the principle that 'in the conduct of public business in Wales, the English and Welsh languages should be treated on a basis of equality', driving local growth.

1.1.3 Growth in demand – reach and range of languages

Translation from and into a wider range of languages and for additional *locales*[14] means that overall demand rises. This section outlines why translation is increasingly commissioned across more language pairs. LSPs visited in research for this book commonly handled projects into between ten and 30 languages, something which helps explain the recent mushrooming of MLVs. Individuals or small groups of translators cannot deliver the expected range of languages or project content needed today. For clients, translation is not usually their core business, so they prefer a 'one-stop shop' than having to deal messily with multiple suppliers.

Why are translations needed in more languages? This change comes in part from users, driven particularly by the Internet. Web users often express frustration when material is not available in their mother tongue or set up their own equivalents where a service is not provided. Bey et al. (ibid.: 52–3) identify two types of motivation here: 'mission-oriented' communities who volunteer to translate clearly defined sets of documents, such as the technical documentation for Open Source (OS) software; and 'subject-oriented' networks who choose to translate material because of shared interests or values (e.g. humanitarian translation). More significant in explaining the rising number of language pairs, however, (and of most relevance for professional translators) is that clients want to reach more customers. Research has consistently demonstrated that web users are more likely to visit a site, spend longer there and, crucially, buy products when a site is available in their own language. For example, a large-scale global survey concluded that, 'four out of five (79.6%) told us they want communications in their mother tongue. [For buyers with low English proficiency], the number of those thinking that language is important or very important jumped to 85.1%' (DePalma et al., 2006: 10). Such research has challenged earlier assumptions that providing websites in English alone was sufficient. To reach and compete in new markets, companies have realized they must localize:

> Today, most exporters face local competitors – consumers in Taipei or Moscow will gravitate toward the product in their own language, not the one in the strange packaging. Companies are finding that *the cost of not translating* poses too great a risk to international sales. (Sprung, 2000: x)

Clients are likely to seek translation across further language pairs in future. Internet usage statistics indicate that continued growth depends on adding users in additional languages. Despite the emphasis on globalization, the 1990s were in fact dominated by a few regions and relatively few language pairs: 'The world economy is far from being genuinely "global". Rather, trade, investment and financial flows are concentrated in the Triad of Europe, Japan and North America' (Hirst and Thompson, 1996/2000: 2). As Table 1.1 shows, there is little scope for further penetration among web users in these established markets. Online expansion is most likely in Africa, Asia, Latin America and the Middle East, where many languages are used and increasing numbers of translations will be needed. These regions are also where the majority of the world's population is concentrated and growing faster, and hence where increasing numbers of potential consumers will be found.

The non-commercial sector also requires translation in an increasing range of languages. As the number of supranational bodies and international organizations has grown, and membership extended, the combinations of languages needed have soared. The original European Economic Community had six founding members and recognized four official languages (Dutch, French, German, Italian) in 1958.[15] By 2007, there were 27 member states and 23 'official and working' languages.[16] This caused decided problems for translation. Recruiting qualified translators for certain language pairs, and the plethora of potential language combinations, posed challenges. There may not be much demand for Latvian texts to be translated into Maltese, even inside the EU institutions, but the service must be available if the need arises. The institutions had to adapt working methods (e.g. increasing use of 'pivot' languages), with potential effects for quality. If translation from Language A to Language B has to go via Language C, further scope for errors is introduced (one EU translator described this as the 'Chinese Whispers' effect[17]).

TABLE 1.1 World Internet usage and population statistics, 2009

World Region	Population (2009 Est.)	Internet Users, 31/12/2000	Internet Users, 31/12/2009	Penetration (% Population)	Users % of Table
Africa	991,002,342	4,514,400	86,217,900	8.7	4.8
Asia	3,808,070,503	114,304,000	764,435,900	20.1	42.4
Europe	803,850,858	105,096,093	425,773,571	53	23.6
Middle East	202,687,005	3,284,800	58,309,546	28.8	3.2
North America	340,831,831	108,096,800	259,561,000	76.2	14.4
Latin America/ Caribbean	586,662,468	18,068,919	186,922,050	31.9	10.4

(Source: Internet World Stats, 2010, www.Internetworldstats.com/stats.htm)

Other less easily quantified developments have affected translation reach. Boucau (2006: 3) identifies as significant 'the widespread trend towards the protection of culture, and therefore of languages, for written documents.' This runs counter to the fear and widespread assumption that English might dominate: 'irrespective of the use of the English language as lingua franca, a further development is also becoming apparent – the protection of cultures and languages. The translation market will without a doubt profit from this tendency'.[18] Some have highlighted the risk of linguistic isolation, where there are sufficient sites for 'netizens' to remain within their own linguistic communities. The Internet might become 'an echo-chamber for like-minded voices [rather than] a powerful tool to encourage interaction and understanding across barriers of nation, language and culture' (Zuckerman, 2008). Zuckerman foresees a future of 'multiple Internets,' divided by different values as well as by language. Even this scenario would involve growth in translation demand, though, as such isolated linguistic communities would presumably expect services and goods in their mother tongues. The scenario can be framed more positively too, with Pym suggesting that localization 'might actively participate in the saving of difference' (2010a: 140).

Political developments (devolution, minority language community activism) have extended translation to previously neglected languages. Steiner originally feared that 'the increasing domination of an Anglo-American Esperanto across the globe looked to be obvious and possibly irreversible', but recognized two decades later that he had been mistaken (1975/1998: xvii):

> Languages are proving more resistant to rationalization, and the benefits of homogeneity and technical formalization, than one might have expected. [. . .] If anything, the dislocation of the Soviet and East European power-blocs is bringing with it an almost fanatical wish for *apartheid*, for self-authenticating autochthony between neighbouring tongues (in the Ukraine, in the Caucasus, throughout the Balkans).

The political commitment to multilingualism in post-apartheid South Africa demonstrates this (South Africans might reject Steiner's depiction of their approach as a wish *for* apartheid). The 1996 Constitution recognizes 11 official languages and makes provision for the use of sign language, minority indigenous languages, languages for religious purposes and 'heritage' languages such as German and Gujarati (Dollerup, 2001: 35). A Language Board monitors and implements the ambitious language policy, with complex effects for translation (ibid.). Such official support for radical language policies has increased access to information across a broader range of languages. Finally, increasing mobility and international travel have also generated new demand for translation for some language pairs, though these developments have arguably been more significant in raising awareness of translation.

1.1.4 *Increasing awareness*

Venuti drew attention to the invisibility of the translat*or*, but the existence of translat*ion* is increasingly visible since the 1990s, sometimes dramatically so, as in the United States of America. There, increased awareness is linked to political developments, as Chriss explains (2006: 9):

> With the start of the War on Terror, translators, for perhaps the first time in history, are being interviewed on television and featured in newspaper and magazine articles, there is active recruitment by the U.S. government, in particular the military and intelligence community, and there is increased public awareness of the role translators and translation play in not only national security but modern life in general.

The review of the events of 9/11 by the US National Commission on Terrorist Attacks also drew attention to translation, explicitly attributing fatal gaps in intelligence to the failure to dedicate sufficient resources to the 'translation needs of counterterrorism agents'.[19]

Where people live in multilingual societies, there has long been strong awareness of translation, or at least interpreting. But for many regions, particularly with the rise of the nation state, monolingualism dominated and translation disappeared from view (Choudhuri, 1997: 439). Globalization has changed this picture. With greater freedom and ability to travel, global reach of some media, the Internet Age and the lowering of international trade barriers, many have been increasingly confronted with a multilingual world. Even in societies which have long been multilingual, such as India, where 'translation is ineluctable' (ibid.: 440), state language policy and greater mobilization around the rights of minority language communities have raised awareness since the 1990s. Greater awareness of translation is also linked to enhanced freedom of movement. Travel, including tourism and business travel, is one of the world's largest industries and has grown substantially since the 1990s, with lowered barriers and increased competition for passengers. Even in the context of increased security and the economic downturn of 2009, the industry accounted for 8.2 per cent of world employment.[20]

Perhaps paradoxically, the *anti*-globalization movement has contributed to increasing awareness of translation. Mobilizing activists and disseminating anti-globalization arguments requires considerable translation, often for language combinations where there is a shortage of trained providers. Such efforts are again informational in nature and operate simultaneously at local, regional and global levels. The movement therefore depends on translation and the communications revolution:

> Coordinating and communicating through transnational networks, activists have engaged in institutional politics, such as global campaigns to defeat the Multilateral Agreement on Investments or abolish the foreign debt, and extrainstitutional strategies, including coordinated global days of action, international forums, and cross-border information sharing. Perhaps most important, activists *think* of themselves as belonging to global movements, discursively linking local activities to diverse struggles elsewhere. (Juris, 2005: 191)

Juris's final point is significant. Translation is more visible in the Internet Age because many 'netizens' expect to communicate internationally and therefore across language barriers. Quah summarizes this 'Internet effect' on awareness (2006: 164): 'A multilingual environment on the web promotes many things, from products and services to understanding and communication between different ethnic communities'.

Mass online gaming offers one useful illustration. Broadband access has given rise to Massively Multiplayer Online Games (MMOGs or MMOs) where tens of thousands of individuals play together in real time online, whatever their mother tongue or location. Their shared interest encourages players to overcome substantial obstacles to communication. The recent nature of this profound change in behaviour[21] makes its ramifications difficult to predict, but it has undeniably raised awareness of translation. Cross-border and cross-language communication is also taking hold in wikis, video and social networking (known collectively as Massive Online Collaboration or MOC), with effects for translation, as Désilets notes (2007: 1): 'Massive Online Collaboration is revolutionizing the way in which content is being produced and consumed worldwide', with 'significant impacts on how we translate content'. For example, source content can easily be shared across multiple translators (Howe, 2008: 11):

> The rise of the network [. . .] allows us to exploit a fact of human labor that long predates the Internet: the ability to divvy up an overwhelming task – such as the writing of an exhaustive encyclopedia – into small enough chunks that completing it becomes not only feasible but fun.

Increasing awareness of translation in the multilingual web environment has also promoted more autonomy among consumers. Growing demand for 'real-time translation' can be attributed to users taking control 'in deciding what information they want when they want it, pulling translated material from the web rather than waiting for publisher-based content' (van der Meer, 2006: 2). The Internet has raised awareness in other ways too, particularly through its role as a 'major driver' for the development of

MT (ibid.: 165) and provision of free tools. The output of these systems has obvious limitations, though as Cronin notes (2004: 22), what is significant is 'not their unreliability but their availability'. Their very unreliability may even improve awareness of professional translation – and, arguably, raise its status. It is often argued that translation is invisible when done well – the so-called pane of glass analogy, with a 'good' translation represented by a clear, smooth sheet of glass, while cracks, scratches or bubbles represent flaws, which draw attention to the enterprise (Chesterman and Wagner, 2002: 28–30; Venuti, 1995/2008: 1). Evident weaknesses of web-based MT output illustrate to non-specialists the difficulty of producing high-quality translation. The explosion in MT use is directly linked to another reason for growth in awareness: the insufficient number of professional translators to meet demand.

Increasing openness and high-profile events have lastly drawn increasing attention to translation for some language pairs. State efforts to raise translation quality in advance of the 2008 Beijing Olympic Games attracted worldwide coverage and discussion of translation provision, both inside China and internationally.[22] Such coverage invariably linked to examples of comic (sometimes apocryphal) mistranslations, raising awareness not only of translation *per se* but also of quality issues in particular.

1.1.5 *Deadlines, speed and rates*

Anyone working in the industry for over a decade has witnessed major change in the delivery and return of work. For most of the twentieth century, usual working practice was for hard-copy STs to be sent by mail or courier to a single translator, who would dictate or type every word of the TT, even if some content had previously been translated. Time for translation – and laborious revision and typesetting – was a significant part of production cycles. By the early 1990s, fax machines were affordable standard equipment for translators in developed countries. Their adoption represented the first major change in translation deadlines. Many translators were apprehensive that 'the translation process somehow has to be as instant as the transmission of a text itself by fax!' (Fraser, 1994: 138). Less than a decade later, fax transmission would seem far from instant. Cheap personal computers and reliable Internet connections further revolutionized expectations about translation speed. Work could now be sent almost instantly to translators. Translation-specific costs for clients and agencies fell substantially, as computing infrastructure was in place independently of specific jobs. Delivery costs (albeit lower than before) were effectively shifted to translators, who now needed a reliable fast IT setup to be able to work at all. Limitations of transfer methods such as email were soon addressed, particularly through the mushrooming of secure FTP (File Transfer Protocol) sites. Even complex large files could be sent quickly and cheaply.

Increasing efficiency in transmitting texts had some effect on the typical view of translation as an add-on, rather than a fully integrated stage in production. Translation traditionally came at the end of the production cycle, so if deadlines slipped, time for translation was squeezed. Translators frequently spot errors in source files, but only late in the cycle, when it can be impossible or complicated to address them. By involving them earlier, unfortunate decisions with significant financial impact can often be avoided, as many interviewees in research carried out for this book stressed. Some companies with in-house provision embedded translators across production structures, rather than housing them in a separate unit, so that linguistic expertise could feed in during design and production.

Translation coming at the end of the production cycle caused other problems for clients. Intense competition among leading software and communications companies, and the desire to upgrade technical products regularly, entailed ever-tighter turnaround times for product releases and pressure to release across different locales simultaneously. Any delay in translation for one language pair could hold up multilingual product release, where an international launch might be planned with substantial advertising revenues committed around the chosen date. Once the translation stage was completed, it was also laborious and expensive to change the source. If an amendment had to be made, translation costs would be significant, even if only a few words had to be altered. Such issues were particularly evident in software and website localization, where frequent updates are essential to companies' success, and in new kinds of customer support environments where ongoing translation is needed.

The Internet Age has brought a change in translation speed more significant than any that went before. Like journalism, translation has had to adapt to rolling deadlines, with constantly evolving ('streaming') content. Entirely new challenges affect translation deadlines, notably the need to provide multiple languages, update frequently, balance global/ translated and local content, automate translation workflows and keep multilingual content in sync with source language material (Esselink, 2001: 16–18). Repeatedly, LSPs interviewed for this book raised these factors as significant for translation quality. A testing challenge is that content which must be translated rapidly is often critical for a client's image (e.g. PR responses to an emerging crisis). Quality levels must therefore be high, despite tighter deadlines. For organizations where 'global communication is critical and time is of the essence in their daily business operations', such as those in the financial sector, 'instantaneous translations of web pages, documents, e-mails and other types of information are crucial' (Quah, 2006: 164). This has led to new approaches to translation, made possible by relatively new tools and technologies. Texts are now commonly split among teams of translators, using tools, reference materials and automated QA procedures to enhance consistency. Some agencies share work across translators in different time zones to keep working 24 hours a day. For language pairs where it is available, MT plays an increasingly important role. Other emerging approaches build in 'user-led' translation, where content is translated quickly in response to user demand.[23]

The need for ongoing high-quality translation has led to new translation approaches, which may spread to other sectors as they become better known. Agile software localization is one example. The methodology comes from software development and emphasizes adaptable, collaborative working methods and shorter timescales ('iterations' of days/weeks, not months/years). There is no end product, just ongoing incremental 'development iterations'. Such approaches make sense when real-world translation needs are considered, such as that of PayPal, requiring 'simshipping in 23 languages with planned product releases every two weeks, marketing pushes every week and unplanned product releases in between', for instance (Dove, 2010). Agile approaches allow for ongoing improvements, and for translators to be involved in each iteration, where appropriate. Crowdsourcing has similarly been explored to meet tight deadlines, drawing on volunteers to translate content. Crowdsourcing approaches may allow new kinds of translation which have not hitherto been possible: CSA has claimed that companies using crowdsourcing were 'not doing so to save money. They were doing so to enter new markets and speed up the translation process.' (ibid.: 62). Co-opting crowdsourced translations in some sensitive contexts (e.g. game localization) might combat counterfeit products, or make translation available in languages of limited diffusion which would otherwise simply not happen.

How have such changes to deadlines affected translators? How many words per day must be translated to make the UK median income, for example? These questions are relevant for quality, for if translators face increased pressure to churn out words, quality is likely to suffer. Establishing an industry average for translator productivity is challenging, however. Different markets and language pairs use different measures – source or target words, characters (e.g. for Japanese), or pages. Page length varies. Estimates can be based on hourly, daily or weekly rates, and the 'average' working day differs from one region to another. Translators perform a range of tasks (e.g. research, proofreading/revision of others' work, bidding for new jobs), and the proportion of time spent on such activities affects productivity. Source content is so diverse that, even for the same individual, the number of words produced in a day can vary enormously. A specialist text in an obscure domain takes longer to understand, research and translate than a repetitive text from a familiar domain. Working conditions have an impact. An in-house translator working on familiar content types, with extensive experience of institutional terminology, generates high-quality output much more quickly than a new freelance supplier translating the same text. Finally, tools and resources available to translators vary widely and can substantially affect productivity.

Translators surveyed for this book estimated output[24] at '2–3,000 words per day or 5–6,000 on an intensive project (but that can't be maintained)', '150 for highly technical to 1,000 per hour for highly repetitive'; the average result was about 2,800 words per day. This includes a wide range of language pairs, domains and working conditions, and tallies with industry surveys. The latest ATA *Translation and Interpreting Compensation Survey* found an average translation speed in target words per hour of 540.[25] Assuming a seven-hour working day spent on translating alone, this gives an average of just under 4,000 words; but the working day also involves other business-related activities. The last UK survey found 'the majority of translators achieve a daily output of 2000 to 3000 words' and warned that 'those embarking on a career would be well advised to base their income expectations on an even lower figure for the first few years in the profession'.[26] A ProZ poll of 1,537 participants in 2010 found that 21.5 per cent did up to 2,000 source words per day, 41.2 per cent managed 2–3,000; 21.1 per cent 3–4,000; and 12.4 per cent over 4,000.[27]

Estimating translators' average annual incomes is harder still. Some translation-related activities (proofreading, notarizing) are usually paid per hour or for a minimum fee rather than per word; translators may earn each rate type in varying proportions. Freelance translators usually have fallow periods with little work, and conversely, busy times when they work long hours, perhaps at premium rates. Many translators will not divulge rates (or range of rates for different clients/jobs). Professional associations may not publish rates surveys in some jurisdictions because they breach legislation (the US Federal Trade Commission investigated the ATA for price-fixing in 1994, following one such survey). The translator's location also affects rates. The latest ATA survey found freelance translators based in the United States of America earned an average annual pre-tax salary of $60,423 in 2006. Outside the United States of America, the equivalent group earned an average of $56,672. Language pair matters. The ATA found that English>Arabic/Danish were paid highest at $0.19 per word; lowest were English>Italian/Portuguese at $0.12 per word.[28] In the United Kingdom, language pair also had a strong influence: translators from English>Scandinavian languages earned nearly 50 per cent more than those from Western European languages>English.[29] Domain specialization finally determines rates. Those in highly technical fields, particularly legal/medical, are consistently remunerated at higher rates than generalists.

1.1.6 Translation content

There has been a major recent shift in what gets translated. In addition to the range of texts which professionals have long translated, new content types such as websites, software, apps, games and audiovisual material comprise an increasing proportion of workloads. Such content poses substantial challenges. The subject matter is frequently more problematic. For instance, when new software features appear, translators may have to research and fully understand their functionality then invent appropriate terms to convey this in the target language, something which involves considerable time, skill and effort. As such products become more complex, this work is increasingly demanding, though this may not be appreciated or appropriately recompensed. Returning to the mobile phone example, user documentation for a smartphone is considerably more complex than that for a mobile from the early 1990s. Translators must translate and adapt new kinds of related content too (e.g. online marketing campaigns). This requires extra intellectual effort. Ever more elaborate features must be communicated simply and persuasively in ever more competitive markets, where brand reputation and clarity are crucial.

Additionally, new content presents non-linguistic challenges, because text is not easily accessible. Translatable natural language content must be distinguished from code and other elements not for translation and extracted from complex file formats. Once translated, the TT must be returned to the native file format and checked in that environment (e.g. because it may be significantly longer or displayed in a different direction). Even deciding which elements to translate can be difficult. For instance, should a hyperlink appearing in a web page be 'translated' to the equivalent target language site, or should the original link to the source language site be retained?[30] The answer depends on surrounding text, translation brief, availability of translated equivalents and client preference, but all involve additional effort. Extracting text from relatively common file types often also requires additional software and skills. Translators interviewed for this book virtually all handled standard MS Office formats (Excel, PowerPoint, Word), but most had to cope with more taxing file types such as PDFs, HTML and XML too. For localization, more complex formats and further tools are required. Most translators also contend regularly, even today, with STs sent as scanned images, faxes or handwritten copy, which cannot be translated in the usual tools without cumbersome conversion or retyping.[31]

Translation projects also commonly entail multiple file formats, with source content repeated across the range. For example, when a new automobile model is launched, translators work on content in user manuals, sales and marketing materials, specialist engineering handbooks, in-house training presentations, PR copy and websites, produced in multiple different file formats. Some content will be repeated across multiple source files and must therefore be identified and translated consistently. End-users (e.g. phone or car owners) expect to access troubleshooting guides or help for complex products in context, by hovering with a mouse over the relevant item or searching online for a key term, for example. Translators and testers must be able to replicate user environments or problems in context, to ensure that translations are accurate. Yet translators are increasingly sent text entirely *out* of context. New content types make translation more challenging because text is presented in isolation. Pym argues that it cannot even be seen as a 'source text in any traditional sense of the term' (2010a: 129). Because products such as software programs are updated frequently:

> Translators no longer work on whole texts, [. . .] but only on the new additions and modifications. The result is a radical change in the way translators are made to think. What they receive is not a text in any sense of a coherent whole. It is more commonly a list of isolated sentences and phrases. (ibid.: 128)

Pym gives the illustration of the English term 'Start'. This might be a noun or verb, a command or location. How is the translator to identify the appropriate translation without 'co-text or context' (ibid.: 130)?

Source content is also created in new ways. Texts are written by teams of contributors, with resulting challenges for coherence and style. Translators interviewed for this book had noticed a rise in technical texts authored by non-native speakers, presenting issues of accuracy and clarity. Texts may be created in content management systems (CMS), then partial content extracted for different purposes/formats. This exacerbates the phenomenon of de-contextualized strings of text being sent for translation. Controlled authoring may help simplify content, but is restricted to a limited range of source languages and sectors and often used in conjunction with MT, rather than benefitting professional translators (Lockwood, 2000; Nyberg et al., 2003).

Pym (2010a: 138–9) and Cronin (2003: 60) highlight disparities in translators' experience of new content types depending on their mother tongue. Pym describes a 'hierarchy of languages' and a 'one-to-many' translation relationship, where production of content is centralized in a handful of languages and regions. Translation then happens from a few source languages, particularly English, to many target languages. Some languages become languages of consumption alone; others are excluded entirely, because they have no standard written form or the number/income of their speakers does not justify translation expenditure. The impact of these developments is sometimes discussed in terms of their effects on users and consumers, but little attention has been paid to disproportionate effects on the world's translators. Cronin argues that, because English is predominantly a source rather than a target language,

> A dual burden is placed on those who do not speak the dominant language. Not only must they translate themselves into English but they must also translate from English into their own language. The translation task then is redoubled in intensity but, because of the nature and direction of the translation, it is erased from public view in the global parochialism of Anglophone monoglossia. (ibid.)

The rise in content from specialist sectors, (e.g. IT) poses challenges. Finding suitably qualified translators is difficult for highly technical content in many of the world's language pairs. Subject-specialist bilinguals are sometimes used instead, often translating out of their mother tongue. MT might seem like a tempting solution in such instances, but 'the validation of a qualified bilingual translator is absolutely necessary' for such critical tasks (Resnik et al., 2010: 127). Resnik et al. see translation as a dichotomy, rather than Pym's hierarchy: 'for most of the world's languages, [. . .] translation is limited to two possibilities: high quality at high cost, via professional translators, and low quality at low cost, via machine translation' (ibid.). Even this dichotomous view is excessively positive: for 'most of the world's languages', MT simply does not exist, and experienced translators may be similarly unavailable.

Emerging types of content present translation challenges because they are not stable, finalized texts. The rise of user-generated content and adoption of Agile localization approaches imply new business models, where content is translated when there is sufficient user demand, rather than the publisher deciding what to translate in advance. Carson-Berndsen et al. (2010: 53) argue that 'Next Generation' localization is needed to address user-led translation needs related to 'increased volume, access and personalization'. Standard translation and localization QA do not map on straightforwardly to such new approaches.

1.1.7 *Translation tools*

Translation tools are often portrayed as a recent innovation, and one imposed on translators rather than freely chosen. As Cronin emphasizes, though, 'translation without tools simply does not exist' (ibid.: 24). The use of tools to communicate text is what distinguishes translation as a profession from interpreting (oral translation). Of course, there is a big leap from paper dictionaries and tools needed to produce handwritten translations to the way translators work today: 'the Information Revolution did not just generate more work for translators, but also new tools aimed at boosting their productivity' (García, 2009a: 201). Professional translators in developed countries are unlikely to survive without PCs, email, search engines and word processing. They typically also need access to fast broadband connections, secure electronic storage for substantial quantities of data, multiple file formats, and basic understanding of DTP and web design. Austermühl (2001: 5) describes the growing 'technologization' of translation: translators must use dedicated tools to be able to work at all. As such tools become embedded in the industry, and offer increasingly complex features, it is commonly assumed that further improving translation speed and quality will mean even more technology, thus perpetuating the 'technologization' cycle.

The tools and technologies in widespread use in the industry today are outlined in Chapter Three. Some translators claimed not to use any translation tools in interviews for this book. Further questioning revealed they meant that they did not use particular technologies, chiefly translation memory (TM), MT and localization tools. All translators used electronic tools, at least for editing, research and terminology. Those who were reluctant to engage with certain tools were almost always senior translators working in-house in large organizations. Various explanations for this reluctance can be offered, based on their own accounts and profiles. In-house translators are not at the mercy of commercial client demands. They have greater job security than freelance translators. In-house translation divisions, particularly in medium-to-large organizations, are often themselves slow to adopt new technologies, given the high cost of equipping staff and often tortuous procedures to agree significant expenditure or adequate IT support. It was noticeable that more experienced staff voiced their rejection of translation tools, perhaps not only because they were sufficiently valued to be able to resist innovations with which they did not agree but also because they had learned their working methods years earlier. Some saw no reason to change when their established methods worked well. Others feared an adverse impact on quality, either because TM tools entailed approaching texts as isolated segments rather than a more coherent whole, or because databases included low-quality entries (e.g. from less experienced colleagues or unknown external translators). Freelance translators could also be critical of modern tools, but were unable to avoid their use. Questioning also revealed different explanations among freelance critics, notably the downward pressure on rates and shorter deadlines they had observed since widespread adoption of the tools.

Concerns regarding the effects of MT on translation quality were most frequent, across translators of all backgrounds and levels of experience. The overwhelming majority found it quicker and less frustrating to translate texts from scratch than to post-edit MT output. Others have previously noted translators' reluctant or fearful attitudes to translation tools (Bowker, 2002: 120), but concluded that the awareness of potential benefits was 'growing steadily'. Tailored training had also helped address the 'negative mindset held by some professional translators' (Quah, 2006: 18). If Quah is correct that tension between translators and machines developed as a 'corollary to new technology entering the translation process' (ibid.), more dramatic opposition may lie ahead, however, as MT becomes more widely integrated. García (2009a: 208) offers a bleak view:

> Soon, if not already, professional translators in the localization industry will no longer translate texts (like their literary counterparts) or segments (as in the TM heyday), but just post-edit machine output.

In García's vision, access to on-site resources (MT-assisted TMs, controlled authoring to provide 'live' translation on demand) will 'entail professional translators working in low-paid, call-centre conditions' (ibid.: 211). Of course, dire predictions as to the imminent impact of MT have been around even longer than the technology itself.

1.2 Quality and today's translation profession

As the above changes affecting the industry have unfolded, quality has attracted increasing attention. While fear of change is a natural human reaction, particularly in situations of extreme adjustment, it can obscure undeniably positive effects. This section reviews why recent changes have implications for translation quality, whether these are clearly negative, clearly positive, or as yet uncertain.

1.2.1 *Quality and increasing demand*

Rapid unplanned increase in demand and the need for more language pairs have placed huge stress on supply. The impact on quality can be acute where there is a dearth of suitable professionals. Some mature translation markets have suffered impossible pressure, affecting quality levels. Insufficient foreign language skills among English native speakers is regularly cited as problematic, for instance. Certain source languages which are now desperately needed have been neglected in recent times. This cannot be resolved quickly: learning languages takes many years and requires training infrastructure, qualified teachers and so on. Increasingly, translators have had to work out of the mother tongue, or between their B and C languages. Unedited MT output may be used because there is no alternative, leading to lower quality levels than users require.[32]

Negative impacts for quality are also seen in markets where professional translation is not financially viable. In the commercial sector, materials are only translated where return on investment (ROI) justifies expenditure. Significant populations have no access to key goods and information; others make do with partial or low-quality translation. In addition, many new markets for translated materials are less well regulated. If faulty translation leads to injury, there may be no legal redress or compensatory mechanisms. Inadequate intellectual property protection sometimes leaves the original provider vulnerable to copyright or patent infringement by unscrupulous local rivals, who can supply cheaper equivalents more quickly than a high-quality translation can be produced.

Conversely, increasing demand has had positive effects for translation quality. Established vendors have brought tried-and-tested methods to new locales, raising expectations generally. Proven approaches to localization and internationalization can be scaled up and spread to new language pairs. A positive corollary of unmet demand is that creative approaches have been found to address the translation gap, which have then contributed insights or new ways of working for the industry generally. The large-scale influx of translators for emerging language pairs has also had a positive impact on quality for established providers. For example, EU translators commented positively in interviews on the impact on quality and efficiency of large numbers of new colleagues in successive accessions. The explanations offered for this were usually either that they came from established translation 'cultures', with high-quality standards as the norm, and so brought high expectations with them; or that their more recent experience of tailored training and commercial experience had equipped them with technical skills and knowledge of cutting-edge practice, which then spread (Drugan, 2007a: 128–31).

1.2.2 Quality and increasing awareness of translation

Growing awareness in recent years has increased availability of translation. Millions of users previously without access to translation can now use MT engines, or may themselves contribute to crowdsourced translation projects. Knowledgeable end-users (e.g. gamers, comic fans) with expert awareness of target language culture and norms in highly specialized fields have also played a role in raising quality levels by reacting to low-quality translations. Where a computer game is inadequately localized, critical reviews can sink the product even before its official release in the target locale. In the past, clients might not have realized that a product's failure was due to inadequate translation, but they will now learn of its impact quickly through online feedback, or through rival unofficial translations produced by users themselves. The end quality of translations is then improved by informed users and improved feedback.

Increasing awareness of translation has a political–ethical dimension, which has emphasized quality issues. Seeing translation as a right has resulted in monitoring of standards and equity of provision in some multilingual contexts such as post-apartheid South Africa and the European Union. Minority language communities have used legislation protecting languages and cultures to lobby for effective provision. Translation failures in such high-profile political contexts as the Iraq War have also focused attention on the importance of quality in critical settings. Increasing attention has been paid in many countries and international organizations to end-users' right to access quality translation, to clients' rights to understand what quality levels they can expect from providers, and to the rights of translators themselves. Chesterman and Wagner stress that codes of practice, Continuing Professional Development (CPD) training, and awareness of translators' and clients' rights have all enjoyed increased attention since the late 1990s (2002: 101–7).

While increasing awareness has undeniably positive implications for quality, there have also been some less clear-cut and potentially damaging effects. Within the industry, there has been a recent focus on what constitutes 'acceptable' quality levels, rather than how to achieve the highest or best quality possible, for example. Where demand is so high, it makes sense to target resources. Concepts such as 'fit for purpose' translation, or 'good enough' translation have thus been supported by leading figures in the industry (Prioux and Rochard, 2007). A threat for translation quality in this development is that a translation's eventual use may not be known when it is commissioned. For example, sufficient levels of translation quality for a draft document intended for in-house discussion are unlikely to be acceptable for use in a press release, but translations are frequently put to uses unintended by their original commissioners, with ultimately damaging effects (Drugan, 2007b: 82).

The emerging 'pull' model of translation (where users request translation of those materials they need rather than ST producers deciding what to translate) can also have mixed effects for quality. The rationale for the 'pull' model is that it avoids unnecessary translation, allowing scarce resources to be focused on producing high-quality output where it is actually required. However, this raises important questions about where commissioning decisions are taken. If comparatively small numbers of users request a particular translation, will this be funded where larger groups are requesting other languages or materials? Who judges which needs are most significant and allocates the appropriate quality levels to the job?

Increasing awareness of translation holds mixed effects for translators' status and visibility. There are some signs of positive recognition of translators' contribution to quality, such as acknowledgement in reviews (e.g. games, film subtitles), and growing calls for translators to 'sign' their work (Durban, 2010: 50–2). The downside of such recognition has been increasing criticism of translators' work, whether justified or not. In the age of wikis and online feedback, users' critical comments where their expectations are not met has meant non-professionals judging translations, usually with no understanding of production conditions. Increased awareness of translation has also drawn negative attention to costs. The question of who pays for translation in healthcare, immigration and justice settings, in particular, has attracted negative publicity in many states in recent years.[33] This attention has resulted in calls to cut funding for translation, and indeed substantial actual cuts in provision in some areas.

1.2.3 Quality and deadlines, speed, rates

Pressure to work faster and for lower rates might seem likely to have entirely negative effects for translation quality, but automation of translation processes has allowed greater consistency, productivity and speedier recall than human translators could ever achieve, making the impact on quality more mixed than might be assumed. Kingscott emphasizes the importance of faster turnaround times for quality in the profession: a high-quality translation delivered a few minutes after the client needed it is useless, but a lower quality one delivered on time can be critically important (1996a: 138). Faster, more secure transmission of texts means that some translation types are now feasible for the first time. This is particularly true in some sectors where time is of the essence (e.g. financial translation). The emergence of specialist 'live' or 'instant' translation services points to a market need that previously went entirely unmet.

The general industry assumption, however, has been that faster translation means lower quality. The little empirical research available corroborates this. Bowker (2005) tested translators working under three conditions: using no TM resources, an 'unadulterated' TM and a TM deliberately seeded with errors. The first group produced high-quality translations but took significantly longer; the second and third groups produced translations more quickly, but with minor quality concerns (for the second group) and much lower quality (for the third group). Bowker concluded that 'when faced with the pressure to translate quickly, translators using TMs may not be critical enough of the proposals offered by the system' (ibid.: 13). Some positive quality effects are linked to pressure to translate more quickly, however. Adoption of tools such as TMs means automated quality checks pick up errors that humans are unlikely to spot (e.g. missed segments). However, the expectation that translators work in large teams to complete jobs more rapidly has less clear implications for quality. While shared termbases and TMs might address issues of consistency across contributors to some degree, no research has yet analysed coherence, style or other aspects of quality of translations produced using such approaches.

Downward pressure on rates might be assumed to have a negative impact on quality, as translators must work faster to make the same income. Tools mitigated this effect, though. Manufacturers claim substantial productivity benefits (e.g. 'increased by 80%' (Drugan, 2007b: 81)). While such levels are unlikely, studies do demonstrate significant productivity increases (O'Brien, 1998; Somers, 2003a). This means that some translators produce similar levels of translation quality for less. Skill levels can also affect translators' productivity. Rates per word do not always reflect quality, therefore.

1.2.4 *Quality and translation content*

Greater complexity of content poses challenges for quality, but new working methods mean its impact has not been entirely negative. The introduction of TM and terminology management tools means repetition of source content across multiple file types/time/translators can be identified, for instance, so approved high-quality translations are recycled and consistency is improved. The importance of consistency in translations is often underestimated outside the industry, but clients and providers were clear that this was one of the main benefits of tools. Clients place a high premium on translators respecting approved terminology. In competitive sectors like automotive translation, this is essential for branding and user friendliness. For instance, to refer to the same concept (traction control), Audi uses 'Electronic Stability Program', BMW opts for 'Dynamic Stability Control' and GM prefers 'Active Handling System'.[34] None of these terms would be *factually* inaccurate, but not using the client's approved term could be confusing, even dangerous, for users, and might infringe competitors' intellectual property rights. Content types such as online help rely on consistency for ease of navigation, especially where material is regularly updated. Investment in creating and maintaining high-quality resources makes sense, as their reuse can be imposed. Improved consistency should then justify the investment over time; though, as Bowker notes (2005: 18), this depends on high-quality input and appropriate database maintenance.

Undeniable negative impacts for quality are found. Translators most often raised the requirement to work on isolated segments of text, without sufficient context to understand the source. Differing rates are generally paid for 100 per cent or fuzzy matches and for new segments.[35] This has implications for quality. Although the TM might contain a match, this could be inappropriate in the new context, requiring complete retranslation. The translator is hardly motivated to attend to this if paid less for the relevant segment. Even complete matches are only acceptable where the TM content is of sufficient quality to begin with. Freelancers repeatedly recounted experiences of querying client TM content on quality grounds but being instructed to re-use the low-quality (even misleading or incorrect) content to maintain consistency. Translators mentioned another negative impact of standard payment approaches: time spent extracting text or working on non-translation tasks such as formatting is effectively unpaid, so it can be tempting to rush translation to make a reasonable return.

Further negative effects for quality related to the rise of intermediaries. Direct clients represented a minority of most translators' workloads, but were much preferred. Only a handful of skilled niche providers managed to work exclusively for direct clients. Translation projects' increasing complexity has led to the mushrooming of translation agencies, who win contracts from direct clients then divide content for translation by teams of freelance suppliers into multiple languages. The standard agency expectation is that translators never have direct contact with end-clients, but communicate queries through PMs. Translators felt that this had negative effects for quality. Agencies themselves raised quality concerns. Increasingly complex file formats can mean that jobs are allocated not to the most skilled linguists but to those who are technically competent. For example, where a client has specified use of a named TM tool, agencies may struggle to find suitably equipped translators. They either have to convert the TM pre- and post-translation themselves (which has implications for quality of both the translation and subsequent TM content), or source new suppliers, whose quality levels are unproven.

Collaborative teams now work on large localization and translation projects. This involves a host of new roles which translators are unlikely to have trained for, such as editing, testing and working on-call (Byrne, 1999). There are negative implications for quality in this approach, particularly where communication between team members is poor, but working in this way can have positive effects too. New members learn from the more experienced. High-quality solutions are communicated across the team; such sharing of ideas is a positive experience for many otherwise isolated freelancers. In interviews, they commented on the benefits of working regularly with certain 'colleagues' whom they had never actually met, but from whom they learned a great deal. They welcomed the chance to solicit feedback from experienced peers. This is rare for many freelance translators, who see little client feedback.

More complex source content for translation poses evident challenges for quality. New concepts present additional intellectual challenges, and may require in-depth understanding of very specialized domains. Clients may be unable to check the quality of target language versions, particularly where they are launching in new locales with little prior experience or in-country staff, leading to clear concerns regarding translation quality and the development of quality control methods such as in-country review (ICR). Yet translators themselves often viewed this type of work positively, valuing the intellectual challenge and autonomy. Since this type of content is preferred to what they described as 'routine' or 'mundane' jobs, translators may engage more enthusiastically with it and produce high-quality work. Translators and PMs also raised quality concerns around non-standard jobs. With the move to standardized workflows, agencies can struggle to place short, one-off client requests in unusual formats, for which a high-quality translation may nonetheless be critical. Chriss gives a typical example: 'Someone scrawled out some message to someone else and this twenty-five word chit of paper is now Exhibit A in an international patent infringement lawsuit. You probably won't know that' (2006: 22). Finally, newer 'pull' models of translation do not fit neatly into standard quality and review processes such as ICR and translate-edit-proofread (TEP). This may impair quality, particularly as speed is usually prioritized for such content.

1.2.5 *Quality and translation tools*

Dedicated tools have clear positive effects for some aspects of quality. They enhance consistency, accuracy and increasingly allow for some elements to be checked automatically, instantaneously and for free, after the initial investment. Automated QC processes outstrip some traditional checks due to human fallibility. A computer never mistakes a comma for a full stop; a human's tired eyes can easily do so. Such errors in translated engineering or pharmaceutical texts can be critical, so this sort of benefit is significant for quality.

Another benefit emphasized by translators and clients in interviews was increased quality over time. Before such tools, if a highly able translator retired or moved on, his knowledge and experience were lost entirely. Appropriate use of TM and terminology tools means his contribution can be accessed by future colleagues. Some translators also indicated that they appreciated the tools' automation of certain highly repetitive tasks, freeing them to focus on new/challenging content and thus improve overall quality.

The contribution of technology to research and preparation is acknowledged by professionals as hugely beneficial for quality. Experienced translators especially stressed the ease of finding information online (e.g. images of technical apparatus searched for in the source language). Understanding such references used to involve time-consuming trips to documentation centres or extensive library or telephone research, often with no satisfactory solution being found. Today, skilled translators can identify target language equivalents in seconds. Online specialist resources were also highly rated, particularly bilingual lexicons and peer-to-peer websites, where translators can raise technical queries. These were particularly valued by those working in unusual language pairs with fewer resources.

Recurrent criticisms of the tools' effects for translation quality were also reported. Translators frequently pointed out that the rationale for their introduction was not a desire to improve quality, but to produce translations more quickly and cheaply. They were clear that the focus on speed and economy meant some aspects of translation quality had suffered. Prominent among such negative effects was the GIGO principle (Garbage In, Garbage Out), recognized by translators and clients. Recycling translated material means that poor quality content is perpetuated. Many translators pointed out that use of the tools was imposed by employers, yet little or no training was provided. Observing translators at work in varied contexts brought home that the majority used a limited range of familiar features and were unaware of key resources. Few freelance translators performed any maintenance operations, for example (Drugan, 2007b: 90–1). This may change as some steps are automated, or improved training addresses the gaps; but the legacy of inexpert use (e.g. inappropriate content/structure) will continue to affect quality. Even proficient users are affected by poor legacy material. Virtually every translator interviewed frequently found low-quality content in matches, whether they worked with in-house resources or external databases. More worryingly for translation quality, most freelance translators stressed that it was not worth reporting such problems; they would either be told that the content was 'approved' so must indeed be used, or would get no feedback at all. There was a clear difference for in-house staff, here: most had reporting structures (e.g. through a 'super-user' for each language pair).

Researchers have pointed out that the GIGO effect is not always due to 'Garbage In'. Because TMs store segment pairs, rather than whole texts, they are in fact a memory of 'sentences out of context' (Bowker, 2005: 15), something which can have various negative effects for quality when they are retrieved. One obvious problem is that sentences depend on one another. For instance, a pronoun might need a different gender in the target language depending on the content of an earlier segment in the ST. This would be presented as a 100 per cent match to the translator, so she might not notice and simply accept the incorrect target segment (ibid.). Worse, translators may not be able to make changes, even if they do notice errors:

> In an update to a manual, segments which had previously been translated and for which 100% matches were found had been locked, but a translator into French explained that, with new segments added in between these approved segments, the gender and number of pronouns needed to be altered for the updated translation to be grammatically accurate, but she did not have access rights to carry out the changes. (Drugan, 2007b: 85)

Translators interviewed for this book frequently stressed the negative effects on coherent style of using a TM, as they are forced to translate segment-by-segment. This was more problematic for some language pairs than others, as standard document structure varied more for certain locales. TMs populated by different translators over many years exacerbated these effects on target style and coherence: '[Each] text and translator will have a different style, and when sentences from each are brought together, the resulting text will be a stylistic hodgepodge' (Bowker, 2005: 16). Translators stressed the need for extreme vigilance and effective revision to pick up such issues. Bowker's work supports this: under experimental conditions, translators indeed missed deliberate errors included in TMs. A final negative effect for quality lay in the imposed use of the tools. A number of outstanding translators simply refused to work on jobs which required the use of certain tools. Some clients and sectors then had to rely on untested translators, recruited for their technical skills rather than their linguistic ability.

Other issues raised in research for this book had mixed implications for quality. Dividing large projects across multiple translators, sharing tools and resources to achieve some level of consistency,[36] was reported as having both positive and negative effects. Positive feedback focused on the 'superior brainpower' of such teams: colleagues could cooperate to resolve queries and avoid duplication of research, for example. Less positive was a tendency to 'level down' to a basic style, or try to pre-empt colleagues' preferences. In-house translators particularly mentioned that, when sharing jobs with certain colleagues, they would anticipate and adopt their preferred style to avoid extensive revision later. One translator referred to this as the 'Lowest Common Denominator' effect; another felt it resulted in 'style pollution'. Some, though, reported the opposite effect, with scrupulous colleagues encouraging them to be more careful. A few clients even mentioned this as a motivating factor in deliberately encouraging the use of teams, as they were believed to respect company 'tone of voice' preferences or house style more dependably (Drugan, 2007b: 81).

The obligation to work at segment level was seen as having mixed rather than entirely negative effects for translation quality by some, particularly in selected domains where the translator's style was less important, or even potentially detrimental. As one localization specialist quoted by SDL explains, 'we are working across cultures where synonyms and "turns of phrase" burden the readers' (ibid.). Translators also stressed the value of automatic warning when segments were missed. Correct use of the tools eliminates this common issue, particularly for technical texts and some file formats where source content might not be easily visible.

Of unclear impact for quality is the recent increase in MT use. Virtually without exception, translators claimed that they would always prefer to translate texts from scratch, often referring to quality as their justification. Hardly any published research thus far compares quality across post-edited MT output and human translations, though Fiederer and O'Brien (2009), the Centre for Next Generation Localization and TAUS have done some early studies. More positively, though, some translators who used MT integrated in TM tools (such as Déjà Vu X, which offers an 'intelligent' combination of TM and MT to fill in gaps in matches) commented they found this feature surprisingly useful, notably at term level.

1.3 Conclusion: Quality and the Internet Age

Zuckerman argues that we are living at a pivotal moment and translation has a crucial role to play in harnessing positive aspects of the Internet Age:

> Many of us share a vision of the Internet as a place where the good ideas of any person in any country can influence thought and opinion around the world. This vision can only be realized if we accept the challenge of a polyglot Internet and build tools and systems to bridge and translate between the hundreds of languages represented online. (2008: n.p.)

Despite his call to develop suitable translation 'tools and systems', Zuckerman goes on to stress that MT, at least at the moment, is not the answer, because if the quality of translations is not sufficiently high, then scope to change lives is limited. This section has outlined recent changes affecting professional translation and the reasons these are important for translation quality. One potentially positive outcome of the massive change affecting the industry lies in the increased attention paid to translation quality. Yet the industry has not generally turned to translation studies research to do this. The next chapter reviews the existing body of theory and academic research on quality and considers why this has not been central to professional attempts to measure, compare and improve quality levels.

CHAPTER TWO

Translation quality: Importance and definitions

2.0 Introduction: Translation quality in theory and in practice

I sometimes wonder how we manage to mark exams and revise translations with such confidence, when we have no objective way of measuring quality and no agreed standards. . . .

CHESTERMAN & WAGNER, 2002: 88

Wagner (Chesterman & Wagner, 2002: 88) identifies the key problem discussed in this chapter. Translation quality is a central concern for translation theory and has been debated in particular contexts for centuries (e.g. translation of religious texts) (Brunette, 2000: 169). Theorists and professionals overwhelmingly agree there is no single objective way to measure quality. Yet every day, translators, editors, revisers, clients and many others nonetheless have to do just this. Chriss sums up the standard view in the profession regarding this dilemma: 'Although theory is important, what can actually be done in the real world is ultimately what matters. [. . .] Ultimately, the market decides what is good enough for the market' (2006: 152). That the industry must perform translation quality assessment (TQA) is recognized within translation studies, though there is often [implicit] criticism of the absence of a clearly enunciated 'theoretical framework': 'models of TQA [. . .] inevitably reflect an overall theoretical framework (or lack of it) and can be discussed in terms of such. On the other hand, TQA is carried out daily, often in an unreflected [sic] and sometimes authoritarian way' (Hönig, 1998: 6).

Given long-standing attempts to define and measure translation quality, why has no standard approach been agreed upon? First, even within translation studies, theorists disagree, even on how many *categories* of models there are. Some classify models according to the broader theories on which they are based, and others according to what the models attempt to measure. Second, different models assess different things. Whether one is measuring and/or guaranteeing quality in the translated product or process, or the competence of the translator to produce adequate translations, will change the nature of the model itself. There is a particular mismatch between industry and academics here. Some approaches focus on quality assessment alone whereas others, particularly in industry, include other aspects of translation quality (e.g. assurance or control).[1] Adding to this confusion, translation quality assurance and assessment share the same acronym. The present discussion uses TQA for translation quality assessment (the more usual sense) alone, and QA for quality assurance. Pym (2003) and Dong and Lan (2010) agree theorists may confuse the picture further by adding ever more components to original definitions, generating what Chesterman dubs 'excruciating typologies' (2002: 89). This makes quality models unwieldy and increasingly likely to conflict with one another. Williams (2004: 7) cites the model devised by academic Daniel Gouadec for the Canadian government's Translation Bureau, *Système d'évaluation positive des traductions* (SEPT), which was never actually used, no doubt because of its comprehensiveness and overwhelming complexity: 675 parameters must be evaluated before a translation's quality can be decided.

Those in translation studies fail to agree on a model, then, but there is also a gulf between theorists and the professionals. During hundreds of interviews and research visits to LSPs for this book, not a single academic model was mentioned as a way of assessing translation quality in the real world. This picture reflects Lauscher's conclusion over a decade ago that, despite an increased focus on TQA in translation studies, 'academic efforts in this area are still largely ignored, if not explicitly rejected by the profession' (2000: 149). There is no agreed approach *within* the industry either, though. Although some generic models exist (e.g. that developed by the now-defunct Localization Industry Standards Association[2]), only a minority use them, often in heavily customized forms. Instead, most LSPs have their own internal approach, sometimes even with disagreement as to the most appropriate model or practice within a single provider. Beyond small-scale awareness of others' methods (for instance, where translators had experience of working for several different employers), LSPs were generally ignorant of others' approaches, and keen to learn how they addressed this contentious area.

One reason for divergence in industry models is that, just as theoretical models evaluate different things, so too do professional ones, partly because there is huge diversity in real-world needs and requirements. For instance, significant specializations (e.g. pharmaceutical translation) are bound by externally imposed quality requirements which would be inapplicable, irrelevant or prohibitively expensive in less regulated sectors. A further reason that professional models evaluate different things, at least on initial appearances, can be a narrow reading of what TQA and QA signify. In interviews for this book, professionals regularly conflated these with revision and editing alone: when asked to explain how they managed translation quality, they simply described how this stage of the translation process was managed. On further probing, many other aspects were in fact included in their approaches to quality. Interviewees simply failed to categorize them as belonging to a coherent overall approach or model. In Chapters Four and Five, these additional features are included, to present a full account.

Perhaps the chief reason that no one model is possible is that, beyond basic features as spelling or completeness, assessments and comparisons of translation quality rely on value judgements. Even on the apparently basic features of spelling and grammar, there is little consensus. This is true in translation studies; but in the profession, too, many agree with Kingscott (1996a: 138) that *all* aspects of translation quality are relative:

> A poor-quality translation, provided it does not positively mislead, which is ready for a businessman on Tuesday before he catches his plane to Tokyo, is far preferable than the accurate + natural idiom translation which is not ready till Friday of the same week; in fact, in such circumstances, the latter translation is worthless. [. . .] Here, then, is the first point to be established, and one difficult for established translators to grasp: Quality is relative.

Mossop offers the illustration of a translator mistranslating 'red' as 'yellow' (2001: 151–2). While undeniably an error, this might be insignificant, if the colour could have been omitted without affecting the end-user. However, if the colour describes a stolen car in a police report, this would be a critical error. Since value judgements and relativity are central, a risk is that of 'prescriptive judgement' (Lauscher, 2000: 162); that is, TQA 'proceeds according to the lordly, but completely unexplained, whimsy of "It doesn't sound right"' (Fawcett, cited in Baker, 1992: xii). Models attempt to address this danger in various ways, but this further variation decreases the likelihood of there ever being one agreed approach.

A final reason that no single model is likely to emerge is that academics and the industry are pursuing different goals and asking different questions when they consider quality. This lies at the heart of the widely noted divide between theory and practice on issues of translation quality.

2.1 The academy–industry divide

The academic Andrew Chesterman and professional translator Emma Wagner are in agreement that 'there can be few professions with such a yawning gap between theory and practice' (2002: 1). They identify translation quality as a significant area of disparity between the ivory tower and the 'wordface'. For Byrne, a gulf remains between theory and practice, with 'a tendency to regard translation errors solely from the point of view of academic studies and translation pedagogy, completely shut off from professional practice' (2007: 2). Theorists often view industry approaches as lacking intellectual rigour or a sufficient underpinning theoretical basis; they are therefore 'marred by impressionistic and often paradoxical judgements based on elusive aesthetics' (Al-Qinai, 2000: 497).

Williams identifies ten areas where consensus is lacking between 'practitioners and theorists' on translation quality (2004: xiv–xvii):

1   Text types: academic models are typically devised with 'literary, advertising, and journalistic translation in mind' rather than what Williams describes as 'instrumental' texts, which represent the bulk of professionals' workloads.

2   'Extraneous factors': should elements such as ST difficulty, deadline or intended end use be included in models?

3   Notions of 'quality': whose takes precedence where there is disagreement? (e.g. between client, translators, end-users).

4   'Language errors' (e.g. style, typos): which should be included?

5   Inconsistency in assessing 'levels of accuracy' and 'fidelity'.

6   Sampling: is it acceptable to evaluate a sample of translated material for errors, rather than whole texts?

7   Focus on error 'quantification': is the number of errors sufficient to rate a translation's quality? How should borderline cases be handled?

8   Rating errors: there is no consensus on what should count as 'minor'/'major'/'critical' errors.

9   Rating overall quality: how are multiple parameters combined to generate an overall rating for a translation?

10   Purpose: models are influenced by whether TQA is being carried out to ensure quality before delivery to a customer, or for internal audit, or to assess students.

A gap is indeed evident between academics and practitioners on some of the above points (e.g. the focus on different text types), but many are equally the source of disagreement *within* the profession or *within* translation studies. For example, there is little consensus inside the industry as to definitions of 'major' or 'minor' errors, and academics disagree on which 'language errors' (if any) ought to be included in TQA. Conversely, there is considerable overlap between some in the industry and some academics on most of these ten points. These factors alone, then, do not account for the perception of a gulf between theory and practice on issues of quality.

Others have stressed further areas of divergence between academics and the industry, however. For Halliday (2001: 13), the two groups have fundamentally different expectations of theory. Linguists believe that theory relates to 'the study of how things are', including 'the nature of the translation process and the relation between texts in translation'; a *descriptive* approach. For most professional translators, in contrast, translation theory is about 'how things ought to be: what constitutes good or effective translation and what can help to achieve a better or more effective product'; a *prescriptive* approach (Halliday prefers the terms 'declarative'/'indicative' and 'imperative' respectively to describe the different approaches). He further argues that 'the main difference between the indicative and the imperative perspectives seems to be that people look at "translation" systemically [i.e. by referring to language as a system], whereas they look at "good translation" instantially' [i.e. as an instantiation, or example, of the system in the text] (ibid.: 14). Halliday therefore sees theorizing of translation quality issues as a particularly pronounced case of the theory–practitioner divide.

Different motivations lie behind different understanding and expectations of theory. For academics, enjoyment of the intellectual challenge and potential for new discoveries are sufficient motivation. Funding providers accept that pure research leads to unexpected outcomes and blind alleys. For professionals, this approach is a luxury. They expect concrete, directly applicable, practical recommendations to justify any expenditure, which is typically provided by clients looking for clear-cut answers to specific problems, rather than being inspired by intellectual curiosity alone. How are practitioners to evaluate which of the conflicting theoretical approaches and models is most useful for their purposes, if any? Quah sees this as a failure of academic theorists, for whom 'solving the problems of professional translators is a matter of interest only when the approaches they have suggested are involved' (2006: 27). Theorists rarely start from professional concerns in drawing up models, but rather devise models from theoretical principles then cherry-pick cases to test them. These test cases are rarely drawn from actual professional translation, but from student assignments or published historical works.

Chesterman and Wagner (2000: 84) argue that these different motivations have led to theorists focusing on different aspects of translation quality. When translation is seen as a service, quality assessment depends on customer satisfaction. '[This view] has had less attention in academic translation studies, but certainly underlies proposals coming from the translation industry, about translation quality standards.' Instead, theorists often propose complex, exhaustive models which are not viable in the real world. Indeed, the very search for a unifying theory or model may be seen as wrong-headed in the profession: 'Increasing pressures on the translation market, [. . .] combined with customers' general lack of understanding of the translation process, mean that systematic, all-encompassing quality assurance is rarely financially viable' (Rasmussen & Schjoldager, 2011: 87). Theorists' recommendations as to how their models might be applied can seem equally unrealistic. For instance, Al-Qinai (2000: 517) indicates that:

> prior to launching a translation for public purposes [. . .], market research via controlled and random groups of informants (or revision committees of TL stylistics) should be conducted to measure such pragmatic considerations as impact, image, acceptability, naturalness and fulfillment of expectations for both ST writer and TT recipients.

While such an approach is likely to have positive effects for translation quality, it would rarely be feasible in terms of deadline or cost.

Academic theory and TQA models are also detached from real-world concerns due to constraints on access. Experiments on real-world subjects and processes are limited by factors including client confidentiality, cost, language proficiency and the need to control and standardize conditions. This means that research and theory have focused on translated products, excluding or in ignorance of translation and QA processes; yet these are clearly important elements, especially for the industry. Academic models are additionally often based on a narrow sample of translations, for two reasons. First, access to linked corpora of STs and TTs is limited; though this is less problematic now, translations are increasingly available online (Pierini, 2007). Second, inevitable limits to researchers' linguistic and domain expertise have meant that a narrow subset of language pairs and subject areas dominate. There is as yet no published academic research on quality incorporating widely spoken languages such as Telugu, or examining technical domains where quality is crucial (e.g. nuclear or space technologies), for instance.

In those cases where processes *are* included (including emerging translation process research), it is typically to hypothesize about how specific translation choices were made, rather than describing or prescribing stages in a business/production model. Lauscher sees this as contributing to the gap between theory and practice: 'As long as our knowledge of actual translation processes remains limited, proponents of scholarly models of translation quality assessment must acknowledge the speculative side of these models' (2000: 161). Another gap between theory and the real world is due to researchers' limited access to professional subjects in situ. When researchers do try to include translation processes, they are likely to recruit student translators as subjects, because they are readily available for free or at lower cost than professionals. Subjects are then observed working in artificial circumstances. Even if researchers endeavour to recreate realistic 'clients', deadlines, commissions or financial incentives, these are inevitably different to the conditions under which professionals produce translations, particularly when the subjects are questioned, filmed or monitored (e.g. using eye tracking technology) while they work. Discussing academic studies of revision, for instance, Mossop (2007: 17) stresses that:

> Most empirical studies are still taking place *in vitro*, usually at a university campus. There is a need to study revision in workplaces, during actual production for the market, since otherwise subjects' decisions may be determined by the fact that they know their output will never be delivered to a client.

Hönig (1998: 15) has also previously underlined the gap between academic and professional motivations on translation quality. He identifies differing motivations for four groups who need TQA:

> *Users* need it because they want to know whether they can trust the translators and rely on the quality of their products.
>
> *Professional translators* need it because there are so many amateur translators who work for very little money that professional translators will only be able to sell their products if there is some proof of the superior quality of their work.
>
> *Translatological research* needs it because if it does not want to become academic and marginal in the eyes of practising translators it must establish criteria for quality control and assessment.
>
> *Trainee translators* need it because otherwise they will not know how to systematically improve the quality of their work.

However, Hönig's list omits key groups, particularly in the profession, who have different, sometimes conflicting, concerns and motivations. Where do clients, PMs, ST authors and editors fit in, for instance? Are all these groups 'users'? Hönig suggests only one reason for each group's need for TQA, but there are clearly other more significant explanations. For example, professional translators questioned on this topic[3] did not indicate a desire to differentiate themselves from amateurs as a motivating factor. Their most common reactions were that TQA was imposed, or enabled them to justify rates, demonstrate compliance with standards, or protect themselves in case of dispute.

House (e.g. 2001: 2) frames academics' motivations as questions. She sees the fundamental question driving academic work on quality as, 'How do we know when a translation is good?' The equivalent fundamental question for the profession would rather seem to be, 'How do we know when a translation is good *enough*?' 'Good' quality translation is not the ultimate goal in industry. Instead, TQA allows the allocation of appropriate resources to different jobs. Particularly given recent soaring demand, the industry has concentrated on the idea of translations which are 'fit for purpose'; good *enough* rather than good: 'fit-for-purpose translation sounds like a business slogan or a DIY sales pitch ('just-in-time', 'cheap-and-cheerful'). [But it is] a conscious attempt to use translation and revision resources intelligently. It is *not a second-class alternative*' (Martin, in Drugan & Martin, 2005: n.p.). When translation resources are limited, aiming for the highest quality translation is wasteful if all that is needed is a summary of content before an imminent meeting.

Beyond these two fundamental questions, more specific questions are raised repeatedly in discussions of quality, whether in academic research or industry forums. A summary of the most common questions points to further divergence between theorists and practitioners. Some questions are indeed shared, with the following of concern to both theorists and practitioners:

- What constitutes a good translation?
- Can theory or TQA make this translation better?
- What impact do translation processes have on quality levels?
- Is the quality of this translation sufficient for its intended purpose?

Some questions seem to be important to academics alone, however, including:[4]

- Why is this translation as it is?
- What features are present in a 'good' translation?

Questions of interest to professionals include:

- How can we justify translation choices to the client?
- Can we measure/guarantee/improve translation quality without understanding the languages in question?
- Does the level of quality in this translation represent value for money?
- Will the quality of this translation damage my reputation/affect sales?
- Can we maintain quality and do it faster?

- Can we maintain quality and do it for less?
- How can different levels of quality be identified? What is acceptable, good, better, best?

A further distinction between theorists and professionals is that academics place definitions of basic terms (such as accuracy or faithfulness) at the heart of their work, whereas these are generally used unquestioningly in professional contexts. There may be a shared shorthand or common assumptions among those who invoke such ideas in their day-to-day work. In-house guides often also provide illustrations which effectively indicate how terms are to be interpreted in particular circumstances. As Pym has suggested, this can be a positive feature for industry, where speed and efficiency are key: professionals may 'have fewer doubts and do not waste time reflecting on the obvious' (2010a: 4).

Some have argued that there is a exceptionally strong divide between particular professional sectors and theory. Pym (2010a) claims that the localization sector in particular operates in mutual ignorance of translation theory, something which is significant for the question of quality, because the localization sector led the development of industry TQA strategies:

> There has been remarkably little debate about localization among translation theorists. [. . . Localization] industry experts have no need for careful theoretical concepts, and little time for extensive empirical research within the frame of such concepts. [. . .] Academics have shown remarkably little inclination to take the localization industry seriously, at least not in any sense that could threaten fundamental beliefs about translation (ibid.: 136).

Is House wrong, then, to claim that 'translation quality assessment presupposes a theory of translation' (1998/2001: 197)? Is the commonly held view that professional translators 'do not always produce convincing theoretical explanations for their translation decisions' (Quah, 2006: 27) justified, with the industry's work on translation quality taking place in a theoretical vacuum? Despite the gaps noted here, theory and practice in fact share much common ground.

Industry models have a theoretical basis, even if they do not make this as explicit as academics do: 'all translators theorize, not just the ones who can express their theories in technical terms' (Pym, 2010a: 4). The models outlined in Chapters Four and Five can be categorized according to underlying theoretical assumptions and views about translation. For example, the idea that translations should read like original STs, written in the target language by an educated speaker, marketing professional or other equivalent of the ST author(s), is entirely uncontroversial in the industry. The openly stated 'ultimate goal' of the localization industry is to provide a product that 'looks like it has been developed in country' (LISA, 2003: 11). Users of the TT should be able to understand instructions, for example, as easily as ST users. This may not always be achievable for reasons of cost or time, but it is the widely accepted goal for which professional translators and clients strive. Such an easy consensus is absent in translation studies, with some theorists joining Venuti (1995/2008: 19–20) in stressing the positive aspects of 'foreignizing' translations or calling for TTs *not* to read like originals written in the target language and translations to be 'visible' as such.

Shared views and connections between theorists and professionals are sometimes obscured by different terminology. Chesterman and Wagner (2002) identify several areas where this is the case. For example, the industry focus on practical QC procedures and theorists' focus on norms in fact address the same concerns and can even be 'translated' to fit into the other's meta-language (ibid.: 94). A different meta-language may explain other apparent gaps. Much of the industry debate on 'fit-for-purpose' translation, for instance, is clearly linked to ideas from *Skopos* theory (Reiss & Vermeer, 1984), even if this is rarely acknowledged, or perhaps even realized. Equally, theorists may not address distinctions between QA and QC directly, as professionals do, but many of the same ideas are found in discussions of translation 'competencies' (Fraser, 2000; Schäffner & Adab, 2000).

Issues of presentation may make the theory-practice divide seem wider than it actually is. Prohibitive charges restrict access to academic debates, particularly for the leading journals, though online publication is changing this picture a little. Professional translators also have particularly high standards for clear communication, usually in their mother tongue, as their reputations and ability to work depend on this. In contrast, many academics must present their theories in their second or third language, due to the academic emphasis on publishing in English. This, and academic jargon, may deter non-academics. There is evidence on both sides of some desire to bridge the gap between theory and practice, though, and this seems particularly true for issues of translation quality. Among others, Hönig (1998: 15) singles out TQA as an area where lack of cooperation is dangerous for both sides:

> If scholars and practitioners do not cooperate in this area they will make it a playground for amateurs – as it often is now. Hundreds of critical remarks about translations are made every day, some of them even get published. [. . .] Very few of these critical, often flippant, remarks are based on much more than a supposed knowledge of the source text language; very often there is no system, there are no common criteria, there is no informed discussion, only an occasional exchange of opinions.

Others offer suggestions as to how the gap can be bridged. Lauscher argues any *rapprochement* must come from both directions, with academics 'inquiring further into evaluation phenomena and into the possibility of prescriptive judgement' and practitioners becoming 'more aware of their respective roles and responsibilities in the translation and evaluation processes' (2000: 164). Like Hönig, she believes TQA offers particularly fertile ground for attempts to bring theory and practice closer together, as 'translation quality assessment and the judgement of translations are a matter of communication, co-operation and consent' (1998: 164). Some academics see signs of progress in the decade since Lauscher and Hönig made their calls, with Hague et al. praising the contribution of functionalist theories in particular: 'The convergence in translation quality assessment since 2002[5] is clearly substantial. This convergence reflects general agreement about the role of extra-textual factors such as audience and purpose, extra-textual factors which have long been basic to functionalism' (2011: 258).

Notwithstanding recent tentative indications of greater mutual collaboration, academic and professional approaches to quality remain largely distinctive so the present chapter outlines these in two separate parts. First, how have theorists approached translation quality? We then turn to the profession. Why is translation quality a critical question for the industry? How are the ways in which professionals approach TQA different to those of theorists?

2.2 Academic approaches to translation quality

Ever since translation studies has been recognized as a separate academic discipline, translation quality has been a significant focus for research. Holmes recognized from the 1970s that 'doubtless the activities of translation interpretation and evaluation will always elude the grasp of objective analysis to some extent, and so continue to reflect the intuitive, impressionist attitudes and stances of the critic' (1972/2000: 190). Dong and Lan see this assessment as valid four decades later: 'translation evaluation [. . .] remains one the most problematic areas of translation studies as a field of study' (2010: 48). Despite the difficulties, theorists continue to focus on translation quality and attempt to overcome the problems. House has called for research to move away from the danger of 'subjective, one-sided or dogmatic' judgements by using large-scale empirical studies to put forward 'intersubjectively verifiable evaluative criteria', reached through the analysis of large multilingual corpora of translated texts (1998/2001: 200). Thus far, no such large-scale research has been published. If realized, such research would still be entirely *product*-based. Examining corpora of texts, no matter how large or linguistically varied, still fails to address the need to include translation *processes* in research and resulting model(s). Others stress that 'subjectivity and randomness' are unlikely ever to be entirely absent from TQA processes, and that 'philosophical problems of meaning, interpretation, fidelity, adequacy, and acceptability' as explored by theorists including Bourdieu, Eco, Ricœur and others are beyond the scope of such models (Williams, 2004: xviii–xix). A range of approaches is therefore likely to continue to coexist in future.

Academics have grouped TQA approaches in various ways, summarized below. However, few theorists have published detailed, reproducible TQA models for human translation with an indication of the text types on which they were tested. Only four specific models, by Al-Qinai, House, Larose and Williams, are widely available. These are outlined here with particular emphasis on how far they are applicable to real-world professional contexts. Many broader approaches in translation theory also relate to translation quality, though do not provide detailed models. These ideas and research themes are finally summarized.

Theorists disagree as to how to classify approaches to TQA. For House (1998/2001: 197–200), approaches fall into three broad categories:[6] anecdotal and subjective, response-oriented and text-based. The first category, anecdotal and subjective, is the only one in which House refers to professional approaches. She implies that all approaches to TQA pre-dating the emergence of translation studies as a discipline sometime in the 1960s fit in this category; that is, those devised by 'practising translators, philosophers, philologists, writers and many others'. She views these approaches as atheoretical, not having as their aim the establishment of general principles. A later 'neo-hermeneutic' approach is finally included in this group. This approach views the 'hermeneutic interpretation of the original and the production of a translation [as] individual, creative acts that defy systematization, generalization and the development of rules' (ibid.: 197).

In House's second response-oriented category fall models based on theories of equivalence between STs and TTs, where target language readers or users of translations have their responses measured and compared to those of ST readers and users. House includes psycholinguistic and 'behaviouristic' approaches in this group, and argues their main weakness is that they all depend on the 'black box' of the human mind and reductionist criteria for assessing quality (ibid.: 198).

The 'text-based' approaches which form House's third category include those of leading theorists such as Reiss and Vermeer. Some of these approaches focus on detailed analysis and comparison of STs and TTs, whereas others focus on TTs alone. House concludes that the approach of all three groups is limited, as 'translation is simultaneously bound to the source text and to the presuppositions and conditions governing its reception in the target linguistic and cultural system. Any attempt at evaluating translations must take this basic fact as a starting point' (ibid.: 199). She proposes her own model as a way of bypassing the trap of being 'anecdotal and subjective', and incorporating aspects of response evaluation and text analysis.

Where do professional ideas about TQA fit in House's schema? Although her focus is translation studies rather than the profession, she does include references to the profession in her first category. It seems unlikely that they would fit there entirely successfully, however, particularly where real-world approaches have worked to surmount the 'subjective and anecdotal'. House states that proponents of this approach normally reject the establishment of general principles for translation quality, yet this is arguably the aim of most professional TQA, albeit on a more limited basis than theorists' attempts to establish all-encompassing models. Perhaps, then, she sees professional TQA as included in response-oriented or text-based approaches? Evidently, some elements of professional approaches are response-based (e.g. measuring reception among target user groups, testing of localized games, ICR); and some are clearly text-based (e.g. translation revision, TM maintenance). These do not cover all aspects of professional TQA, however. Where does the professional emphasis on production processes and standards sit in House's classification, for instance? Perhaps, with her fundamental insistence on theory as the prerequisite for all TQA, she believes that applied professional approaches should not qualify for inclusion at all. Alternatively, she may believe that professional approaches span two or more categories, as it is presumably possible to combine an 'anecdotal and subjective' approach with text-based TQA, for example; and her own model indeed aims to integrate two of the approaches.

Chesterman (2007: 117–46) identifies five distinct categories of TQA in academic research, of which four are relevant here (the fifth, pedagogical assessment, is restricted to translator education). The first category, retrospective assessment, focuses on 'the relation between the target text and its source text' (ibid.: 123) and is similar to House's third category of text-based assessment. Chesterman includes House's approach in this category. The second group, prospective assessment, 'looks forward from the target text to the effect this has, or is designed to have, on its readers, rather than back to the source text' (ibid.: 128) and corresponds to some degree to House's second category of response-oriented approaches. Chesterman includes in this group Nida's suggestions (1964) on 'sameness of effect' rather than 'sameness of form'. The third category, lateral assessment, is not truly present in House's schema, beyond its limited crossover with her response-oriented approaches. In this group, Chesterman includes approaches which measure translation quality by comparing translated texts with original (non-translated) parallel texts in the target language (ibid.: 133). Corpus linguistics approaches to translation evaluation fit in this category. Finally, Chesterman recognizes the role played by what he terms introspective assessment (ibid.: 136); that is, attempts to understand the decision-making process during the translation process. His categories, then, include some approaches ignored by House. They are inclusive of professional approaches, though Chesterman himself concedes that the 'view of translation being a service', which dominates in the industry, is not much discussed in academic theory (2002: 84). And again, professional models would often combine two or more of the approaches which Chesterman separates into different groups.

Williams adopts another means of classifying approaches to TQA (2004: 3–19). Unlike House and Chesterman, whose categories are based on what is included in the assessment, Williams focuses on the methodology adopted to carry it out. Also unlike House and Chesterman, he explicitly includes some professional models in his classification. He identifies only two categories of approach: models with a quantitative dimension and non-quantitative models. Within each category, he then identifies several subgroups. He finds that almost all models share a common feature: 'categorization of errors lies at the heart of each approach' (ibid.: 3).

In an apparent contrast to House, who implies that professional models fall in the 'anecdotal and subjective' category, Williams places real-world models in the 'quantitative' category. He recognizes that some professional approaches involve quality controllers or evaluators 'determining' or 'characterizing' errors or the weight accorded to quality assessment factors (ibid.: 4–8), but significantly, his account of professional methods notes that they do attempt to quantify and objectify their approach. Two theoretical approaches are also considered by Williams to have a quantitative dimension. The first is based on discourse analysis theories, though this is restricted to evaluating student translators and literary texts alone (ibid.: 9). The second 'teleological' approach, that of Canadian theorist Larose, aims at TQA being 'objective and reliable [as] the real objectives not of the author but of the translation contract issued by the client are taken into account' (ibid.: 10). Williams places almost all academic theories on TQA in his second category of 'non-quantitative' models, including those of House, Nord and Reiss. Within this two-part classification, Williams notes a divide between approaches which are 'standards-referenced' (i.e. those which establish fixed standards which must always be met; these map partly onto Chesterman's first two categories) and those which are 'criterion-referenced' (i.e. those which identify specific objectives which must be met for a given text; these map partly onto Chesterman's first category and House's text-based approaches) (ibid.: 3).

Williams' stress on the role of quantitative methods and accounting for some professional models would not necessarily, however, convince House and other theorists that such approaches are not subjective: the criteria or standards, as Williams recognizes, still require interpretation. Terms such as 'essential element' are subject to different judgements so, though errors may be quantified, a degree of subjectivity remains in identifying these and applying associated models.

Schäffner's discussion of theoretical approaches to TQA identifies two main categories. An early reliance on a 'linguistic' model of translation is presented in contrast to a broader group of later approaches (textlinguistic, pragmatic, discourse, functionalist) (1998b: 1–3). In the linguistic model, 'the TT is compared to the ST in order to see whether the TT is an accurate, correct, precise, faithful or true reproduction of the ST' (ibid.: 1). This seems to be linked to the text-based category identified by House, though the ambiguity of terms such as 'accurate' also associates it with her anecdotal and subjective category. The second, broader category of later theoretical approaches, though not defined in relation to TQA in any detail in Schäffner's account, apply 'partly different criteria' to TQA. The significance of their contribution is that 'they have changed the focus from translation as text reproduction to text *production*' (ibid.); that is, they introduce situational/cultural aspects, as stressed in the various categories focusing on translation reception.

Lauscher also divides theoretical approaches to TQA into two broad groups: equivalence-based approaches and functional approaches. Equivalence serves as 'a descriptive and prescriptive category for defining the relationship between source and target texts, and for distinguishing translations and translating from other types of texts and text-producing activities' (Lauscher, 2000: 151). This group would therefore map on to others' text-based categories, but might also address the processes involved in translation and Chesterman's lateral assessment category. Such approaches include those of Nida, Reiss and others. Lauscher's functional approaches are closer to House's 'response-based' or Chesterman's 'prospective assessment' categories, being based on 'the assumption that translating is not so much determined by the source text as by factors relating to the target culture' (ibid.: 156). Her categories only cover academic approaches, as she sees a clear divide between these and real-world application: 'scholarly approaches to translation evaluation have not yet been able to provide help for practical quality assessment because they do not account for the reality of translating and translations' (2000: 158).

No translation scholars have previously suggested classifying approaches to translation quality according to whether they are theoretical or applied, where applied means not just tested on a few selected cases to measure a model's strengths and weaknesses, but applied on a regular basis in the real world. On the whole, this is because professional approaches are either excluded from translation theory or given no more than cursory attention, with a few notable exceptions such as Larose and Williams. Yet the approaches in industry are markedly different to those of theorists, often attempting to integrate aspects of translation quality which are excluded in the theorists' narrower focus on TQA alone. A new and useful way to classify approaches might be precisely to separate those which are purely academic and those which are designed, adopted and refined based on ongoing applied professional experience. The remainder of this chapter takes just such an approach. Summaries of the leading *theoretical* approaches to TQA which have dominated in translation studies are presented first, then professional, *applied* approaches are outlined in Section 2.3.

Given the strong focus on translation quality in research, there are surprisingly few published models. Theorists have instead tended to critique others' (sometimes inferred) approaches or tease out what various translation theories seem to imply for TQA. Others have restricted their focus to particular aspects such as translation revision. The four detailed TQA models presented in academic research thus far (by House, Larose, Al-Qinai and Williams, in chronological order) are outlined first. Next, broader theoretical approaches to translation quality are summarized. Though none of these contributes an applied TQA model, they illustrate which aspects of quality have been important for translation studies, and some contribute practical suggestions for particular aspects of TQA.

2.2.1 House's (revisited) model of TQA

The foremost TQA model in translation studies is found in the work of German scholar, Juliane House, since the 1970s. Her approach has, of course, been refined in reaction to feedback and so has evolved somewhat over the decades (House, 1997: 101). The first summary is based on the original model, then an account of her updated approach is given.

House based her model on pragmatic theories of language use and research from other disciplines (Halliday's functional and systemic theories, register theory, stylistics, discourse analysis). The concept of equivalence is central: 'translation is constituted by a "double-binding" relationship both to its source and to the communicative conditions of the receiving linguaculture, and it is the concept of equivalence which captures this relationship' (ibid.: 29). She stresses two possible approaches to translation: *overt* (where 'the function of the translation is to enable its readers access to the function of the original in its original linguacultural setting through another language') and *covert* (where 'equivalence is sought in and via the vessel of the new language for the function that the original has in its linguacultural setting'). In other words, covert translations are not intended to be read as translations at all. A key concept for translation studies drawn from House's work is that of the *cultural filter*. This is an 'empirically established [filter] to adapt the target text to the communicative preferences of the target audience' (Lauscher, 2000: 153).

How does this work in practice? In her account of the 'operation of the [original] model' (ibid.: 43–65), House outlines three stages:

1   *Analysis of ST and Statement of Function.* House analyses her chosen ST to identify key features across five areas: *medium, participation, social role relationship, social attitude* and *province.* These are drawn from Crystal and Davy's system (1969: 66), which breaks the 'notion of situation' down into analysable features. House presents many of these features as 'self-explanatory' and

only elucidates on those which she sees as 'need[ing] explanation' (ibid.: 38), but her understanding would seem to be as outlined below.

Medium can be simple or complex, and in House's model refers to whether a text is 'writing to be spoken as if not written, to be spoken, not necessarily to be spoken, or to be read as if heard' (ibid.: 40).

Participation can be a 'monologue' or 'dialogue', each of which can be simple or complex; a ST may also be some mixture of both. As an example of 'complex participation', House suggests a 'text produced by only one person (a "monologue") [which] nonetheless contains features which would normally be assumed to characterize a dialogue, e.g. imperative forms or question tags' (ibid.: 39).

Social role relationship is House's term for the relationship between ST 'addresser' [i.e. author(s)] and 'addressees' [i.e. readers, users or audience]. This can be 'symmetrical' (based on a relationship of equals) or 'asymmetrical' (where there is some relationship of authority).

Social attitude relates to levels of formality. House recognizes five levels of formality: frozen, formal, consultative, casual and intimate (ibid.: 41), though she gives little detail as to how she assigns a particular level to a text or part of text.

Province is a very broad category, referring to 'the text producer's occupational and professional activity', 'the field or topic of the text in its widest sense of "area of operation" of the language activity' and 'details of the text production as these can be deduced from the text itself' (ibid.: 42), including register.

Within this five-part analysis, relevant 'dimensions of language use' are considered, such as the syntactic, lexical and textual 'means' employed. House also considers the language *user* (e.g. geographical origin and social class of the ST 'addresser', time of the text's production).

After these steps, an overall summary of the 'statement of function' of the ST is provided.

2 *ST and TT comparison*. House next compares the ST with the TT across the five dimensions of medium, participation, social role relationship, social attitude and province. She analyses the TT and compares it to the ST to identify errors. Errors can be 'overtly erroneous' (breaches of the target language system, mismatch in 'denotative meaning') or 'covertly erroneous'. The second type of error refers to any 'mismatch' between the five dimensions of the ST and TT, as a translation text should 'fulfil the requirement of a

dimensional [and] a functional match' (ibid.: 45). House points out that 'overtly erroneous' errors have traditionally attracted far more attention in TQA, as it is more straightforward to identify these. 'Covertly erroneous' errors or mismatches between the dimensions 'demand a much more qualitative-descriptive, in-depth analysis' (ibid.) and have thus been neglected, in her view.

3 *Statement of quality.* Following the detailed comparison of ST and TT and identification of errors and mismatches, House produces an overall 'statement of quality' for the given translation.

House has argued that criticisms of her original model fall in four categories (ibid.: 101): the nature of the analytical categories and the terminology used; lack of intersubjective verifiability of the analyses; the 'limits of translatability' and the distinction between 'overt' and 'covert' translation. House revises her model to address those criticisms she felt to be justified, notably by adapting her terminology and reviewing the number of 'dimensions', and incorporates research which appeared in the decades after her first version appeared. The revisited model also has three stages:

1 *Analysis of the original.* The revised terminology and presentation are more simple and direct, building on Hallidayan linguistics and focusing on *field*, *tenor*, *mode* and *genre*, instead of the earlier medium, participation, social role relationship, social attitude and province.

Field includes the field of activity of the ST, topic, content and subject matter.

Tenor describes 'participants', the addresser and addressees and any social relationship between them, including such aspects as the addresser's 'temporal, geographical [and] social provenance' (ibid.: 108–9). Instead of the old five 'levels of formality', only three 'styles' are now used: formal, consultative and informal.

Mode includes both the old medium and participation, that is, the 'channel' (spoken, written) and the former monologue/dialogue distinction.

Genre is not defined in detail, but presented as '"in between" the register characterization and the textual function' (ibid.: 110) and used 'in its everyday sense, [with] some restrictions' (ibid.: 159).

After the original is analysed in these four dimensions, an overall summary of the 'statement of function' of the ST is again provided.

2 *Comparison of original and translation.* Again, House analyses the translation and compares it to the original, looking for errors and mismatches. She considers these in the four new 'dimensions' of field, tenor, mode and genre.

3 *Statement of quality.* Following the detailed comparison of original and translation and identification of errors and mismatches, House again produces an overall 'statement of quality' for the given translation.

House's original model (1977) was tested on eight pairs of STs and TTs: 'a scientific text, an economic text, a journalistic article, a tourist information brochure, [. . .], an excerpt from a sermon, a political speech, a moral anecdote, and a dialogue taken from a comedy' (ibid.: 48). All STs were in English and the TTs were in German. The revisited model was 'implemented' on four text pairs of STs and TTs: a 'children's book', an 'excerpt from an autobiography by a Nobel prize winning scientist', a section of Benjamin's 'famous essay' on the discipline of translation studies and a passage from a controversial history text and its even more controversial translation, Goldhagen's *Hitler's Willing Executioners*. Three of these originals were again in English and translated into German; Benjamin's original was in German and translated into English.

Besides the criticisms levelled at House's model by academics,[7] professional translators and those performing TQA in the real world are likely to raise other issues (though it should be recognized that practitioners are not her target audience). First, the sample on which she tests the models is restricted, focussing on only one language pair and a total of 12 original texts, 11 of them translated in the same direction (EN–DE) and all of them short.[8] How far is House's model applicable when TQA is being performed across dozens of languages, on STs of many hundreds of thousands of words which evolve as the translators work, where the original is likely to have been composed by multiple unnamed authors and updated repeatedly over some years? Second, few of the 12 STs chosen to test the model are representative of those on which professional translators typically earn their living; nor do they include complex text types and formats with inherent challenges for quality, such as websites or software. Third, as House seems to acknowledge, the time needed to apply the model makes it unworkable in the professional context. She leaves future 'detailed practical realization and empirical testing' to 'experienced translation teachers' rather than to practising translators, who might have been assumed to be the natural test bed for her approach (ibid.: 167). Fourth, House works from originals and their translations with little indication as to how much access she had to the commissioner's brief, the context of production of the original or the conditions in which the translation was carried out. Her deductions about 'addresser' and 'addressees' do not seem to be based on concrete information about the translation process (e.g. deadline; tools and resources available) or client specifications, both of which are central to professional approaches. House does not suggest she had contact with the original authors or translators of the texts. Rather, her outline of their 'personal (emotional or intellectual) stance' and other such attributes seems to be inferred from her reading of the STs and TTs. Finally, the purpose of House's model is to find faults. Although she does comment briefly on how far the ST and TT match or are 'functionally equivalent', her emphasis is on spotting mismatches, whereas the professional emphasis is on approving a translation as an adequate or acceptable product. Related to this, a feature commonly found (and valued) in professional TQA is where a translator has improved on a poor or inaccurate original, for example by correcting figures or enhancing clarity in user instructions in the target language. House's model would presumably penalize professional translators for such improvements by categorizing them as mismatches between original and translation.

2.2.2 Larose's teleological model for translation assessment

Canadian theorist Larose first outlined this approach to TQA in his *Théories contemporaines de la traduction* (1987; this discussion is based on the 2nd edition from 1989). While most of the text is a survey of translation theories intended for pedagogical purposes, with no particular focus on issues of translation quality, the latter third is devoted to a discussion of TQA and includes a detailed model. His approach was then further developed in a series of articles. The objective or purpose of any translation is central to assessing its quality (1994: 362). Larose is unusual among theorists in his acknowledgement of broader aspects of translation, beyond textual comparison alone. His focus on the objective of translations means he recognizes that the context in which translation occurs, client brief and so on are essential factors in translation quality, though he nonetheless fails to include most of these in his detailed model. He divides his overall approach into two domains: 'extra-textual' ('l'ensemble de facteurs qui exercent des pressions sur le textuel') and 'textual elements' (1989: 222). Although Larose's account of extra-textual elements does not directly include such aspects as translator competence or, unsurprisingly, the use of today's electronic tools, his attempt to broaden his model to embrace extra-textual factors remains pioneering. For example, he acknowledges the potential influence on TQA of factors relating to the *assessors* themselves, noting that such factors as the age, gender or level of experience of the assessor may all have an influence, as will the conditions in which TQA is carried out and the information at the assessor's disposal (1998: 163).

Larose moves away from 'naïve' debates on defining good or bad translation by focusing on assessing 'efficacité' (1987: 362–3), that is, how far the translator's purpose matches the original author's intention, rather than the preferences of the assessor (ibid.: 288). With this in mind, he discusses the translation process at some length. He identifies three main stages which are relevant: *interpretation* ('procès', whereby the translator endeavours to understand the meanings of the source text), *production* ('pratique', at which point the translator 'pins down' and communicates one meaning) and final *product* ('produit', the translated text which can be evaluated) (1994: 362). Unlike House and Al-Qinai, he stresses the importance of diversity, rather than claiming his model is applicable to all contexts. A range of possible approaches to TQA is valid and likely to endure: there are different ways of translating and different purposes for translations, so different ways of assessing translations (1989: 196).

How does the teleological approach work in practice? This is not always as clear as in the models presented by House and Williams, especially as his later work does not relate the approach directly to translation. For example, in a 1989 article, he presents a fairly detailed grid approach to assessing product quality, but the products he chooses as test cases are not translations but different types of cars and a particular model of skis (ibid.: 372–3). Larose's later discussions of quality therefore offer only implied approaches, with no detailed stages, sample texts or translation-specific criteria, so the model might be applied, replicated or criticized.

Larose's focus in TQA where he does apply a model (1987) is on the text itself, where he differentiates between three different levels, placed in a hierarchical structure:

1 *Microstructural*. The lowest level, this concerns 'forms of expression', graphic, syntactic and lexical elements, at the sentence or sub-sentence level.

2 *Macrostructural*. This level refers to the semantic structure of discourse content, above the sentence level, and includes cohesion.

3 *Superstructural*. The highest level, this refers to the overall structure of discourse, including the narrative or argumentation structure.

The approach also involves identifying extra-textual factors relating to the translation's purpose, notably overall client or other requirements which the translator is aiming to fulfil. These are, however, gleaned from a reading of the ST and TT, rather than through access to the actual client brief or directly questioning the translator. The ST and TT are then evaluated separately in relation to these three levels, bearing in mind the overall 'objectives' of the author and translator. The two higher super- and macrostructural levels apply to the narrative and argument organization, text type and function, and overall structure. Larose's hierarchy is then used to weight translation errors. The functional or structural importance of any error is key: an error's significance is increased by its 'niveau de pertinence dans le texte' [level of importance/relevance in the text], and by the level at which it occurs, with microstructural errors of less significance than those at the two higher levels (1987: 237). Larose presents his grids for reuse or evaluation at the end of his discussion. Although he states elsewhere that his main interest lies in translation assessment for professional contexts (1998: 164), he tests his approach on classical literary translations, from Aristophanes' *Lysistrata*.

Aspects of Larose's approach would be welcomed in the professional context. His strong emphasis on the context in which translation and TQA are performed in the real world is unusual in theory, and he demonstrates sound understanding of professional constraints and the working environment. Larose acknowledges the professional emphasis on producing translations which read like original target language texts. His model allows for cases such as translations improving original texts. He recognizes that the number of criteria for assessing a translation must be restricted if any TQA approach is to be viable in practice (1998: 175). Unlike some approaches where the emphasis is on finding errors or mismatches between ST and TT, he stresses that TQA must not be confused with translation revision: TQA is an overall statement of a translation's quality and can be positive, rather than finding fault (ibid.: 166).

However, practitioners would be likely to question various aspects of Larose's approach. Although he offers a detailed account of the context in which translation and TQA take place, his own model does not really account for these factors or accord them much significance in rating translations. The focus on STs and TTs omits to include real-world client specifications or the actual working conditions in which translations were produced. Larose follows a similar approach to House in that he works from the text up, rather than having access to the conditions of production. His later work provides no clear detailed model which might be tested or applied, and where he himself applies his earlier model, he does so to the translation of classical literary texts in one language pair rather than to professional translations. He suggests that his approach could be adapted to be applicable to professional contexts, but does not do so. He sometimes uses rather negative terminology when discussing professional translation in comparison to literature or classical texts, contrasting the 'canonical work' with the 'pâle texte utilitaire', for instance (1994: 362). Finally, though he recognizes repeatedly that a crucial factor for TQA models in the real world is that they must be efficient and able to be applied without requiring unreasonable amounts of time or resources (1998: 175), his approach is itself time-consuming and not sufficiently clearly related to professional translation to be applied in its original form.

2.2.3 *Al-Qinai's 'empirical, eclectic' model for TQA*

A later attempt to devise and test a TQA model is found in the work of Al-Qinai (2000). Al-Qinai himself categorizes his model as 'eclectic', basing his approach on a textual analysis which takes account of a wide range of features, specifically 'textual typology, formal correspondence, thematic coherence, reference cohesion, pragmatic equivalence and lexico-syntactic properties' (ibid.: 497). While he acknowledges some theorists' concerns regarding attempts to evaluate translation as a product rather than translating as a process (i.e. by analytic comparison of ST and TT with no consideration of 'the procedures undertaken by the translator to resolve problems' (Hatim & Mason, 1990: 3)), he nonetheless bases his model on just such a comparison of STs and TTs, rather than integrating translation processes or information on the context for production.

The theoretical underpinnings of Al-Qinai's model are also eclectic. He draws on House's original model and approach, and states that empirical objectivity rather than subjective impressionism should be the goal of theoretical approaches, including his own (Al-Qinai, 2000: 498). He differentiates his approach from that of House to some extent, however, by distancing himself from theories of equivalence. His preference is to evaluate the 'adequacy of a translation rather than the degree of equivalence' (ibid.), and this is to be achieved through a consideration of 'textual/functional (or pragmatic) compatibility (i.e. quality of linguistic conversion)' (ibid.: 499). To do this, Al-Qinai identifies seven sets of 'parametres' (sic) which he believes to be suggested in the work of other theorists (Hatim & Mason, House, Newmark & Steiner). These are:

1   *Textual typology (province) and tenor*

    Here, Al-Qinai includes the linguistic and narrative structure of the ST and TT, and the textual function, which might be 'didactic, informative, instructional, persuasive, evocative' (ibid.).

2   *Formal correspondence*

    By this, he implies a comparison of ST and TT in terms of presentation (e.g. length, 'arrangement', paragraph division, punctuation).

3   *Coherence of thematic structure*

    How consistent are the ST and TT in terms of 'thematic development'?

4   *Cohesion*

    Here, Al-Qinai implies a focus on the TT: how far is a translation 'out of focus' due to inappropriate reproduction of source language 'rhetoric and sequence of thought'?

5   *Text-pragmatic (dynamic) equivalence*

    Does the TT achieve a similar 'intended effect' as the ST (e.g. through 'fulfillment of reader expectations')?

6 *Lexical properties*

This category covers register and linguistic features (e.g. jargon, idioms, collocations). ST and TT are compared to establish translation strategies where 'style shifts' are indicated due to differences between source and target languages (ibid.: 511).

7 *Grammatical/syntactic equivalence*

ST and TT are compared with regard to word order, agreement (number, gender, person), etc.

Al-Qinai offers no justification for his selection of these seven parameters, nor does he explain why they are essential for an empirical evaluation of translation quality, whereas other features can safely be excluded. Instead, he illustrates how he intends for these parameters to be applied by presenting a sample textual analysis of two pairs of original English texts and their Arabic translations, taken from Baker's coursebook on translation, *In Other Words* (1992: 71, 80). The first is a 1989 advertisement for the Austin Rover Metro car and the second an undated advert for the companion Metro Sport model. Each ST is of fewer than 150 words. Al-Qinai states that the purpose of applying the model to these texts is to 'test its viability [. . .] with the aim of highlighting points of correspondence and divergence' (2000: 497).

How does Al-Qinai's model work in practice? He runs through each of the seven parameters in turn, defining his understanding of each concept with reference to translation theory and then comparing the ST with the TT to note points of correspondence and divergence in approach and assumed effect. Throughout, there is a particular focus on 'style shifts' or linguistic gaps between written English and Arabic, with translation choices frequently explained by generalizations (e.g. 'compared to Arabic, English generally prefers to present information in relatively small chunks using a wide variety of conjunctions and a highly developed punctuation system to signal breaks' (ibid.: 507)). Several tables are used to illustrate claims (e.g. he counts the type and frequency of cohesive devices in the ST and TT). Frequent short quotes from ST and TT are given, though the Arabic is rarely presented alongside an English back-translation or gist, making it impossible for non-Arabic speakers to assess specific judgements or claims made in the textual analysis. Following the detailed consideration of each of the seven parameters in relation to ST and TT, Al-Qinai presents a 'holistic view' as a final assessment (ibid.: 516). In this, he summarizes six main points of divergence and adaptation between the original and its Arabic translation. He does not rate the translation as a whole according to any scale, or even on a pass/fail basis, but makes it clear that this was not his goal:

> Instead of passing sweeping value-judgements on the overall quality of [the] TT, it would be more sensible to screen the points of equivalence

and the points of divergence at various levels of analysis in line with the model we've proposed in this study. (ibid.)

In his conclusion, Al-Qinai stresses that 'reception of [the] TT is the ultimate assessment of quality' and proposes that any translation for 'public purposes' ought to be subject to market research to check that the ST writer and TT recipients have their expectations fulfilled (ibid.: 517). He recognizes that follow-up studies are indicated, to test his approach on a greater variety of texts, language pairs and text types and to establish responses of 'monolingual and bilingual "critical judges"' to pairs of STs and TTs (ibid.).

Al-Qinai includes the translation profession in his model more than House does, with recognition, for instance, that a 'shoddy poorly-written, poorly-structured ST' ought not generally to be translated as a 'shoddy poor TT' (ibid.: 498). His use of real-world translations to test his model also points to a concern that his approach be applicable to practitioners' work, rather than of interest for translator training or theory alone. His focus is also more positive than that of House: he aims to establish points of convergence between ST and TT, as much as to indicate any mismatches.

However, Al-Qinai's approach is likely to attract professional criticism. Tested on a very limited sample of fewer than 300 source words in only one language pair/direction, there was no access to information about production of the original text or translation process (brief, deadline, working conditions, tools and resources used), nor any attempt to question the translator(s) regarding specific choices or client requirements, which are likely to have been particularly detailed and stringent in this domain. The texts were already dated when the model was applied to them, having been published 11 years beforehand, something which is significant in automotive advertising, where expectations move on quickly. More seriously, for the professional context, the time required to apply the model in its current format makes it unworkable. For under 300 ST words, Al-Qinai takes over 16 pages to evaluate the main aspects of his seven parameters. House provides clear back-translations throughout, so her judgements can themselves be judged by readers, but Al-Qinai omits to do this for most examples. Deductions are made regarding translators' motivations with no access to information about how clients might have altered the TT post-translation, perhaps following just the sort of market research for which he calls. No overall statement of adequacy is given for the translation (admittedly, this is not his aim), but this is what the profession, and clients, need. Several other important questions remain unanswered. First, are the categories weighted or of equal importance? If a translation performs strongly on some parameters but not others, how is it to be judged overall? Second, if a translation contains more 'convergence' than divergence, is that sufficient to declare it acceptable? Presumably not, as Al-Qinai states in his conclusion that the only true judgement of translation quality is based on reception of the TT. This begs an obvious question for practitioners: why apply this model at all if the measure of a translation's success is market research or how the translation is received by sample users? Why should commissioners or clients not simply move straight to those tests and omit this kind of evaluation altogether?

2.2.4 Williams' argumentation-centred approach to TQA (ARTRAQ)

Williams draws on argumentation theory, a branch of discourse analysis, to develop a framework for TQA intended to complement existing 'microtextual' approaches (2004: xvii). Williams sees professional models as microtextual because he believes they 'tend to focus on discrete lexical and morphosyntactic units at the subsentence level and to be applied to short passages of texts' (ibid.). His aim is to build on the approach of theorists, including House and Larose, whose models try to 'enhance TQA validity and reliability [. . .] by integrating a macrotextual, discourse (textological or text-linguistic) perspective, along with relevant aspects of pragmatics, into the assessment process' (ibid.). His approach is distinctive because it aims to extend the work of other theorists who, as we have seen, typically address 'journalistic and literary documents in a student-training context' rather than 'instrumental translation in a production context' (ibid.: xviii) – that is, professional translation.

Williams' approach involves analysing an ST and TT to assess the 'transfer of argument'. In his view, this necessarily broadens the usual professional approach to the 'macrotextual' level, involving examination of 'the messages conveyed in the text, and of the reasoning on which they are based' (ibid.). Williams argues this can address concerns around determining any acceptability threshold, that is, the level of errors which can be tolerated in a given translation. His model focuses on the relationship between 'level of seriousness of error and full-text analysis, using argumentation theory to determine what is important in the messages conveyed by the text and defining "major error" accordingly' (ibid.). Unlike House, Larose or Al-Qinai, Williams applies his model with reference to translations produced in an institutional context. With Larose, he explicitly acknowledges the standard professional goal of producing 'a translation that reads as though it was in fact originated in the target language' (ibid.: xix).

How does this work in practice? Williams runs through his original approach and its theoretical underpinnings, provides definitions of key terms such as 'major error' and then devises a preliminary TQA grid, which is tested on four pairs of STs and TTs: two Canadian government texts on statistics and energy, and two criminology and legal texts. Adopting a markedly more realistic scenario than House, Larose or Al-Qinai, Williams uses unrevised translations of varying lengths, submitted by freelance translators to real-world clients. His choice of text types is also deliberate, with two texts of an 'argumentative, even polemical' nature (ibid.: 69) and two statistical texts with more factual, less polemical content, in order to test whether his model is valid for texts with no obvious reliance on argumentation.

Williams' approach has four stages:

1 *Analysis of the original.* Each ST is analysed to establish its 'argument schema, arrangement and organizational relations' to identify what part(s) of the document contain 'essential messages' (ibid.: 73).

2 *Analysis of the translated text.* Each TT is examined without reference to the ST to assess its 'overall coherence', determine whether overall arrangement is preserved or appropriately modified, and establish any problems relating to readability or acceptability as a target language text. Williams points out that this procedure is used in industry, with the Ontario Government Translation Services assessing TTs in this way, for instance.

3 *Comparative assessment.* The next stage involves comparing ST and TT in relation to 'argumentation parameters' identified as important by Williams. These are argument schema/arrangement/ organizational relations; propositional functions/conjunctives/other inference indicators; types of arguments; figures of speech and narrative strategy (ibid.: 73–4). Williams provides definitions of each of these parameters and illustrates their relevance for TQA.

4 *Overall quality statement.* The final stage involves producing a statement of the overall argumentation-centred TQA, and comparing the results of this with existing real-world 'quantitative-microtextual' TQA approaches such as SICAL. Williams uses the acronym ARTRAQ for his scheme, though provides no definition (presumably ARgumentation-centred TRAnslation Quality?).

After this test, Williams presents the changes and refinements he feels are indicated to optimize his model. He investigates the possibility of incorporating a 'rating scale' in his model, then provides a detailed appendix with a sample TQA, clearly showing how his ARTRAQ grid-based approach might be applied in practice (ibid.: 153–7). This includes a return to the standard industry QC distinction between critical, major and minor defects, but here, these are defined in relation to the 'usability of the translation [where a defect] impairs the central reasoning of the text' (ibid.: 133), rather than less clearly defined notions such as accuracy or fidelity. Williams concludes with a 'mathematical model' (ibid.: 139), which he intends to become a useful criterion-referenced tool and quality standard. He proposes four standards in his grade scheme:

1 *Publication standard.* The text accurately renders all components of the argument schema and meets the requirements for all target-language parameters and other selected core and field- or use-specific parameters. It contains no critical or major defects.

2 *Information standard.* The text acccurately renders all components of the argument schema and meets requirements for selected core and field- or use-specific parameters. It contains no critical defects.

3 *Minimum standard.* The text accurately renders all components of the argument schema. It contains no critical defects.

4 *Substandard.* The text fails to render the argument schema (contains at least one critical defect) and/or does not meet requirements for one or more core or field- or use-specific parameters.

The approach is presented as 'modular', with the option to add other grades or standards, according to client needs or further analysis of specific text types:

> For example, if it were determined that correct terminology, not grammar, style and usage, was the key parameter for certain scientific or technical texts, then the quality of the text exemplifying the 'scientific/technical translation standard' would have to be defined accordingly. (ibid.: 145).

Williams addresses the translation profession more consistently and directly than other theorists. He asserts real-world applicability as an objective for his model, claiming his final version represents 'an approach that covers all the significant elements in instrumental translation and places emphasis on quality according to translation function and end use' (ibid.: 152). The desire for practical applicability is also apparent in his choice of actual professional translations as samples to test his model, and in his recognition of the need for a scalable, flexible approach in different contexts (ibid.). Professionals are likely to welcome his adoption of a grid summarizing results, which is quickly grasped and offers a clear overall translation rating. He addresses many professional concerns, notably in his recognition of criticality, attempts at objective definitions and objective application of assessment criteria, acceptance of the importance of standards and new approach to contentious terms such as major error. The argumentation-centred method is also sufficiently flexible to allow for cases where translations improve on the ST without penalizing translators for mismatches.

However, practitioners are likely to question or reject aspects of Williams' approach. Like both House and Al-Qinai, his focus remains on the translation product with little or no consideration of the processes involved, context of production or access to the producers, whether for the ST or translation. Williams himself acknowledges these limits: his model 'links assessment to the objectives of the ST author, the target text, and the client, *where these objectives are known or can be extrapolated from the texts in question*' (ibid.: 129; my emphasis). His focus on texts alone, rather than broader aspects of translation quality, also means that key aspects of professional approaches such as translator competence, workflow and tools are left unaddressed.

Williams is unusual in his selection of real professional texts on which to test his model and some of these are substantially longer than those used by other theorists (e.g. one ST of 11,000 words). However, these are still limited in number and text type, and again, only one language pair (French–English) is assessed. Williams states that his translation samples were chosen for their ability to illustrate the applicability of his model to technical texts which might not appear to be based on argumentation or 'polemic' (ibid.: 69), but he nonetheless only considers whole texts with fixed linear structures. Does argument structure matter equally for all text types found in professional translation? If not, how should practitioners decide when to apply this model? How far is the argumentation-centred approach valid in the modern professional context of translators working in teams on subsections of texts, sometimes with no access to the surrounding context; or to translations of stand-alone segments and frequent updates, as in the localization industry? How might the model be applied where the ST evolves, perhaps over decades, with multiple ST authors translated by many translators, sharing resources such as translation memories over time? Is the model still relevant when texts sent for translation may be authored in content management systems, for later extraction of subtexts to be used in different formats independent of the original argument structure? How can it be applied to online translations, which may be accessed in a variety of sequences depending on individual users' decisions as to where to click or navigate, or to the translation of computer games, where both source and translated material may appear in a vast number of permutations of combinations or orders?

Applying this model is again time-consuming, something of critical concern in the professional context. Williams recognizes this, but contends that actual 'assessment in the field would drop much of the explanation and detail given' for testing purposes (ibid.: 73–4). He claims that 'the weighting of parameters has enabled us to generate an aggregate TQA without requiring too many calculations,' (ibid.: 150) but this is of course a subjective assessment. Professional users would need to be convinced that the model was at least as time-efficient as existing procedures, or that it brought sufficient additional advantages for quality and ROI to justify switching to the argumentation-centred approach. Also of concern to many in the industry would be Williams' observation that TQA 'would ideally entail detailed examination of all passages containing key elements of the argument schema', as serious defects might otherwise be missed, no matter how competent the translator (ibid.: 134). Williams thus seems to suggest that sampling is not appropriate, however long or short the text; or at least, that if sampling is to take place, this should be on the basis of the argument structure and content rather than other parameters. He recognizes that 'it is true that this does not necessarily make for efficiency. It *may*, however, obviate the need to assess the whole translation' (ibid.: 151; my italics). Conversely, it may, of course, imply a need *to* assess the whole translation, depending on the argument structure found in the initial analysis.

Two chief areas for concern are likely to dominate professional reactions, though. First, is Williams justified in replacing linguistic or 'microtextual' features with argumentation as the main criterion on which to assess translations? Even if both sets of features are combined in some way, as he implies in his revised model, is this important or relevant for all translation jobs? If argumentation is such a significant factor, why have so few real-world approaches thus far emphasized it? The second issue which is likely to cause alarm in the professional context is that all four test texts are judged 'Substandard' when his revised ARTRAQ model is applied to them (ibid.: 147). This might mean that all four sample translations were indeed inadequate, though two had been judged 'Satisfactory' when the original model was applied (ibid.: 124). It could instead mean that few, if any, translations are likely to meet the requisite standard across all features in the ARTRAQ model, which would raise professional concerns as to excessive rigour. Williams does not present revised translations to demonstrate how the original STs might be adapted to attain the higher quality levels in his model, or indicate how long such revision would be likely to take. No attempt is made to ascertain whether clients or end-users would find such revision or ultimate quality levels essential or useful, again raising concerns over the efficiency and viability of the model in practice.

2.2.5 *Other theoretical approaches to translation quality*

The models devised by House, Larose, Al-Qinai and Williams are unusual in translation studies because they have been tested. Each is presented in sufficient detail to be replicated or evaluated by others, and provides details of how sample translations were assessed. Many other translation theorists have also offered suggestions as to how TQA ought to be carried out, or have teased out the implications of the foremost translation theories for translation evaluation. However, these other approaches have either not presented detailed models or tested their suggestions, or have been explicitly directed at the training of translators rather than application to 'real' translations. The leading examples of these contributions to translation studies research are now outlined.

An early theorist to focus on TQA was Reiss, whose ideas were first outlined in 1971[9] and have had a wider influence in translation studies than the 'tested' models outlined above. Drawing on theories of equivalence, she proposes a two-step approach to TQA (Lauscher, 2000: 152):

1 Analysis of the TT to evaluate the 'appropriateness of target language use'.
2 Comparison of ST and TT to establish the degree of equivalence between these.

A translation is good for Reiss if it achieves 'optimum equivalence', that is,

> considering the linguistic and situational context, the linguistic and stylistic level and the intention of the author, target text and target text units have the same 'value' as the text unit in the source language. (1971: 11–12; cited in Lauscher, 2000: 151; translation by Lauscher)

Reiss states her aim is to move away from the sort of anecdotal and subjective approach later criticized by House, yet many of her key terms have been criticized for depending on just such a subjective interpretation. Lauscher points out that defining 'optimum equivalence' is contentious, for instance (ibid.: 152).

Reiss's text-based approach involves deducing the translator's intent and determining the translation strategy by working backwards from the ST and TT, rather than through access to the translation process or direct contact with the translator. She proposes a 'comprehensive, systematic model of text analysis for both translation and translation evaluation' (ibid.) and, like Larose and Williams, argues that word- or sentence-level comparison of ST and TT is insufficient. She also integrates the macrotextual level and focuses on the text's overall function. The text type of the ST is the most important variable (2000: 114). Reiss also includes 'extra-linguistic determinants' in her approach, that is, the conditions which determine translation decisions, though these are again gleaned from an analysis of the text rather than direct access to the translator or process. In her view, there are always subjective limits to translation criticism; she sees both translation and TQA as hermeneutic, subjective processes. As House points out, 'exactly how language functions and source text types can be determined, and at what level of delicacy, is left unexplained' (1998/2001: 198). Reiss's later work with Hans Vermeer (1984) further emphasizes the purpose or *Skopos* of the translation and develops the concept of adequacy in translation where equivalence is not possible or appropriate. No detailed explanation of how this would work in practice is supplied, however, leading many later theorists to criticize their approach. For instance, House stresses the failure to indicate how exactly the *Skopos* is to be assessed, or how to determine in practical terms whether a translation is adequate or equivalent (1998/2001: 198–9).

Nord built on Reiss's approach, proposing an important model for text analysis based on function and purpose (1991). Nord sees her approach as applicable to professional as well as literary translation or translator training, though her principal concern – and the rationale for the book – is the last of these (1991: 2). She suggests STs be analysed in detail prior to translation by asking 76 questions, so the function of the texts can be determined (this would become 'largely automatic' in the professional context, though (Pym, 2010: 48)). Nord grades translations in relation to the purpose of the translation 'initiator' and that of the TT. Her approach is again text-based, but with the focus above the word or sentence level. The text as a whole (macro level) 'must be regarded as the crucial criteria for translation criticism' (Nord, 1991: 166). Unlike House, Nord recognizes that a professional TT might have a different *Skopos* than the related ST. She refers to this as 'instrumental' translation, where the end-user may not be 'conscious of reading or hearing a text which, in a different form, was used in a different communicative action' (ibid.: 73). Analyses of three sample texts and their translations illustrate how her model might be applied, but Nord concludes that none of the translated texts would pass: they all fail to 'meet the requirements set by text function and recipient orientation' (ibid.: 231), something which would again cause concern in the professional context. Her approach to analysis has been criticized for lack of precision in its potential application for TQA purposes, with Williams asking how she would produce an overall assessment from specific comparisons, 'particularly where her judgement is based on the nature of the errors, not their number' (2004: 13), for instance. Its exhaustive set of parameters and features has been particularly questioned, notably with regard to analysis of the ST. For Pym, 'Nord cannot be accused of having left much out. The problem is rather that she has put everything in' (1993: 186).

The work of Reiss, Vermeer and Nord is frequently grouped with that of other theorists under the heading of functionalist approaches to TQA. Schäffner sees this set of approaches as moving translation assessment from rating translations as 'good' to seeing them as 'functionally appropriate' (1998b: 1). Although they differ in emphasis or detail, they are united by the belief that 'the purpose of the TT is the most important criterion in any translation' (ibid.: 2). Also associated with this set of approaches is another German theorist, Hönig; again, his focus is mainly on pedagogical approaches to TQA rather than the profession (1998: 15).

A closely related focus for theory in relation to translation quality has been the concept of translation norms. Drawing on sociological and philosophical approaches, theorists have pointed to norms as a potentially more positive way to consider translation quality. For Nida, the translator is, famously, 'severely criticized if he makes a mistake, but only faintly praised when he succeeds' (1964: 155). Recognizing the norms operating in translation in given contexts allows evaluators to move away from the idea of translation quality as simply the absence of errors (Chesterman & Wagner, 2002: 89). The theorist most closely associated with this focus in translation studies has been Toury, whose general definition is as follows (1999: 15):

> Norms have long been regarded as the translation of general values or ideas shared by a group – as to what is conventionally right and wrong, adequate and inadequate – into performance instructions appropriate for and applicable to particular situations, specifying what is prescribed and forbidden, as well as what is tolerated and permitted in a certain behavioural dimension.

Norms operating in a given *translation* context can be used to explain or account for translation decisions retrospectively, but also to indicate prospectively how translation *should* be performed. Most theorists looking at norms have focused on literary translation, comparing the different norms operating in different target languages or cultures at different times, for instance (Chesterman & Wagner, 2002: 91). Chesterman (1997, 2002) relates the concepts more directly to professional translation, identifying four 'fundamental norms that together define what is meant by translation quality' (Chesterman & Wagner, 2002: 92–3):

1 The *acceptability norm* states that a good translation is one that fits closely enough into the appropriate family of target-language texts.

2 The *relation norm* governs the relation between the source text and the translation. It says that between the two texts there must be a relation of 'relevant similarity'.

3 The *communication norm* says that the translation should be optimally intelligible, that it should help the original author and/or sender to communicate the appropriate message to the readers.

4 The *accountability norm* [is best put negatively]: the translation should not contain any evidence that the translator has been disloyal to any of the parties involved in the communication.

He concludes that these norms provide 'four positive quality criteria for the translation product: appropriate target-language fit, relevant similarity, optimum intelligibility and manifest loyalty' (ibid.: 93). While this approach would speak to the professional desire to use TQA to approve translations, it remains entirely theoretical at present. The positive quality criteria are not related in concrete terms to any TQA model that might actually be applied, nor does Chesterman provide a sample illustration of how this might work in practice. His co-author, professional translator

Emma Wagner, does however indicate how closely these norms map on to real-world industrial standards and QC procedures, suggesting this may be an area where theorists and practitioners have identified a common concern and approach (ibid.: 93–5).

More recently, some translation theorists have moved their focus away from text-based approaches to the translator. This is a potentially promising development in bridging the gap between theorists' and practitioners' concerns, as real-world approaches to translation quality have long included translator competence. Within translation studies, however, there has been a basic lack of consensus on defining competence, with Pym holding to a 'minimalist' definition, while a growing group of theorists have preferred a more detailed set of subcategories (Hague et al., 2011: 245–6). For Pym (2003: 489), translation competence is 'the ability to generate a series of more than one viable target text (TTI, TT2 . . . TTn) for a pertinent source text (ST) [and] to select only one viable TT from this series, quickly and with justified confidence'. In contrast, other scholars have emphasized long lists or complex schemes of 'subcompetences'. For the PACTE group (Process in the Acquisition of Translation Competence and Evaluation), for example, there are five subcompetences for translators: bilingual, strategic, instrumental, knowledge about translation and extra-linguistic (2003). Bell (1991) agrees on the number of competences but not their nature, listing target language knowledge, text-type knowledge, source language knowledge, real-world knowledge and contrastive knowledge. Kelly (2005) identifies seven different competences: communicative and textual, cultural and intercultural, subject area, professional and instrumental, attitudinal or psycho-physiological, interpersonal and strategic.

Research on competence has understandably focused on training future translators. Efforts have on the whole been directed at defining competence, helping students achieve agreed levels of competence and reliably testing these, rather than professional concerns. Schäffner and Adab's volume on *Developing Translation Competence* (2000), for instance, has three parts (defining, building and assessing translation competence) and is almost exclusively focused on theory and training. Later work by Hague et al. (2011: 251–3 and 257–8) has begun to compare theoretical and pedagogical approaches to competence with those used in two professional contexts (the US government and American Society for Testing and Materials); and Dong and Lan have used theories on translation competence to test widespread assumptions regarding the superiority of translation into mother tongue (2010: 47–9). However, as Dong and Lan have pointed out, the various definitions of translation competence or criteria for assessing this have not been validated by empirical experimental research (ibid.: 48).

More specific aspects of TQA which have been important focus points for theorists include revision and editing, particularly the work of Canadian practitioner and theorist Mossop, though some theorists, with Larose, have argued that revision has no place in discussions of TQA (1998: 166). Mossop himself addresses part of his influential text on *Revising and Editing for Translators* to Quality Assessment (2001: 150–4). He recognizes the distinction between the two while clearly believing that both activities *are* of relevance for any discussion of professional translation quality. Also relevant for TQA is theorists' work on error categories and attempts to weight or categorize different error types, notably Pym's (1992) distinction between binary errors (objective, factual) and non-binary errors (subjective, value-judgements).

A final significant strand in academic work on translation quality has long been found in MT research. Some of the earliest approaches to TQA were developed to assess the quality of fully automatic (as opposed to human) translation, with little crossover between 'scientists and linguists' until relatively recently (Quah, 2006: 29, 35). This has been of limited usefulness for human professional translation contexts. Where human translation has been included in MT research, it has been to use human translations as a reference against which MT output can be compared and evaluated. Human translations are seen as the 'so-called "gold standard"' (Fiederer & O'Brien, 2009: 54). Little or no distinction is made by MT researchers between *different* quality levels produced by human translators: reaching the standard of human translation at all is the aspiration for MT systems. Rarely, MT researchers and theorists have attempted to devise models to evaluate both human and machine translations (Carroll, 1966). With the focus firmly on assessing and improving MT output, or on comparing different systems, though, this field of research has not thus far contributed much to assessing or improving quality in professional human translations.

2.3 Professional approaches to translation quality

Quality is assessed and compared constantly in real life. Those commissioning translations expect to be able to judge what they are investing in, even when they cannot understand either the source or target language. Practitioners have therefore always had to explain, justify and defend quality levels, without being able to point to a close comparative reading of ST and TT. But particularly since the 1990s, the translation profession, like other service providers, has been increasingly focused on quality. A proliferation of international standards now affects most industries (Nadvi & Wältring, 2004). The changing context in which professional translation is carried out has also had an impact, as explained in Chapter One. The next sections explain why the industry sees quality as an important concern; and second, how it has been approached.

2.3.1 *Why quality matters for the industry*

Academic research on translation quality has concentrated on TQA, on product rather than process or context, and on relatively narrow testing of the theories and models proposed.[10] In contrast, the industry approach to quality issues is all-embracing. As well as assessing quality post-delivery, professionals have explored how quality can be measured, improved and achieved efficiently and consistently at all stages of the process, even before the translation proper begins. Their emphasis is not on evaluating translations in isolation, but on comparative assessment, proper allocation of resources and a range of other concerns generally absent from theory.

One of the main driving factors behind the attention paid to quality in the profession is the awareness of how often it causes problems and first-hand understanding of the serious consequences. Regular clients invariably had previous negative experiences, with little apparent scope for redress. Agencies and in-house revisers offered horror stories of freelance translators 'outsourcing to their granny or their goat'[11] at busy times and working out of the mother tongue or their areas of competence against contract. Translators complained of abysmal source files, being compelled to use low-quality terminology or TM resources, or having their translations post-edited by incompetent agencies or in-house staff, with the translator's identity still attached to the new content.

Unlike academic theorists, professionals' focus on quality is also likely to be externally imposed. Concern for translation quality is in large part client-driven. Because the profession is not regulated, most clients struggle to identify skilled suppliers. Translation degrees or professional qualifications do not guarantee excellent translations. Many such qualifications are assessed by essays on translation theory rather than hands-on practice. For the majority of the world's languages and specializations, formal qualifications simply do not exist. Even tried-and-tested suppliers with outstanding credentials may not produce high quality levels consistently. As Chriss explains (2006: 140–1),

> This makes the people who hire translators nervous, since they don't know what they are getting, and they've either been burned themselves or heard stories of others being burned by bad translators. This is a situation economists call asymmetric information: there is no easy, reliable way to figure out which translator is worth hiring or working with, and which should be avoided at all possible costs.

Clients, of course, want to know *before* investing significantly in translation that quality levels will be sufficient. This goes some way to explaining the different emphasis for professionals and academics. TQA, the focus of academic interest in this area, is necessarily performed post-translation, whereas clients require assurances in advance that suppliers can produce the goods, then ongoing project updates on how targets are being met. Agencies and translators have to bid against others to win projects by demonstrating they can provide optimal quality levels to deadline at competitive prices, and then be able to report to clients on key performance indicators as translation takes place. Yet the clients themselves often cannot judge the quality of the translations returned to them: the entire reason for commissioning the translations is that the client is unable to produce the material in the target languages. Proving the quality of a translation service is thus increasingly challenging in today's context of multilingual projects, where the goal is simshipping in dozens of languages.

Varied translation needs also make it harder than ever for clients to accurately judge quality today. The industry is a diverse one: how is a new client, or a regular user of translation branching into new sectors or languages, to judge whether Agency A or B will better meet their requirements? Is a freelance translator sourced from the directory of a national translators' organization fine, or does the job require an EN 15038-certified supplier or sworn translator in some jurisdictions? Would raw or post-edited MT output be quicker, cheaper and sufficient for a particular need? Does it matter what tool a supplier uses to produce and maintain resources? The explosion of the translation market and an expanding number of languages required by leading clients means they can rarely rely on an existing roster of known suppliers. Clients also need to be able to test quality levels for entirely new types of work, such as localizing online support, perhaps for locales with little history of providing translation services.

Clients in some sectors are themselves subject to strict quality conditions and legal requirements to document QC, which they must in turn require of their translation suppliers. For this reason, clients including 'medical-device manufacturing, pharmaceutical companies, law firms, financial institutions, auto makers, and many businesses where user-safety or legal-liability concerns loom large' have particularly pushed a focus on translation quality issues (Sprung, 2000b: 173). Moreover, such clients are often *required* to provide documentation in translation, so represent a significant share of the market for professional translation services. Applying their standards and techniques across the board might seem one obvious way to generally improve quality standards in the industry. However, this would be counter-productive. Costly and time-consuming, it would place translation out of reach of the majority of clients or mean target language versions were not available by the deadline; regulated industries often lose significant sums due to translation delays:

> Though translation usually represents a small proportion of product-development expense, glitches in translation quality and turnaround time can create problems out of all proportion to the cost of such services. (ibid.: 173)

Sprung cites a manufacturer of endoscopic surgical equipment, whose products have a short market lifespan and for whom 'every week of translation time that could have been spared represents significant lost revenues' (ibid.: 174). The aim to produce *sufficient* translation quality, but avoid overkill, thus means measuring and allocating appropriate resources – but no more – to each job, and much effort has gone into identifying methods to assess and scale resources in practical, reliable ways in the profession (Prioux & Rochard, 2007; Drugan & Martin, 2005).

All this means that TQA remains important in the profession, but is not the only or main focus when considering translation quality. TQA has a role to play, and clients do require this, as Mossop (2001: 150) explains:

> [TQA] may be used for performance appraisal or promotion purposes [. . .], to select the contractor who will be given a job, or as a point of reference if the translation submitted is rejected and the freelance complains about the financial penalty. [. . . Government organizations that run a translation service may require] a formal, 'objective' assessment system in order to justify, for example, removing a given person from a roster of qualified freelances.

Like theorists, professional TQA integrates an error-based approach; but a further important distinction between theory and practice is found here. In the real world, errors have consequences. For freelance translators, the most common consequences are a withheld fee, or payment only after substantial (fee-free) reworking and reputational damage. More serious consequences are also possible, including legal action against translators where errors have an impact on clients or users. Two studies of court rulings and legal journals, looking for instances where translators were found liable as the result of poor translations, failed to identify any such cases (Ansaldi, 1999; Byrne, 2007). Nonetheless, the risk of translators being prosecuted for inaccurate or dangerous work is deemed sufficient for most translators' associations to provide professional indemnity insurance, and both Ansaldi and Byrne conclude that the absence of known precedents in the public domain should not lure translators into a false sense of security. For clients and end-users, the consequences of translation errors can be severe. Byrne (2007: 4) stresses the implications of inadequate translations in legal, political and commercial terms. He offers real-world examples where translation errors were:

- costly for commissioners (e.g. an EU call for tenders which had to be withdrawn due to translation errors);

- 'oppressive' (e.g. where minority linguistic communities are misinformed);

- damaging to client reputations (e.g. a banking crisis, resulting from a mistranslation);

- dangerous, or even fatal, for users (e.g. 'fuel' mistranslated as 'petrol').

For some specialist fields (e.g. the translation of tests or exams), errors can have strong financial, legal or social ramifications. One test-provider interviewed for this book cited an instance where incorrect use of the Castilian Spanish term *ordenador* instead of the Latin American Spanish terms *computador/computadora* incurred the expensive and socially disruptive retesting of an entire year's cohort of children. The impact of poor translations for providers of standardized psychological, psychiatric or medical tests, or psychometric tests used in recruitment, would be significant. Providers of such materials therefore insist on detailed QC procedures throughout the translation process (Sireci et al., 2006).

Many large-scale commissioners of translations have faced new requirements to outsource a higher proportion of work for reasons of efficiency or policy. This has meant a concomitant need for increased QA procedures, because translation is performed by external suppliers rather than by established in-house staff familiar with content, workflow and resources. The drive to outsource translation has also led to a greater focus on measuring quality because in-house divisions increasingly need to be able to demonstrate they add value, by providing higher quality than outsourcing (Lönnroth, 2005). Clients increasingly raise the prospect of integrating MT in translation workflows too. When deciding whether to adopt MT, clear cost-benefit analyses are usually carried out before projects, and these hinge on issues of quality. Chriss (2006: 153) offers the illustration of automobile specifications needed in eight target languages. His hypothetical example would take at least 20 days and cost around $2,000,000, using large teams of human translators working at high output levels (5,000 words per day). He estimates the equivalent investment in MT at $35,000 (hardware and software for each language pair). The initial MT investment would acquire tools which could be used at no additional cost for future projects. Indeed, the software would gain value over time, once user dictionaries become populated with client-specific terms. In contrast, relying on human translation, even with substantial translation memory or terminological resources, would involve similar outlay for every future project. The MT approach would also be significantly faster, two days plus post-editing time.

The decision to use MT might seem a straightforward one when presented in such stark financial terms, but time and effort for post-editing to reach adequate quality levels is hugely variable. Durban (2010: 255) cites the chainsaw metaphor – invaluable for chopping lots of wood in a hurry, but no use for paper, your fingernails or a steak at a business lunch. Equally, employing a surgeon to use his scalpel when you need a forest chopped down quickly would be pointless. The analogy is an apt one: different translation purposes and content require different tools and eventual quality levels. How good will the MT output quality be for given texts, end uses and language pairs, in comparison to human quality translation?

How much post-editing work will be required to reach the level needed by the client; are resources available to perform this post-editing efficiently; is it therefore cost-effective to adopt MT in the given context? Such questions lie at the heart of present industry concerns and involve careful assessment and comparison of quality levels.

The industry has also had to respond to clients' growing awareness of different quality levels. When a client is aware that Google Translate provides a target text for free, professionals have to be able to explain exactly how their service offers additional quality. For De Sutter, this has meant a greater focus on quality generally: 'Many companies seek refuge by positioning themselves as "high quality providers" and strive toward a conscious commitment to quality as a differentiator' (2005: 22). Initiatives such as the Cheating Translators website (www.cheatingtranslators.com/), which allows clients or users to check how likely it is that a translation has been produced using a free MT system, are evidence of growing willingness and ability to check quality levels.

Finally, quality management is the focus of an entire series of ISO standards developed since the late 1980s, the ISO 9000 series, affecting a broad range of industries, including translation. The extent of the impact of such standards is demonstrated by the huge rise in certification: in 2000, the year it was established, 457,834 certificates were awarded for ISO 9001 (quality management systems), and by 2009, there were 1,064,785.[12] A range of other such standards relating to translation is in place internationally. These have meant increased attention to quality at all stages of the translation process, further emphasizing one of the main differences between theoretical and real-world approaches.

The main standards recognized by LSPs interviewed for this book[13] were:

- ISO 9000 series (various numbers have been used at different times, notably the now-defunct ISO 9002 standard). These focus on documented quality management processes for service sectors, not translation per se. Certification and ongoing auditing are required. Quality procedures are defined by the certified company itself, then documented and made available for inspection;

- DIN 2345. Established in 1998 by the German standards body, this was one of the first translation-specific standards. It set out responsibilities for clients and LSPs, and specified qualifications for translators and certain quality processes, based on a client-provider contract, but is now subsumed into the CEN standard. LSPs nonetheless continued to mention its provisions regularly, particularly those working with the German language;

- (C)EN 15038:2006 (European Committee for Standards, released June 2006): Translation Services: Service Requirements. This aims to establish a single pan-European standard specifying translation services. It focuses on the competence of translators and revisers and defines QC procedures to some extent, though again, the emphasis is on clients and LSPs jointly defining processes prior to translation;

● ASTM (American Society for Testing and Materials) F2575 – 06 Standard for Quality Assurance in Translation. This standard is again specific to translation, offers guidelines for 'all stakeholders', including clients, and aims to provide a framework for agreement on defining processes which will lead to the desired level of quality in the end product. It specifies parameters, including some relating to translation quality, to be considered before translation begins;

● National Standard of the People's Republic of China GB/T 19363. 1–2003 Specification for Translation Service. First implemented in 2004, this is also translation-specific, and was developed with reference to the CEN and DIN standards. It applies to large-scale LSPs and clients, not freelance translators. It gives a comprehensive account of a wide range of 'quality features' (from translator qualifications down to the dress code for receptionists) and meticulously details some linguistic quality elements (e.g. specifying how foreign names must be translated into Chinese).

Even where providers are not bound by formal international standards, a growing emphasis on quality management in important client sectors has affected translation. Leading management theories, particularly Total Quality Management,[14] Kaizen[15] and Six Sigma[16] have had a significant impact on translation, especially in some sectors and language pairs. The influence of these theories on the translation industry's approach to quality is hardly surprising, as they began life in sectors which rely heavily on translation (automotive, communications), so the methods spread naturally.

What has the increasing focus on translation quality meant for industry definitions and approaches? The next section considers the professional understanding of translation quality and outlines the broad approaches taken for measuring, comparing and ensuring quality levels, in contrast to academic work on TQA. These are developed in more detail later, with case studies as illustrations, in Chapters Four and Five.

2.3.2 *Industry definitions and accounts of translation quality*

The professional view of translation quality is all-encompassing in comparison with the usually narrower focus on TQA in translation studies.

The terminology in general use in the industry reflects this difference. Several terms are commonly used to classify approaches to ensuring and measuring quality. Significantly, the terms TQA/QA themselves are generally used with a different sense in the industry, referring sometimes to translation quality assessment but more often to quality assurance; QE (Quality Evaluation) is also widespread.[17] This encapsulates the core difference between theorists' focus on assessing quality post-translation (looking at the product), and the profession's concern to assure clients, both before and during the process, that a mutually acceptable level of quality will be provided. TQA remains important, but as only one element in a broader overall approach.

The prospective aspect of QA is highlighted in the ISO definition of the term. QA is 'part of quality management focused on *providing confidence* that quality requirements *will* be fulfilled' (ISO 9000:2005 3.2.11; my emphasis). An important distinction is made in industry between QA (assurance) and QC (Quality Control). QC is distinguished from assurance as 'part of quality management focused on *fulfilling* quality requirements' (ISO 9000:2005 3.2.10; my emphasis). This distinction is one commonly recognized by translation professionals. In localization, for example, 'quality assurance is defined as the steps and processes used to ensure a final quality product, while quality control focuses on the quality of the products produced by the process' (Esselink, 2000: 146). There are differing views within the translation profession as to how QA and QC are best managed, of course, but the detailed attention paid to processes in the real world represents a marked difference with theory.

In concrete terms, QA refers to systems put in place to pre-empt and avoid errors or quality problems at any stage of a translation job. QA is typically understood as the global approach to translation quality (Mossop, 2001: 92). It encompasses all other aspects of achieving and measuring quality, including planning, QC and TQA. QA involves defining processes for all stages of the translation job, including post-translation review and extra-linguistic elements. It therefore concerns not only translators, but all those involved in delivering translations to clients. Strong claims are often made, particularly in relation to official standards, that getting such QA processes right means that any eventual assessment of product quality becomes redundant: 'When the work processes are maintained and controlled according to approved procedures, the final product will meet the customer's product quality requirements, regardless what type of product was manufactured' (Gaal, 2001: 4). Thus the ISO standard 'is not concerned with the contents of the translation' (Ørsted, 2001: 444).

This is not to say that process is valued in the profession at the expense of the product, however, because the process typically involves QC too, even if standards do not emphasize this or detail how precisely it should be done. QC means checking aspects of the translation product; it thus includes TQA.[18] This is usually done after the translation stage is complete, but aspects of QC may be performed on a rolling basis during the process too. Mossop sees translation revision as the 'highest degree of QC' (2001: 84), but many other elements are included in the term and QC need not involve full revision. For instance, what is often referred to in the industry as 'linguistic testing', would be part of QC. This might mean a target-language speaker with no knowledge of the source text checking that the text display and consistency of the translation are adequate. For some specializations, functional testing of the translated product would also be included in QC (e.g. in localization, checking the user interface or that links work). DTP is included in QC too; this would again often be done by a non-linguist (e.g. checking that fonts, images and page layout are displayed correctly in the target files).

Further relevant key terms in widespread use in industry again demonstrate the different focus in the real world. These include Quality Planning and Quality Improvement. As in many quality management philosophies, translation quality is not seen as an end goal in the profession or something which is merely to be assessed, but an ongoing process which can always be refined, improved or achieved more efficiently (i.e. the same quality level at reduced cost). All these aspects are included in the professional understanding of quality management, resulting in a broader overall conception of translation quality.

How are QA, QC, planning and improvement done in practice? As the industry emphasizes process as well as product, it is helpful to consider translation quality during the three main stages in any translation process: pre-translation, translation and post-translation. A general overview of the translation process is presented below, detailing the various features the industry takes into consideration in ensuring and assessing quality. No LSP's approach would involve all steps, particularly as some are not applicable to the range of providers: freelance translators will not adopt processes in place at agency level, for instance. Comparing these stages to the focus in academic TQA is instructive, as it demonstrates how much broader the professional concept of translation quality is. Just as for academic models, criticisms can and have been made of the various strategies, of course. These are not addressed here, but in Chapters Four and Five, where the strategies are presented in context and in more concrete detail via case studies.

Pretranslation stage

Before a translation project is even announced, professionals invariably have standard operating procedures in place which can be adapted to each project or client. In interviews and work-shadowing placements, it was evident that LSPs from individual freelance translators through to large-scale providers relied on established procedures to ensure certain quality levels, often without recognizing or articulating openly that they did so. The following were aspects of professional pre-translation processes with effects for quality:

- Pricing: bidding for job, often including sample translations to demonstrate quality levels offered in advance; allocating resources within budget; agreeing remuneration with suppliers;

- Planning: agreeing appropriate processes and deadlines with clients and suppliers, including how QC should be managed and which added-value services are included with translation (e.g. DTP); identifying key performance indicators for use during project; setting up appropriate file management processes and storage; receiving and agreeing client brief or localization kit; agreeing query structures (e.g. lead translators, client contacts); pseudo-translation; kick-off meeting (especially in localization);

- Human resources: identifying client needs then appropriate testing, recruitment outsourcing or assignment of linguistic and other staff (revisers, PMs, software engineers);

- Source file preparation and QC: internationalization support and advice to client; internationalization testing; terminology extraction; feedback on ST quality; adaptation or pre-editing of ST prior to translation; preparation and review of 'pivot' language ST where appropriate prior to multilingual translation;

- Terminology resources: research; preparing resources; integrating client resources with existing personal or in-house databases; term validation;

- Translation resources: hardware; software; translation memories; alignment of previous translations; MT; style guides;

- Project management resources: databases; software; division of large-scale projects;

- Training for suppliers (translators, terminologists) to ensure they comply with standards, resources are used appropriately, agreed workflow is respected or client specifications are followed. Such training might be project-specific, client-driven or ongoing (CPD).

Translation stage

This is defined here as beginning when the source files are sent to the translator(s) and ending when the unrevised translation is returned to a reviser, agency or client. The following were aspects of professional translation processes with effects for quality:

● Research: understanding source content, specialist terminology or target language norms (e.g. using product or testing software in the source language); querying content with clients/authors/agencies;

● Preparation of resources: checking localization kit or client brief; import of terminology or translation memory data; installing or setting up software for use in project (e.g. fuzzy match parameters);

● Translation: drafting; use of translation tools; post-editing MT output; generation of target files in native file format;

● Monitoring: project spending; maintaining control of agreed project budget; meeting interim deadlines;

● Planning: review and reallocation of resources where necessary to stay on schedule and within budget;

● Self-checking: translator's own review processes following the first draft (e.g. proofreading, spellchecking, tag and terminology verification checks, testing of generated target files in native file format);

● Participation in feedback cycle: responding to client feedback during project.

Post-translation stage

The professional approach is broader than TQA alone. TQA is carried out with a view not only to rating retrospectively the quality of particular translations, but to feeding into an ongoing quality cycle. Identifying quality problems post-translation allows LSPs to pre-empt these for future projects. The post-translation stage is defined here as beginning when the translated draft target files are returned by the translator, usually to a reviser, agency or client. The following were aspects of professional post-translation processes with effects for quality:

● QC processes, prior to project completion: consistency checks; compliance with client resources; copyediting; editing; functional testing; ICR; linguistic testing; product checking; proofreading; review; revision; sampling; spot-checking;[19]

● Translator feedback: return of results of proofreading/revision/ review for error correction; updating of terminology and TM resources;

- TQA/QE processes, prior to and/or post-project completion: application of tools and metrics (aiming at unbiased/replicable judgements); rating of translators' work;

- Project management processes: invoicing; archiving of resources; secure storage; ownership issues; feedback;

- Project review: post-mortem; feedback cycle (to clients and suppliers, including positive feedback on performance); client presentation; client/user satisfaction surveys; ongoing review and refinement of processes for future related projects.

One caveat to this presentation of the industry's general approach to translation quality is that it is based on a traditional model of translation stages. Recently, the industry has witnessed the emergence of non-serial models of translation, with more flexible, ongoing processes where translation is embedded in production, such as in Agile localization projects. These emerging approaches represent only a tiny proportion of projects overall, however, and are considered further in Chapter Five.

2.4 Conclusion: Real-world translation quality models

As can be seen in the above lists, the professional approach to ensuring and measuring translation quality goes far beyond TQA alone. Quality must often be assessed during the lifetime of projects, aspects of TQA are sometimes imposed and professionals performing TQA have different motivations than theorists do. The industry is a diverse one, not least in terms of supplier size, and a range of standards and regulations apply to different LSPs. Interpretations of TQA or QE processes differ substantially from one LSP to another, and the various approaches have advantages and failings, just as theories do. Client needs and preferences also have a significant affect on LSP interpretations of quality processes. The range of real-world approaches can however be classified in two broad models: top-down and bottom-up. Chapters Four and Five describe the range of real-world professional approaches to translation quality in more detail, and comparatively, within these two models. The strengths and weaknesses of each approach are considered for different translation scenarios.

The profession increasingly relies on automation, whether to support production of high-quality output or to improve consistency and objectivity in evaluating quality. The next chapter considers how the main tools in widespread use in the industry have affected translation workflow and quality.

CHAPTER THREE

Tools, workflow and quality

3.0 Introduction: The impact of translation tools

The potential impact of electronic tools on translation and localization has previously been considered to some extent (Cronin, 2003; Pym, 2003, 2010a). The tools' design and main features have also been outlined, though most published accounts are now dated (Austermühl, 2001; Bowker, 2002; Esselink, 2000; Lagoudaki, 2006, 2009; Quah, 2006). Limited research has been published on the impact of electronic tools on translation quality (Bédard, 2000; Bowker, 2005, 2007; Drugan, 2007b; García, 2009a; Teixeira, 2011; Torres-Hostench et al., 2010). Most of this limited body of research was produced 'in vitro' on university campuses, using small cohorts of student translators, rather than professionals working with familiar, self-selected tools in their standard working conditions (Olohan, 2011: 353). The tools have only been in widespread use since the late 1990s (Bowker, 2005: 14), with uptake varying significantly in different sectors and language pairs, so it has only been possible to assess their impact in the real world relatively recently (Drugan, 2004, 2007a,b). The research which has been published so far is also limited by:

- language pair: almost all studies consider only European/Scandinavian languages;[1]

- tool selection: for example, all the published research on TM use, with the exception of the author's, refer to SDL Trados (or earlier versions), whereas multiple tools are used in industry. No studies of more specialist tools (e.g. dedicated localization software such as Alchemy Catalyst) were found;

- combination of tools: few translators use only one tool. They typically draw on research, terminology and TM tools and their own custom-built resources. This is difficult to replicate or allow for in lab conditions;

- user groups: existing research considers only translators, proofreaders and revisers. As an increasing range of specialists take on more significant roles in the industry, studying these groups in isolation risks missing important effects of tool use for quality, as there are now many other players contributing to the final product.

The present study attempts to address these gaps by drawing on research in vivo, including translators working with languages which have been less studied (Arabic, Chinese, Japanese, Russian and 'smaller' languages such as Latvian, Norwegian and Welsh). Professionals were observed in their usual working conditions, producing live jobs for paying clients or in-house managers, to real deadlines. This approach clearly entails other problems, not least subjects' awareness of the researcher's presence. It is likely that translators were more self-conscious than usual and paid more attention to issues relating to translation quality, for instance. Nonetheless, when combined with the published research carried out in more controlled conditions, this approach offers new insights into the effects of electronic tools.

Workflow emerged as a relevant issue when considering quality during research. It is addressed here because practitioners repeatedly attributed changes in workflow processes to the tools' influence. As the various translation and quality standards emphasize, getting processes and workflow right helps create conditions in which acceptable levels of quality will be achieved in the eventual product. Changes to translation workflow are therefore likely to have affected quality, whether positively or negatively. The next section lists the main categories of electronic tools in widespread use in the profession today, stressing those features which are relevant for translation quality. Their impact on translation workflow, quality management and assessment is then summarized, drawing both on the limited studies published thus far and the original research carried out for the present book. Finally, the impact of electronic tools is considered in relation to professional models of translation quality.

3.1 The translator's workbench

The concept of the translator's workbench or workstation refers to the bespoke combination of electronic tools assembled by each user. Until recently, many translators relied on a basic set-up of word processing, Internet browser and email. Quah summarizes a typical workstation today as integrating 'translation tools and resources such as a translation memory, an alignment tool, a tag filter, electronic dictionaries, terminology databases, a terminology management system and spell and grammar-checkers' (2006: 93–4). The growing diversity of roles in the industry also means that tools are increasingly used by people other than translators. A 2006 survey of nearly 900 LSPs from 54 countries found that 82.5 per cent of respondents used translation memory tools, for instance (Lagoudaki, 2006: 12–13), despite including groups like interpreters who were unlikely to need all tools. LSPs of different sizes use different tools, depending on the scenarios in which they typically work, language pairs and specializations. Few if any will use all tools listed here. Electronic tools are outlined in roughly descending order, with the most widely used[2] listed first. They are grouped by functionality, because software providers offer different combinations of features. An exhaustive list of proprietary software is not supplied, as this information is widely available and changes frequently when new tools are launched or existing ones upgraded, but sample tools are suggested in each category for illustration purposes.

3.1.1 Project planning, preparation and management tools

Because projects vary drastically in scale and technical requirements, a wide range of tools is used in the industry for planning and management. Individual freelance translators may rely on an Excel database or electronic calendar to keep track of their commitments, or use the basic project tracking functions bundled as standard with some TM tools. In-house Project Managers (PMs) need more sophisticated applications which handle multiple complex projects concurrently and automate support tasks, including some relating to management of translation quality. The PM's toolkit is usually built around a dedicated project management application. Some companies use generic software not specifically designed for the translation industry (e.g. Microsoft Project), though this may be customized to suit local needs. A second group of translation-specific PM tools are linked to proprietary translation software such as TM and localization tools (e.g. Across Language Server, SDL WorldServer). These have the advantage of integrating translation and terminology resources, so PMs can more easily analyse new jobs against previous projects and cost these according to matches in existing databases. A third approach is to invest in a dedicated stand-alone translation project management tool (e.g. LTC Worx, Projetex). These have additional functionalities and usually support multiple translation and localization tools or formats. Finally, larger LSPs may design their own bespoke tool (e.g. Lionbridge's Freeway platform). All these tools are scalable for projects handling two languages to up to

40 or more. An increasing number are interactive cloud-based applications, accessed through portals using the SaaS (Software as a Service) model, rather than being purchased and installed locally. This means that both clients and suppliers can interact with the project management tool, perhaps by generating an estimated quote for a new job without human interaction or using an online chat feature to discuss a project with other suppliers.

PM tools typically include the following functionalities:

- automated workflow processes, prompting and supporting the PM through various steps in business, process and linguistic management;

- project information storage from the RFQ (request for quotation) stage, then automatic quote generation based on parameters entered by the PM;

- standard template generation (e.g. for quoting, invoicing, progress reports, job tracking sheets);

- time management and planning features, allowing PMs to schedule and coordinate various activities included in a project, working back from the client deadline;

- prompts for and documentation of compliance with quality management processes, based on a project quality plan in line with client requirements or external standards where applicable. This stipulates which quality checks will be completed. These are prompted and signed off as they are actually carried out. A related work schedule for revision, proofreading and engineering quality checks can also be automated. Tools can generate standard sign-off forms for particular processes or stages;

- support for ongoing project coordination (e.g. reviewing deadlines as a project evolves);

- monitoring of project progress (e.g. live statistics on how many words have been translated or revised).

PMs interviewed for the present study were enthusiastic about an imminent 'one-stop shop' model for management and translation tools. In some newer versions, project management is supported alongside client and supplier needs. For instance, translators are automatically notified to 'check out' files for translation, revision or proofreading as they become available, thus locking them for editing by others contributing to the project, and reducing the workload and risks for the PM. If the source files are amended during the life of the project, the same translator will be notified automatically so she can review the changes and make suitable amendments to her translation, if necessary. Such approaches also allow PMs to monitor suppliers' productivity, hours worked and speed of translation and revision for particular projects and clients.

PMs, translation managers and freelance translators must be able to generate accurate word or character counts for new source files to bid for commercial jobs, and to plan timing and resources in all contexts. This is challenging when projects might involve hundreds of source files in multiple file formats for each language pair. Obtaining an accurate word count might take days of repetitive and boring work. Relying on manual opening of files to do this risks source material being missed. Dedicated tools (e.g. WebBudget) therefore generate accurate word counts for complex file types such as HTML or XML, which standard tools cannot process effectively, as they frequently miss 'hidden' translatable text, or conversely, include text or code which is not for translation. Dedicated tools can process multiple file types in batch mode and allow identification of repetitions. These come in two forms:

- Internal repetitions, that is, where a segment of ST is repeated within a new project. The same phrase may appear many times (e.g. as a header, link, in body text) across multiple related files. Clients typically expect to pay full rate for the first translation, then a lower rate or nothing for subsequent exact matches.

- Leveraged from previous translation projects, that is, where a segment or longer section of text in the new project has previously been translated and is contained in the client's reference materials (e.g. a TM sent with the new project). These are handled in a range of ways. They may be 'locked', if the client is sure they should not be retranslated; in this case, the translator may not even see the relevant parts of the source files. They may be counted as 100 per cent matches for quoting purposes, but left visible to translators, so they have context for translating surrounding text. They may be counted as 100 per cent or fuzzy matches but charged, albeit at a lower rate than new text. Some clients recognize that even exact matches ought to be checked in context in new files.

Word count tools are not always available or suitable for certain file formats. Other methods include performing word counts in the native file format, using the word count functionality in a TM or localization tool, exporting text to another application for counting, or using a dedicated word count tool designed for a particular file type; the latter is particularly common with PDF files.[3] Even with these methods and tools, some text may be excluded, notably text saved as images or content retrieved from databases for dynamic server pages (this is usually missed so has to be exported and counted separately).

Dedicated PM tools are used in conjunction with a supplier database for large projects. This typically lists suppliers' contact details, rates, availability, specialization, previous experience, language pair, quality ranking, location (relevant if based in a different time zone) and previous client/agency feedback. For large-scale projects, PMs call on teams of translators for each language over many months so assigning work to suppliers can be a complex operation; again tools can partially automate this task.

Pre-translation preparation of source materials is again supported by a number of dedicated tools and functionalities. This might include:

- Alignment. Where previous translations are related to the new project and may provide matches, but are not available in a suitable TM format, previous source and target files can be automatically aligned to create a new TM or be imported into an existing one. This is non-trivial and has implications for reference material quality. Any post-translation alignment must be checked carefully, ideally by a linguist who understands and speaks both source and target languages, as alignment may be inaccurate, affecting TM quality.

- Source file preparation. For large multilingual projects, the source may be pre-edited prior to translation. Pre-editing includes 'restricting vocabulary and grammar before the translation process can take place [and . . .] checking the source-language text for errors and ambiguities' (Quah, 2006: 44). This can avoid later quality problems across multiple target languages. A controlled language[4] may be used so MT can be applied more successfully or to cut down on variation across languages. Tools can test for compliance with a controlled language (e.g. HyperSTE).

- Source file import and file conversion (e.g. from a range of file formats to one suitable for use in a TM tool). In localization, filters or parsers may be needed to extract translatable text from non-standard formats (Esselink, 2000: 414). These stages are often carried out by agency staff prior to distribution in the appropriate format to translators and again may require specialist or bespoke tools.

Further project support tools may also be used in certain conditions (e.g. CMS for planning and version control of documentation).

3.1.2 Research tools

No matter how qualified or informed in specialist fields translators are, the nature of material needed in translation is such that new content, terminology and concepts will inevitably need to be understood in the source language then effectively rendered in the target language. Where material is new to the translator, he must learn about the field or product and identify appropriate terminology for the target language. Entirely new concepts may have been invented in the source, so translators have to coin equivalent new terms, which might involve substantial research (e.g. marketing, patents, legal issues). Until recently, in-house translators had substantially superior research resources than their freelance colleagues. Documentation centres were common in translation divisions, often staffed by specialist linguists who could prepare terminology lists or carry out research on translators' behalf. In-house staff maintain an advantage in some contexts. Translation divisions of hi-tech companies visited in research might have privileged access to beta-versions of products which they could test to help identify appropriate terms to describe new features, for example. Some manufacturers base translators on production sites to afford them such access or ship new products (e.g. cameras, printers) to secure storage within the translation division, so linguists can use the products and understand the features to be communicated to new users.

The Internet has nonetheless considerably levelled the playing field for freelance translators and was by far the most popular response when LSPs were asked in interviews what research tools they used for the present book, even where access was limited by slow connection speeds or restrictions on usage (e.g. in the PRC). It is now much quicker to carry out research than pre-Internet, particularly for terminology and technical translation where there are excellent specialist online resources. A significant change is that access to resources and data is much more open through Internet tools, rather than controlled by libraries, geographically remote or stored inaccessibly within companies. The vast majority of translators used Google as their main search engine in Internet Explorer, with local variations in some regions.

The most common research tasks related to terminology. Translators searched in both source and target languages to understand source meaning and identify the most appropriate target term. Virtually all translators first searched local resources (client or personal termbases, CD-ROMs) then progressed to online resources if these offered no hits. Authorized resources (e.g. Microsoft bilingual glossaries) and highly specialized online term lists were the next port of call. A range of translators' and technical writing forums were popular, sometimes through specialist subject networks or professional associations. Many linguists did also refer to less authoritative resources such as the ProZ.com KudoZ forum and tools such as Web Term Search (this can be configured to check the official EU IATE terminology resource and other databases, Google's MT engine and ten different search engines in one step). A few translators mentioned more recently established dedicated search and storage tools (e.g. TermWiki).

Understanding or verifying the sense of source content was the next most commonly cited reason for carrying out research. Again, the Internet was invariably seen as the most useful tool. The positive impact of image searches was repeatedly highlighted: where a technical or ambiguous term is used in the source, an image can often help translators establish an object's size or orientation, which prepositions should be used in relation to its placement, etc. Also helpful were online user forums for technical specialists in the source language, client websites, and intranets, where access was granted.

Checking target language usage, especially in new or emerging contexts, also requires research. Previously translated files or documents in the target language and client reference materials were checked first, as these would give an indication of preferred style and register. Internet searches were then tried. A minority of translators had used corpora[5] other than the Internet, with a few having created their own monolingual or bilingual corpus for specialist domains in which they translated regularly. Electronic corpora allow users to search for non-translated examples of usage in the target language, particularly collocates (words that typically co-occur in natural languages). Other uses include understanding definitions in context. Corpus analysis tools (e.g. WordSmith Tools) allow translators to search large corpora quickly and effectively:

> Consulting printed 'parallel' texts in the target language – in order, for example, to search for terminology or look for idiomatic phraseology – is of course something that translators are very familiar with. Consulting digitalized corpora by means of corpus analysis tools enables them to exploit large quantities of text far more rapidly and systematically. (Wilkinson, 2005: n.p.)

Most such tools include a concordancer, a feature familiar to translators from TM tools. This allows users to find all entries for a search term or phrase in a corpus then displays hits in context, including the sentence or phrase around the search term. Clicking on a hit takes users to a longer section of the text, to view more context or detail. A few translators who translated out of their mother tongue were particularly positive about the value of such tools.

3.1.3 *Terminology tools*

LSPs need to access specialist terminology quickly and reliably. Specialist glossaries may be provided by clients, found or purchased via professional networks or built up by translators, in-house units or agencies themselves. These are large and must be frequently updated, so dedicated tools to populate, manage and access them are standard. Terminology tools have four main functions, two or more of which may be combined in an application: term extraction; storage and management; search, retrieval and insertion; term checking. Term extraction tools can be used to create new monolingual, bilingual or multilingual term lists, or to populate existing termbases. These may come bundled with TM applications (e.g. the Create Lexicon feature in Atril DVX), or be purchased as add-ons or stand-alone tools (e.g. SDL MultiTerm Extract, AlchemyAPI). An increasing number of stand-alone tools were developed for term extraction needs in other contexts (e.g. Search Engine Optimization (SEO), indexing online content). Such tools automatically scan electronic corpora such as TMs or webpages and identify candidate terms for human review before import into term lists or termbases. They adopt a statistical approach (selecting terms based on their frequency in a corpus) or a linguistic (rule-based) one. They were found to be of limited usefulness in the industry. While specialist terminologists did use them, mainly to create monolingual source term lists, the few translators who had tried them saw them as 'useless' for their purposes. Their accuracy was found to be limited for most languages. The expense of most tools and time needed to review and reject inappropriate candidate terms meant LSPs rejected them as less efficient than other termbase population methods.

Terminology management systems (TMSs) can again be acquired as stand-alone tools (e.g. SDL MultiTerm) or come as standard in TM and localization applications (e.g. the Atril DVX Project Lexicon). These were among the most widely used tools for LSPs of all sizes. A TMS allows creation, storage and management of specialist terminology in a searchable and exportable format. Termbases are usually created and stored as multilingual resources, but any combination of monolingual or bilingual data can be extracted for particular freelance or project uses. Terminology can be imported from multiple file formats, though this may require laborious conversion. Entries in TMSs are highly customizable, with most now supporting images/video alongside linguistic data, a feature of growing importance in technical fields where new product information must be shared with linguists. The tools can store whatever linguistic information the termbase creator requires. Wizards at the termbase setup stage prompt for a vast range of potential fields in most tools (e.g. context, definition).

Once created in a TMS, termbases are used for searches, retrieval, active terminology recognition and automatic insertion of terms while translating. TM systems work with bilingual termbases, identifying source terms as the translator works through segments and automatically suggesting or inserting appropriate target terms. If a source file term has no corresponding entry in the termbase, most systems will allow translators to add it with its target equivalent 'on the fly'. An increasing move to 'live' termbases, posted on intranets or available online, means all translators for a language pair can access the most current version of terminological resources without laborious export/import.

The final function of terminology tools relates to QC. Post-translation, filters can check for translator compliance with approved terms and consistency across translated files, then carry out an instant find-and-replace for any non-approved terms.

3.1.4 *Text editing and input tools*

The overwhelming majority of professional translators visited for this study entered text in TM or localization tools for virtually all jobs. Most still worked directly in the native file format at least on occasion, typing over the ST. This was particularly true of those who worked with MS Office formats, some of which were seen as poorly supported by TM tools (PowerPoint was flagged most). Translators who usually worked in a TM tool sometimes worked in the native file format when the ST was very short, a one-off assignment or in a file format not supported by their TM system.

Only a small minority entered text via voice recognition tools, even where access and support were available. Dragon Naturally Speaking was the only tool observed, mostly in conjunction with DVX or SDL Trados for TM. While DVX users reported no problems working in the TM editor, Trados users preferred to have the TM running in the background to check matches on screen, but would enter their translation in the native file format. All had encountered technical problems when they tried to work directly in Trados via voice recognition input. Adopters of this approach belonged to two main groups:

- translators who had previous experience of dictation decades earlier, when they used Dictaphones then audio-typists typed their translations for hard-copy editing;

- those who avoided typing because they suffered from or were concerned about repetitive strain injury.

One translator with a physical disability found this input method more efficient. A few claimed they could work noticeably more quickly. Only translators working with European languages were found to use the tool, though Dragon claim their software supports others, including complex scripts. Computing hardware performance was an issue and most users had had to buy additional RAM.

A very small number of translators, all in-house, worked directly in a CMS, with a TM running to access matches, but also sometimes to make sure linguistic support was sufficient. A related recent development is that of web-based editing environments which include TM and terminology resources (e.g. Lionbridge Translation Workspace). In this model, translators do not buy tools or work on local installations but log in to request jobs and carry out the work online in the text editor mandated by the provider.

3.1.5 *Translation memory tools*

LSPs who participated in research for this book agreed these are the 'most significant' tools for translators (García, 2009a: 199). TM tools arguably require less effort of translators than terminology tools do. Each time the tool is used as the translation environment, which is increasingly the default practice for all jobs, the translator automatically feeds the database. Using a standard workflow, many users were able to avoid laborious conversion and other tasks. TM systems integrate various kinds of support, including for terminology, which can be accessed through a concordance feature even if no glossary is available. Most provide a customizable editing environment with access to the main features translators need via a single screen, allowing them to work with complex file formats (e.g. tagged files) relatively straightforwardly. During the 1990s, the range of tools mushroomed. Current versions are faster, more stable and ship with more features as the standard (e.g. alignment, PM features, localization support, batch processing, automatic QC checks). The interface and workflow are significantly more intuitive than in early versions. Universal character encoding through Unicode means that any written language is available in most tools and multilingual projects are well supported. The tools' cost has fallen substantially, and several free or OS versions are available (e.g. Omega T).

SDL Trados remains the market's leading tool by some length, but LSPs included in research for the present book commonly used several tools in response to client demand. Other tools dominated in certain sectors or domains (e.g. STAR Transit in automotive translation). Over ten different TM tools were observed in use. Very few translators were found to use TM tools with Macs. Wordfast is designed to work in the Mac OS as well as Windows, OS tools can be used and there is one free CAT tool, Appletrans, for Mac users; but the only Mac users observed in this study used Boot Camp (which allows a Mac to run as if it were a PC) or a parallel desktop add-in to run Windows software with one of the standard TM tools. Both these workarounds required additional memory to run effectively. Some versions of TM tools can be used 'live' on networks (e.g. SDL Trados Studio 2011 Professional), so translators share linguistic resources in real time, seeing other suppliers' translations and terms as they work. A similar approach is now available via emerging cloud-based tools (e.g. Lionbridge Translation Workspace).

TM tools mirror terminology tools in their four main functionalities, two or more of which may be combined in one application:

- Creation of databases of translated content. TMs match source and target segments of natural language text. The database is populated as the user works: each time a new segment is translated, the source and the human-generated target are linked and added to the TM. The TM can also be populated by importing client data (i.e. TMs containing previous translators' work) or by aligning previous translations available in machine-readable format;

- Storage, management and maintenance of matched segments. LSPs and clients can leverage substantial productivity gains by combining TM content from different projects. However, this has implications for storage and management of content. Effective maintenance is essential to ensure continued value (e.g. where clients change a translation, the TM should be updated and the original suggestion deleted, so clients do not have to make the same change again);

- Search, retrieval and insertion of previous translations. Where a source segment has previously been translated, the target segment should be suggested to the translator whenever it recurs, so she can review and accept it or choose to retranslate. To do this, TM tools all analyse new source files, identify matches in the database and automatically suggest these to the translator when she arrives at the relevant segment. Security features allow approved segments to be locked for editing in most tools. Where no match is found, several tools now offer the option of MT integration, to 'fill in' untranslated segments for post-editing. Tools are increasingly customizable (e.g. in STAR Transit, translators can create rules to mine their own TMs for sub-segment matches);

- Translation checking. Most TM tools now support standard editing features such as autotext, autocorrect, grammar and spellchecking as text is entered. An array of automatic QC functions allow instant checks for such elements as formatting, placeables, tags and terminology, either as the translator moves from one segment to the next or in batch mode after translation is complete. WYSIWYG or preview features allow translators to view source and target files in context during translation in most tools. Some allow for translation QC, including revision and proofreading, to be performed in the TM system or automatically update the TM with any changes introduced at the QC stage.

3.1.6 *Quality assurance tools*

A 2007 study of QA tools used in industry found them to be 10–15 years behind TM tools in their development and functionalities (Makoushina, 2007: 4). STAR Transit was the first TM tool to offer quality checks, from 1998; the dominant tool, Trados, only introduced such support from 2006. A few stand-alone QA tools appeared around the same time (e.g. QA Distiller). Such tools automate those QA tasks suitable for automation; fortuitously, these are generally the ones which are monotonous, repetitive and time-consuming. Despite their late arrival on the market and limited features in many cases, the tools thus found a receptive audience. Makoushina found 88 per cent of all LSPs employed either a stand-alone tool or the QA add-ins bundled with TM tools (ibid.: 17), and among the LSPs visited for the present study, only a handful of freelance translators did not use at least some QC functionalities of their tools. All these checks are performed rapidly or instantly, at no cost (following the initial investment). They are consistent and reliable: a machine will not miss a small error after processing hundreds of thousands of words, but humans are fallible, particularly when tired or working under time pressure. The checks are performed in electronic formats and so, sometimes, save time on generating target files, transferring data across formats and printing costs. Substantial variability exists across the tools, however. Their support for certain languages is weak or non-existent (current dedicated tools were all designed for European languages; LSPs working with character-based scripts and right-to-left languages were often scathing about support for their language pairs), and many file formats cannot be checked.

The most basic level of QA using tools is checking the TT in the native file format (e.g. MS Word), using the standard spell-check feature, searches for anticipated errors or client-stipulated checks, font consistency checks, etc. Many translators populated auto-correct lists to check for known weaknesses as they entered text. Terminology management tools (e.g. SDL MultiTerm) may be accessed from other file formats via toolbars, allowing term consistency checks. Some translators ran native format spelling checks even where they also had access to more sophisticated QA tools because they knew clients did so. If a client who does not speak the target language finds errors using an automatic spelling check, it can undermine confidence in the quality of the translation.

TM tools offer more sophisticated automated checks, including bilingual checks, where the source and target segments are compared against one another to identify translation errors. Automated checks often depended on high-level user awareness and confidence (e.g. creating macros to identify common errors for checking). TM tools usually support the following checks, though performance is variable:

- compliance with project glossary;
- compliance with user- or client-set blacklists (e.g. unacceptable terms or entries);
- consistent translation of terms;
- correct number formats (e.g. decimal point in the source should become a comma in the target for many languages); correct/preferred currency formats; automated measurement conversion (e.g. feet to metres);
- different number of sentences in ST/TT: this can be legitimate, but might indicate duplicates or missed text;
- omissions (e.g. empty TL segment);
- identical segments in ST/TT: these may be untranslated;
- inconsistency of content (e.g. identical segments in the ST have been translated differently in the TT);
- partial translation: presence of source terms or characters in TT. This may identify untranslated material (e.g. Chinese characters in an English segment);
- punctuation: different punctuation marks in matched ST/TT segments (allowing for known language differences); correct spaces with punctuation marks (e.g. in French, a space before the colon); double punctuation marks (e.g. extra full stop); missed quote marks/parenthesis, etc.;
- segments of substantially differing lengths in ST/TT: text may be missing, or a translator may have failed to delete extra text when copying and pasting;
- tags: same number in ST/TT, correct order, complete;
- unopened segment (never opened in the TM tool): this can reveal hidden text or that a translator missed translatable text;
- untranslatables: elements in the ST which should not have been translated but were altered in the TT.

More comprehensive stand-alone tools are in widespread use in the industry to measure and sometimes to correct errors automatically (e.g. ErrorSpy). These support multiple file formats and TM tools. All the above checks are likely to be well-supported but there is more flexibility for users and clients to set checks and some known linguistic issues may also be included (e.g.

calques). While the TM tools and native file formats are designed to check for errors so they may be corrected prior to delivery, the stand-alone tools also have a comparative function. They thus allow agencies to measure and compare the quality of test translations, for instance.

A final set of automated tools for QA requires additional human input. Tools in this group (e.g. BlackJack) are designed to support human evaluators by prompting, recording and scoring measurement of TQ. They are based on metrics, such as the SAE J2450 standard (developed for translation in the automotive industry) and the LISA QA metric. Metrics aim to define a consistent standard against which quality can be measured by identifying error types, weighting these and then counting the number of errors in each type in samples of translated text. Errors are usually classed as critical, major or minor and points are attached to each type and the level of severity. The tools spot some errors automatically, or can be used in conjunction with other automated tools, then human evaluators check the TT against the ST to identify those which cannot be checked automatically, using templates based on the metric. A final score is automatically generated for the translation or sample, usually by dividing the total score for errors by the total number of words in the ST. In the LISA model, this is known as the Translation Quality Index. An advantage of this approach is that it allows for formatting, functional and language QA (Koo & Kinds, 2000: 147). Weighting and scores can be varied (e.g. for each job or client): users can change the total number of error points allowed, how these points are distributed among error categories, how error types are defined, etc. Although not fully automated, the aim of these tools is to replicate the impartiality of machine evaluation: 'the basic ideas driving the [LISA] QA Model's approach are *repeatability* (one person doing the same work twice should obtain the same result) and *reproducibility* (two people doing the same work should also obtain the same result)' (ibid.: 148).

Lastly, bespoke QA tools were fairly widespread, particularly in agencies and larger LSPs with good IT support (e.g. in the localization sector). Some were based on the LSP's own in-house quality metric or QA checklists and workflows, while others used or adapted existing industry metrics.

3.1.7 *Conversion, exchange and storage tools/approaches*

Although their importance is largely ignored outside the industry, these tools and features make possible its current scale and form. Until very recently, translation capacity was dictated by how much data could be transferred and at what speed. Relying on faxes and other hard-copy formats imposed significant limits on how much translation LSPs could handle. The spread of email, zipped file formats and FTP sites, followed by intranets, vastly increased server capacity and, more recently, cloud computing have enabled the industry to take on projects of previously unimaginable size, to translate material that was previously untranslatable and to work at entirely different rates.

Conversion of files across different formats is essential for all LSPs. Even freelance translators can rarely work in native file formats alone with no conversion. Commonly, translators need to receive, translate and return a range of proprietary MS Office formats, common TM and terminology formats, and other specifications (e.g. RTF files, which must be converted into another format prior to translation). Almost all translators interviewed in research reported receiving source materials in hard copy format. Most converted such materials to electronic format by scanning and conversion to machine-readable format via OCR', with the exception of very short, faxed or handwritten texts. Clients may produce files for translation in new or unusual formats, requiring LSPs to convert these in order to take on the work. Standards for data exchange allow interoperability. Text must be separated from formatting using filters to enable 'tool neutral' formats. Multiple exchange formats are now in place for terminology (e.g. TBX – TermBase eXchange format), translation memory (e.g. TMX – Translation Memory eXchange format) and localization (e.g. XLIFF – XML Localization Interchange File Format). A range of tools support such conversion so LSPs can import and export data in shareable formats (e.g. MultiTerm Convert for terminology). The development of exchange formats again dates back only to the late 1990s, however, and conversion still entails quality problems. Many LSPs insist translators use a stipulated tool to work on their projects, as they find too many quality issues otherwise.

Data must be exchanged at various stages in any translation project. Clients send source and reference materials (e.g. localization kits) to LSPs, usually in native file formats. After project preparation, the PM provides suppliers with source files, reference materials, project details (e.g. client specifications, deadlines, instructions on communication and queries, order in which files should be translated, style sheets), a running version of the application if localizing and, sometimes, access to any specialist tools needed. This is a non-negligible step. A project may involve exchanging hundreds of files in multiple formats with each individual supplier, so efficient tracking is essential to avoid duplication or missed files. The quantity of data transferred often rules out basic methods (e.g. emailing zipped attachments). This causes particular problems in hi-tech sectors such as localization and subtitling, where file size is substantial and the number of files significant. Until very recently, subtitlers expected to leave files downloading overnight so they could work on them the next day, for example.

During and after a project, secure and logical data transfer and storage are essential. The contract may specify secure archiving of the job, particularly where the LSP and client have an ongoing agreement or there is any risk of subsequent litigation (Byrne, 2007: 8). Data must also be accessible quickly for distribution and re-use when needed. As content volumes increase, this raises significant issues. For instance, are increasingly large TMs, containing decades worth of translation in dozens of languages, best organized and archived according to subject, client, format, date, job or supplier? Or is one massive database with filters to extract the information needed for particular jobs a better approach? In large organizations with thousands of suppliers, such issues pose substantial challenges. As these are new issues for the industry, there is no clear best practice. Research for this book found hugely varied approaches to managing data, at all levels. A related issue is whether to convert data prior to archiving, to avoid 'locked-in' data syndrome (e.g. the danger that resources might become unusable or require substantial reorganization if you switch tools). Cloud computing is being proposed in many sectors as a possible solution to some such issues, but there is general wariness in the industry and among clients on this strategy, not least because of concerns about confidentiality and ownership of resources.

3.1.8 Machine translation tools

There has long been an imbalance between academia and industry with regard to where they focus their respective efforts and attention on translation tools. For Quah (2006: 2), while MT tools were swiftly rejected as insufficiently useful by the industry, 'the majority of publications from the literature on translation technology are about the development of machine translation systems, primarily involving experimental systems'. Although the concept of fully automatic translation existed much earlier, MT research and the development of tools began in earnest following the Second World War (ibid.: 58). Various approaches to MT have since been tried, with researchers' and developers' attention focusing on rule-based (RBMT), statistical (SMT), example-based (EBMT) and hybrid (HMT) systems at different stages.[6] However, a recent tipping point in the translation industry has seen the 'strong reemergence of Machine Translation in response to TM's inability to cope with the increasing translation needs of today's digital age' (García, 2009a: 199). The MT tools available at this time of heightened need were themselves benefitting from important steps forward, notably in the availability of data in suitable formats to make the tools more useful (Koehn, 2005: 79). In the professional context too, MT tools, particularly SMT and HMT systems, are now attracting serious consideration for integration in translation workflows.

All MT systems allow users to enter text in one natural language in electronic format then almost instantly receive a translation into another natural language supported by the system. SMT systems (e.g. Google Translate) apply statistical methods to huge bilingual corpora to generate likely new translations. Google has revolutionized the popularity and credibility of SMT systems, effectively by using the entire Internet as a corpus. For many reasons, Google Translate itself is not appropriate for use in the professional context, however. First, even this tool supports only a tiny number of the world's languages. Because it relies on the availability of huge online corpora of natural language, performance is variable (e.g. weaker for languages where the online corpus is limited). Research has also found that SMT is much more domain-dependent than RBMT systems, so performs less well in specialized or technical domains (Koehn, 2010: 537); such specialist texts are the ones most likely to be translated by professionals. Only basic text formats can be entered, whereas clients expect LSPs to handle multiple complex file formats. More important than any of these drawbacks, however, is the use to which Google can put any text entered in its tool: Google effectively owns the rights to any text entered. For most commercial jobs, LSPs agree to abide by client contracts respecting confidentiality and copyright of data sent for translation. Even where there is no explicit agreement with the client, LSPs are clearly not the owners of the ST so are not entitled to pass ownership to Google (Drugan & Babych, 2010: 4). This is not to say that LSPs never use it, of course, though no LSP visited for this study admitted doing so for commercial translation jobs. Other SMT approaches, or much more commonly, HMT systems (e.g. Systran in its later versions) were the tools most widely found in use in the industry. Hybrid systems bring together combinations of rule-based, statistical and example-based approaches. Providers like Asia Online design custom HMT engines for clients, usually directed at a specific domain or specialization and language pair(s). Such tools integrate client glossaries, can usually be associated with TM or localization tools and bypass confidentiality/ownership issues.

When using MT, pre-editing of source files is recommended to improve output quality. For anything other than basic gisting purposes, human post-editing is usually also needed. This happens increasingly through the integration of MT and TM tools (e.g. SDL Trados with Systran, the combination available, in customized form, in the EC). Where TM and MT tools are combined, the TM is first searched for any match. If there are no hits in the TM, MT output is either automatically proposed for missing text, or available at the translator's request. Some TM tools now offer the possibility of using Google Translate to do this (e.g. Wordfast Pro), despite the concerns noted above, but most integrated systems are based on proprietary solutions. The human translator then reviews and edits the segment and confirms the translation before sending it to the TM for storage and later reuse. In both research and the industry, serious attention is now being paid to identifying scenarios where MT + human postediting might be cheaper or faster than human translation, or allow new markets to be reached. Recent versions of TM tools now ship with MT integration, at least for some language pairs. Clients are driving this change in the industry: many who long rejected MT are now using it or considering its use.

3.1.9 *Localization tools*

Localization remains a 'little-known and poorly understood phenomenon outside of the relatively closed circle of its clients and practitioners' (Dunne, 2006: 1), both in industry and academia. The sector's complexity and the range of activities typically involved in a localization project mean that the 'closed circle' is also unusually diverse in make-up. It relies on contributors from language, computer science and business backgrounds, subjects which have traditionally been studied in isolation (ibid.: 1). Localization usually refers to the translation and adaptation of specific content types: it is translating 'for the screen, not for the printer' (García, 2009a: 200). When the sector first developed, its focus was translating software and the supporting materials associated with programs (e.g. online help). Website and game localization grew in importance during the 1990s. More recently, the need to localize mobile and cross-platform apps has posed new challenges for the sector.

TM and TMS tools are standard in the localization industry, but are insufficient to support the file formats and activities needed in most projects. Dedicated localization tools (e.g. SDL Passolo) are needed to extract translatable text from user interfaces (e.g. dialog boxes or menus), translate the text while referring to client terminology and TM resources and export then test localized files. Most localization providers use several tools and custom filters, features or workarounds, as they frequently translate innovative file formats or content which standard tools cannot support. Esselink (2000: 361) indicates that typical projects involve support from TMS, TM, MT and localization tools, plus working in the 'native creation tool' for several file types (e.g. marketing material, software binary files), and the creation of filters using scripting languages. Some providers rely on in-house tools (e.g. Microsoft LocStudio) and workflow systems which they have developed independently to meet these needs.

Dedicated localization tools allow translation of natural language text in software user interfaces. In addition to terminology and TM integration, they offer resource editing, validation features and quality checks (e.g. spell checks, compliance checks). Even more than TM tools, they require users to translate isolated 'strings', rather than longer segments or entire texts. However, they usually enable translation in WYSIWYG mode, so translated text can be viewed in the user interface in the target language. This allows translators to verify ST sense in context and perform such tasks as resizing elements or repositioning edit boxes where necessary. For instance, if the English term 'Cancel' appears in a prompt, the German equivalent 'Abbrechen' is 50 per cent longer, so the element or button in which the target term appears may have to be resized. The tools also support project testing steps such as generating a pseudo-translation. Pseudo-translation is automatically replacing source text with a meaningless sample of accented characters or complex script to establish in advance whether problems are likely to arise during localization proper. For example, the English phrase 'pseudo-translation' might be rendered as 'psèùðò-trànslátìóñ' to test European languages and 'よるぽろぼょうれりべゆるやべれめよゆ' for Japanese. This step is important to estimate likely differences in length, height or font, so time and resources for DTP and checking can be built in and costed.

A significant challenge in the sector is that pace of change generally outstrips the development of support tools. Recent demand for translated apps is one example. High-quality translation is essential if new apps are to be successful in foreign language markets and avoid being supplanted by local equivalents, but the ST content is by nature specialist or in niche fields, often written in US slang or the shared meta-language of a dedicated fan group. Users increasingly want to use games and apps across platforms (e.g. play a Facebook game on a laptop then switch to playing on a smartphone), presenting extra and novel technical challenges. Depending on the application being localized, relatively unusual languages may dominate. For instance, the blocking of the site in the PRC means that Facebook games are more often available in Turkish than in Chinese, despite the imbalance in number of speakers of those languages.

3.1.10 *Subtitling tools*

The Internet Age and digitalization of resources have led to a spike in demand for multilingual subtitling, particularly in the past decade, with the increase of online video content and use of multilingual subtitles for SEO. While subtitling of foreign-language feature films, training materials or monolingual captions for deaf and hard of hearing viewers have been supported for some time, the proliferation of online video and newer recent content types (e.g. DVDs, web captions) are more technically challenging and quick to evolve, so have meant more complex tools and new workflows. Subtitling is quicker and cheaper than dubbing so is used more widely and across more platforms, but presents additional challenges for translators than other text formats. Specialist tools (e.g. Swift) have developed to support essential functionalities (e.g. timecoding), and to allow subtitlers to adjust on-screen elements (e.g. fonts, positional or alignment information). Subtitling audio content in another language requires both translation and substantial editing, as reading speeds are much slower than speech processing. The tools use algorithms to calculate maximum screen time per subtitle and enable text to be cued at the appropriate moment. File size is significant and a wide range of file formats must be supported for different broadcasters and platforms. Confidentiality and copyright can be significant limiting factors affecting how subtitlers work, curbing the integration of free MT engines, for example, though some OS tools (e.g. Subtitle Edit) do support this.

The tools can be likened to localization tools in that they allow the translator to view the subtitles in context, aiding comprehension and enabling appropriate technical and linguistic changes. However, cost, availability and standard workflow in the industry have meant linguistic and QA steps are often separated, with translators sent intralingual subtitles (i.e. in the same source language as the spoken dialogue or narration) for translation in templates, independent of the software. Translators insert the TT in the template, sometimes without access to the accompanying film. The translated templates are returned to in-house support staff, who import the subtitles and prepare the display of translated material. These non-linguists are unlikely to understand the subtitles, causing issues with output quality (Flanagan, 2009: 85). Recent developments suggest these tools are likely to evolve in similar ways to TM and localization tools, with attention turning to integration of MT and corpora of previous subtitles to support translation (ibid.: 86–8).

3.1.11 *Collaborative translation tools*

Recently developed tools bring together several of the above technologies to support emerging types of collaborative translation. Increasing translation demand has led clients to consider alternative strategies to translate content or harness expert users in the target language to contribute to local versions. Such tools (e.g. Lingotek) provide cloud-based, prompted working environments, integrating resources such as MT output and TM matches for users without training and experience. Some integrate additional functionalities (e.g. project management) in the interface, accessible to all contributors and clients. Some established tool providers have released collaborative working environments (e.g. SDL Cloud Translation Solutions), and a few newer tools (e.g. Wordbee) claim to support even more complex translation types, including localization and subtitling.

Integrating crowdsourced translations with MT support and review by experienced professionals where appropriate increases translation capacity. These tools allow contributors to a project to work over a live network, seeing others' contributions in real time and sharing resources. Review and comment features build user and client feedback into the work cycle. Suggested uses include co-opting specialist staff in the target language of client companies to translate or post-edit, thus harnessing technical and client-specific expertise. A similar approach is that adopted by Facebook, where an in-house tool was developed to enable users of the site to collaborate in producing, correcting and rating translations, sometimes for later review by in-house or professional staff. This enabled the site to localize huge amounts of data much more quickly and cheaply than would have been feasible under traditional workflows or business models.

3.2 The impact of tools on workflow

Translation projects vary enormously in size, complexity and context, but almost all share five broad stages in workflow:

1 Pre-job planning and bidding for work;
2 Award of contract and agreeing project conditions;
3 Project management during the life of the project;
4 Project completion and return to client;
5 Post-project review and management.

These stages take different forms in certain settings. For instance, while translation 'clients' in some large organizations expect in-house departments to 'tender' for work, others bypass job costing procedures and simply allocate work to suitable staff. There will usually still be a comparable pre-project planning stage, however. Though they may take a slightly different form, then, these stages are found, even in contexts where electronic tools have not yet had much impact on the translation sector (e.g. developing countries with poor IT infrastructure). However, tools have developed to support and, where possible, automate each of the above stages, with various effects on workflow in most translation markets.

   Without tools, certain job types common today would simply not be possible. The combination of PM and localization tools, for example, enables translations across multiple languages and in complex formats which would otherwise be impossibly time-consuming or expensive. To achieve this, however, tools 'systematise the translation process so that it can be standardised and protocols can be implemented' (Torres-Hostench et al., 2010: 255). This has both positive and negative effects. Since the tools' integration in the industry, there has been observable change in its make-up. They both enable and encourage the scaling-up of translation processes. They encourage much larger projects, huge multilingual teams of translators and other specialists, the appearance and growing importance of larger MLVs to manage the huge volumes of information, increasing outsourcing and an inevitable new emphasis on project management.

Management processes have become more complex, resulting in a substantial new cohort of translation PMs. This means that increasing resources must be devoted to management, rather than directly to linguistic aspects. Tools also support a much greater range of file formats, with the industry now expected to service multilingual publishing, DTP and a range of other specialized services which individuals and smaller LSPs cannot provide. There are financial and support implications of providing the growing number of tools needed to service the range of client requirements: freelance translators cannot afford all the tools clients may require.

What does this mean for typical workflow? Translators are now part of much bigger teams, with tools automating more project processes and often dictating how translation fits in. For instance, if subtitling and web localization have to be integrated into a larger translation project, there is substantial impact for timing and QC. Bottlenecks can affect deadlines and delivery if such projects are not well-managed. Some argued during interviews that the increasing reliance on electronic tools has led to the development of a 'two-speed' industry to some extent. Poor infrastructure and patchy uptake of tools in some locales mean that the picture looks quite different in some markets and there are significant concerns regarding access to information as a result. Translators had mixed reactions to such developments. Some saw the increasingly large scale of project management as positive, freeing translators to work on linguistic aspects while PMs took over the business side. Others expressed concerns that, as in any large-scale model, there is a danger that a 'one size fits all' approach develops, and everyone is shoehorned into a standard workflow that may not be the most appropriate for different project needs. A closer look at the five stages in the management of most translation projects indicates how tools have affected each one.

Pre-job planning and bidding for work relies intensively on tools, particularly for large projects. When a PM receives an initial request for quotation from a client, he must evaluate resources required to cost and bid for the job. Tools make this process largely automatic. Quoting and file handling are sometimes also fully automated at this stage. Some LSPs provide instant online quotes. More commonly, however, this stage involves planning efficient working methods for the project and includes estimating:

- the volume of work at different stages, including non-linguistic aspects. Here, TM and localization tools support the process, for example, by analysing project content against client reference materials and establishing their likely usefulness across multiple languages;
- software, hardware and any training requirements;
- required deliverables and any value-added services;
- QA requirements.

Once these steps are complete, a project management fee is added and a quote generated, often automatically, even for projects involving dozens of languages and running over many months.

If the bid is successful, tools next support the PM in agreeing project conditions. Final source files are delivered to the PM for pre-processing. Where final versions are not ready, TM and localization tools allow work to begin on beta versions. Translators are then alerted to changes in the final versions for checking and editing. This has implications for translation workflow, as extra translation and revision stages may be needed. Batch processing (analysis, pre-translation) of multiple file types prior to translation allows the PM to cost input for each language and select suppliers. All PMs interviewed for the present book stated that rates and ability to use required tools were the main determining factors in selecting suppliers. Quality of work was relevant and might mean those charging higher rates were employed, but they would usually be reserved for challenging content, certain clients or when all other suppliers were already engaged. Such considerations also have an impact on project planning (e.g. identifying the complexity of content, booking suppliers' time to make sure they are available at the relevant project stage). At this stage, workflow for the project will be forecast in more detail and resources scheduled.

The importance of source file analysis was repeatedly stressed by PMs. If this is neglected, substantial extra work is likely to be needed later in the project, when time is at a premium. For instance, if an ST error is spotted after translation has been carried out for most languages, the PM must go back to dozens of translators across multiple languages and arrange for correction, usually with additional payment. PMs and lead translators highlighted the importance of resolving unclear content (e.g. acronyms, ambiguous pronouns) before sending files to suppliers so the same question is not raised repeatedly, or different solutions selected for each language. File conversion issues can have an impact on workflow at this stage. If there are problems with the smooth exchange of data, vital information may be lost so that alignment, access to the files in the TM tool, later QC processes, etc. do not work properly, delaying progress. At this stage, the impact of translation tools can be seen clearly: translators' very ability to take on certain jobs is determined by the formats they can receive and support, processing power and ability to comply with client or LSP workflow.

A significant impact of the tools on workflow is seen in the 'parcelling' of translation jobs across multiple translators. Tools mean that suppliers in the same language pair can share TMs and terminology resources. Large jobs are then split to increase speed of production. Manufacturers claim such use of their tools 'guarantees consistency of language style' across different translators (Drugan, 2007b: 82). This facility has been seized on by the industry to enable LSPs to meet tight release schedules and is now standard. During the translation stage, tools also increasingly allow tracking, monitoring and feedback. Previous paper tracking systems have largely given way to electronic tools to manage such monitoring, with many contributors to this study pointing out this allowed them to spot problems much earlier than previously and allocate additional resources where suppliers or particular language teams might otherwise delay a project.

Use of tools such as TMs can also dictate or cause problems in workflow, necessitating workarounds. In several tools (e.g. STAR Transit), the conversion of files for translation is performed by the PM pre-project. Translators then cannot export translated files for proofreading or revision outside the TM tool, but must return the files to the PM for export, creating an additional stage in the workflow. Some LSPs found it frustrating to have additional steps imposed in this way and translators felt it posed challenges for their own QC. Revision and editing were frequently the stages where the tools were felt to create an extra burden, often because they imposed an interface for the checks or made it unnecessarily complicated for the TM to be updated.

Once translation, QC and final testing have been completed, agreed deliverables are returned to the client. Post-project, there is usually a review of processes and possibly a client presentation or summary, which may feed back into databases (e.g. the supplier database may incorporate feedback on individual performance).

The workflow in the project stage in the above summary (i.e. post-contract through to delivery to the client) is referred to in the industry as TEP (Translate-Edit-Proofread) and has long been seen as the standard approach. The arrival of the tools and their impact on this workflow is perhaps best seen in the increasing redundancy of this acronym. If the TMS, TM, localization and QA tools are used in the ways recommended (and sometimes imposed) by their designers, the TEP stage would be significantly expanded, along the following lines:

1 Pre-edit ST;

2 QA of ST;

3 Preprocessing (may include pseudo-translation, sample translation);

4 Test (sample product, e.g. software in pseudo-translated format; workflow as well as translation);

5 QA of process and sample product; review planned processes and agree QA plan;

6 Translate ST;

7 QA of sample TT;

8 Return of QA results to translator for revision of TT;

9 Edit/revise amended TT;

10 QC of amended TT;

11 Proofread;

12 Generate final target files;

13 QA of process and final product;

14 Post-delivery review of QA process, updating and review of resources (TM, TBs).

These stages are not relevant for all projects (e.g. pre-translation testing is common in software localization but relatively rare in other domains). However, Makoushina (2007: 14) found that, despite variation across projects, there was clear evidence in the industry of greater integration of QA processes throughout the translation cycle. 12 per cent of LSPs applied QA procedures on source files and at the end of each TEP stage; 32 per cent did not QA source files but applied QA processes at the end of each TEP stage. Only 28 per cent restricted TQA to the traditional stage, applying them only to the final files. The most common response, however, was that the process 'depends on the project'. Client preference has a determining role in workflow, particularly in certain technical sectors. This finding is consistent with practices observed by the author. While LSPs had 'out of the box' workflows for application to projects where no client preference was expressed, special cases with exceptional levels of QA were found in virtually all settings. One exception was where LSPs were ISO certified or had signed up to other standards; they might then be obliged to implement QA processes at agreed stages, even where clients had not requested them.

Koo and Kinds (2000: 147) describe in detail one localization vendor's application of the LISA QA model and associated tool in conjunction with a defined translation sampling method. They explain the benefits of such amended workflow: 'early sampling has allowed early feedback and error rectification – critical in the fast-moving localization business' (ibid.: 151). In this approach, critical, major and minor errors are defined and scored prior to project commencement. If a single critical error is found at any stage, the work is rejected and returned to the supplier. Major/minor errors are weighted and counted, then a Pass/Fail score is allocated for the whole job. They found unexpected side effects for both future workflow and translation quality. Compiling data on error types found in projects allowed them to identify trends, helping suppliers avoid repetition of such errors in future jobs (ibid.). Illustrating the different effects of QA in translation theory and the real world, they list a sequence of potential consequences, with 'in extreme cases, translators [being] pulled off the job' (ibid.: 156).

The expanded workflow outlined above is modular (stages can be added or removed, according to client preference, for example). Even with such flexibility, it is unlikely to dominate in the way the TEP model did, however, as other workflow models are emerging simultaneously. First, as already noted, there are a number of sectors where the very concept of the defined translation project is becoming passé. Rolling translation of websites and software are increasingly seen as continual processes. Where they have defined stages, these may happen concurrently for different iterations and language pairs. This is having an impact on the tools which support workflow too (e.g. new features and greater flexibility). Second, increasing use of MT + human post-editing has implications for workflow. If MT is integrated, are new QA processes needed? If so, when are they best integrated? Does sampling for QA at different stages still make sense? A significant issue for the industry where MT is integrated relates to pricing, and this too has implications for workflow. If suppliers are paid different rates depending on how much post-editing a segment requires, how can this be calculated (and projects costed) in advance? MT output may be the equivalent of a 100 per cent TM match for some segments, but will require translation from scratch for others. Using a TM, PMs can predict with high accuracy in advance what percentage of a source file will need to be translated from scratch (and remunerated accordingly), but this is impossible in advance with MT output.

Bowker (2002: 139) summarizes the double nature electronic tools' impact: 'As technology advances, new types of translation work are being created. [. . .] These new types of translation work, in turn, are prompting the development of new types of technology'. In translation workflow too, this two-way relationship can be observed, and is likely to lead to result in ongoing evolution in industry approaches. The greater integration of QA processes in the standard workflow thus far can be seen as one way the industry has responded to concerns regarding the tools' potential impact on quality. The next section outlines these concerns and findings on tools' impact on quality in more detail.

3.3 The impact of tools on quality

All studies of the impact of electronic tools on quality have recognized the limitations of research in this area. Evaluating translation quality itself is challenging, but adding complicating factors of process-based research, working conditions and relatively new technologies compounds the difficulty. It is probably impossible to create entirely rigorous scientific conditions for such research. For instance, subjects must either be aware they are taking part in research on translation quality and tool use (in which case, they are likely to pay particular attention to certain factors or steps, potentially distorting results), or researchers must observe them under false pretences (an approach of dubious ethical standing, and which may have unintended distorting effects, depending on the alternative reason the subjects are given for their participation). A few studies have nonetheless been carried out, with their limitations acknowledged. For example, Spanish researchers recently investigated the hypotheses that 'translations resulting from different processes are different' and 'the use of CAT tools has an impact on the final translation' (Torres-Hostench et al., 2010: 256). Their TRACE project to evaluate these assumptions is however at an early stage and findings remain inconclusive, not least because they have tested only the effect of different tool *interfaces*; translators in their experiments worked with empty TMs.

The results of existing research are combined here with observations of real-world contexts carried out for the present book. Experimental findings, real-world observation and industry concerns reveal recurring patterns, concerns and observations, which would together seem to confirm certain impacts on quality. A weakness in this approach, however, is that published research on quality has focused virtually exclusively on TM and MT tools, with some limited attention to QA tools. For the majority of tools, then, the suggestions below come only from observations carried out for the present study. The impact of the tools on translation quality can be both positive and negative, and both types of impact are now summarized.

3.3.1 *Proven effects*

Basic effects of the tools on quality are undisputed. First, text in some applications and formats would not be translated at all, certainly not into as many languages, if specialist tools were not available to extract text straightforwardly and make the ROI worthwhile. Workarounds to enable translation could be used, but are linked to more errors (e.g. hidden text being missed), and both costs and time for translation would be considerably higher. Second, the impact on productivity is measurable and significant in many cases (O'Brien, 1998; Somers, 2003a; Yamada, 2011). Where repetitive texts or updates are translated using the tools, there are clear gains in turnaround speed when performance using the tools is compared with other working methods. Manufacturers tend to overestimate this benefit (Drugan, 2007b: 81), but widespread observation and translator experience confirm a real impact on productivity. Although academic approaches rarely include speed of translation in their accounts of translation quality, it features high on the list of industry criteria. Meeting client deadlines is a fundamental, sometimes the most important, aspect of quality when translation is viewed as a service (Kingscott, 1996a: 138).

3.3.2 *Tools and users*

Technology is used in unintended ways. Tools designed to support translation depend on both human users and the quality of resources. They can therefore have unforeseen or unintended effects on quality. As with any tool, the GIGO principle (Garbage In, Garbage Out) applies. If poor quality resources are integrated in TM databases, for example, these have an ongoing impact. Bowker has demonstrated that translators accept matches without noticing or correcting errors (2005: 18). This risk is exacerbated in two conditions: where inexperienced translators are using tools; and where translators are working under time constraints (i.e. almost always). Even experienced, observant translators may miss small errors such as a misplaced decimal point. One translator observed for the current study demonstrated how easily this can happen: a 90 per cent fuzzy match was proposed, with a change to one term clearly colour-coded. The translator amended this term and moved onto the next segment, without spotting that another small change (punctuation, in this case) was also needed. Even if translators spot errors in TM content, they cannot always correct these. Translators repeatedly complained that poor quality content was locked, and thus imposed for the new translation; or that when they tried to correct errors, their suggestions were rejected because consistency across projects was prioritized. An EC translator volunteered the term 'health and safety' in illustration. In most EC databases, 'safety and health' is preferred, but national UK legislation refers to 'health and safety'. Where a translator is not vigilant, accepting the proposed translation might mislead, hamper links to national legislation or even harm the legal standing of the TT.

TM tools introduce new types of error, but rely on human users to spot and correct them (Makoushina, 2007: 4). It is easy to miss the small changes required in fuzzy matches (e.g. pronouns, figures, tags). The tools can only highlight differences: humans must evaluate the content and decide whether changes are appropriate. Translators stressed the difficulty of spotting every such change, especially when tired or working with TMs containing poor quality segments which required a lot of editing. The importance of adequate maintenance of TM and terminology databases, and need for freedom to override inappropriate matches, were stressed by most users. Otherwise there is a real danger that poorly aligned segments, or poor quality segments entered by previous translators, are perpetuated. In interviews for this book, it was apparent that, while translators were aware of the need to store only high-quality data, very few carried out TM maintenance regularly. A majority of freelance translators were unable to demonstrate how to use their chosen tool(s) to do this. To some extent, the widespread lack of awareness of how to carry out TM maintenance in the industry can be attributed to workflow: translators do not do this because they assume clients or agencies will furnish them with properly maintained databases for each job. Yet when clients and agencies were questioned, they were often surprised that translators expected this to be their responsibility. TM maintenance was regularly seen as an 'admin' or routine job, performed by staff who were not even bilingual.

User vigilance regarding quality of database content (e.g. for TMs and termbases) has secondary effects for the application of automated QA tools. When QA tools perform automatic compliance checks, they are limited by the resources used. They cannot detect the cause of an error, simply its presence. For example, if an inappropriate term is in the termbase and the translator corrects this in the TT, the TQA tools will class the translator's correction as a 'wrong term', because it does not match the client database. The tools' limitations need to be clearly communicated. For example, any QA tool based on applying metrics can only measure error levels, not correct them. QA tools are restricted too in what they can measure. They cannot spot many linguistic errors, and all rely on effective human input to spot the false positives they invariably return. Although tools 'speed up QA processes and increase translation quality to some extent, their error level is still high, which means people who perform QA spend most of their time deciding whether an error reported needs to be corrected or not' (ibid.: 38).

Unrealistic client and user expectations of MT affect translation quality, not least in the plethora of badly translated websites, whose creators believed that free MT without post-editing was sufficient to produce foreign language versions. Even MT plus human post-editing/translation is inefficient for many scenarios and likely to lead to quality issues:

> Improper use of MT systems for the wrong types of documents, will make MT a costly, inefficient and time-consuming exercise. Machine translation has been proven to be effective only when used by vendors to translate very controlled input that has been carefully planned for by the post-editing team. (Esselink, 2000: 395)

For many reasons (to speed up or lower the cost of translation, to permit translation into underserved languages, to allow translation of texts which would not otherwise provide sufficient ROI), increasing numbers of clients are looking to MT + human post-editing. The impact on quality of this working method is thus beginning to be explored (Fiederer & O'Brien, 2009). In a fairly limited but controlled experiment, clarity and accuracy levels of post-edited MT output compared favourably with human translation, but when style was considered, there was a clear preference among evaluators for human translation (ibid.: 69). One significant potential impact on quality of such approaches is likely to be the dearth of linguists with experience of post-editing MT rather than translating from scratch. Translators questioned in research for this book had little or no experience of this working method. Those who used TM tools which could propose MT output for unmatched segments had usually disabled the feature, as they found the suggestions insufficiently useful to be worth the time to read them. The few who did use it claimed they mainly used MT output for terminology.

A related trend noted in research for this book was that, whenever technology moves forward significantly, it is often the technically competent or confident, rather than linguistic experts, who take on translation jobs. Particularly in areas such as app localization, few professional translators have the experience or technical understanding to perform the work. Where clients required the use of a particular tool or ability to handle certain formats, relatively inexperienced translators in the supplier database, or even new providers deliberately recruited for the project, can be used, rather than tried-and-tested translators with a track record of producing work of the required quality.

3.3.3 *Human error*

Translators are known to make certain errors (Mossop, 2001: 1–2). Revisers and proofreaders have always checked for common error types (e.g. missed text, incorrect figures). A strength of tools is their ability to prevent or signal many errors. TM and localization tools reliably extract source material and present it to the user for translation.[7] Most tools record completed segments as the user translates, and if text is skipped or partially translated, they flag this. ST figures are identified as placeables and automatically inserted in the TT in the user's preferred format (e.g. €1.000,00 in the ST becomes €1,000.00 in the TT). This improves reliability and quality, particularly for figure-heavy texts, but depends on appropriate human input. Users can choose to omit post-translation QC or override error messages, so the defects picked up by such checks will still be missed. Most translators interviewed for this study noted that such errors were very hard for humans to spot reliably, but potentially critical to quality. 'Translators, even those who write superbly, are notoriously lax with figures, but an error such as "The patient must not eats for two hours" is not life-threatening, whereas writing 15mg instead of 1.5mg is' (Kingscott, 1999: 200). Human revisers miss such errors, especially in long files containing lots of figures; tools never do. A live illustration of this was observed during research. Despite working under observation in a scientific domain where accuracy was critical (aeronautical engineering), a translator and reviser carrying out laborious oral revision both failed to spot an incorrect decimal point. When this was highlighted, they were unsurprised, agreeing it was 'just impossible to catch every error'.

Conversely, tools make some human errors more likely and introduce new ones, such as partly amended sentences when text is cut and pasted (Mossop, 2001: 25–6). Many such errors relate to segmentation. Rather than approaching a new ST as a whole text, translators are presented with short text extracts out of context. Various quality problems have been suggested or proven in relation to this. Localization leads to 'lower qualities of text and communication', for example (Pym, 2010a: 137). How does this happen in practice? First, segmentation increases faithfulness to source language norms at the expense of the target language. Researchers have shown that translators working in a TM tool violated target language punctuation rules more than when working in MS Word (Torres-Hostench et al., 2010: 270). Translators who used TM tools confirmed in interviews for this book that it was also tempting to follow ST structures and syntax. To remedy this, many relied on full-text self-revision, ideally on paper, of the draft translation. However, they recognized that such checks might be sacrificed under time pressure. Another solution demonstrated by professional translators was to view the whole ST or longer sections (e.g. a document page) while translating, either via two screens (one apiece for the TM editor and ST), preview functions or a hard copy of the ST. Very few worked exclusively in a TM or localization tool with no access to the source. When a challenging segment appeared, they switched to looking at the whole text before entering their translation back in the TM tool.

Another consequence of segmentation which affects quality is the 'sentence salad' effect (Bédard, 2000: 45). Because pairs of segments are sent to the TM then later proposed to different users translating new texts, perhaps years later, various translators' and ST authors' different styles are merged. Bédard argues that no ST is likely to be written in this way, and that the quality of translated texts will therefore be inferior in comparison. In fact, CMS and other tools do often now merge segments of STs compiled in different contexts. Professional translators were aware of this potential effect (referring to it as a 'pot pourri', for example) and again suggested a reading of the whole draft text as a necessary step to avoid it.

When matches are proposed to translators, various kinds of human error can affect quality. Chief among these is the temptation to accept matches without sufficient questioning or reworking for new contexts. Where a 100 per cent match is proposed, translators acknowledged the risk of accepting it uncritically, or having it imposed (locked). Some clients refuse to pay for 100 per cent matches, further removing the incentive for the translator to amend segments. This leads to errors in various ways:

- In new texts, gender, pronouns and other features of the ST may be different and require alteration in the TT, even where the two ST segments were identical;

- Different usage or client preferences might make changes necessary (e.g. some style guides mandate –ise endings in English, where others require –ize; both might exist in the TM or termbase);

- A TM segment may contain errors. These should be corrected for the new TT. Interviewees mentioned this was a particular problem for novice translators, who might assume TM entries were accurate, rather than challenging experienced colleagues' work.

Translators' concerns on these points were confirmed by Bowker (2005: 19), in experiments with student translators as subjects. She found that proposed matches were accepted, even when errors had been deliberately sown in the TM.

3.3.4 *Consistency/efficiency in the translation process*

Project management, planning and preparation tools are directly linked to quality because they prompt QA processes consistently across all languages. Automated workflow removes variability and reduces reliance on individual suppliers to follow QA processes, which might be sacrificed in the face of tight deadlines. The tools enable tracking and monitoring during the life of a project, which can both improve efficiency in the translation process and catch quality issues to be addressed sufficiently early. Centralization of resources and online tools also increase efficiency, which has secondary effects for quality. For example, in larger projects, PMs typically take on client liaison, passing on translator queries. Some tools force responses to any query to be shared automatically with all translators working on a project, meaning that those suppliers who had not noticed an issue with the source files benefit from the queries raised by more critical or questioning colleagues.

Conversely, the tools' imposition of consistency in the translation process was viewed as having a negative impact on quality by some of those interviewed. PMs felt they were encouraged, even obligated, to adopt workflows that were not the most efficient, as it was easier to slot new projects into the standard model than configure the tools differently, particularly where a project was a one-off. Some volunteered that this meant they simply skipped or checked off certain stages for certain projects. Efficiency was also questioned, with translators and PMs seeing some stages in the translation process as unnecessarily cumbersome when working with the tools (e.g. time needed for laborious conversion of different formats, maintenance).

QA tools are often used in conjunction with PM tools and have some clear positive effects for consistency and efficiency in the process. PMs and unit heads commented on the usefulness of QA procedures being applied as a standard stage in workflow, as this meant that all translations were checked with no stigma. One unit head indicated that it was sometimes difficult to raise quality issues with senior colleagues, but the manifest impartiality of the tools made this less sensitive. In an experiment on his own translations, Gerasimov confirmed that even established translators working in familiar domains and following QA procedures could benefit. After applying automated TQA tools retrospectively to translations which had passed through his own, revisers' and clients' quality checks, he found multiple further errors which had passed unnoticed into TMs and been returned to clients. He concluded, 'no matter how experienced the translator is and what human quality assurance methods s/he uses, TQA tools are able to decrease the number of mistakes and improve the overall quality of translation' (2007: 25).

However, QA tools can confer a false sense of security by focusing attention on those quality aspects which can be easily checked. When clients are told that the translation process involves such QA checks, they may not understand the implications and assume stronger guarantees than in fact apply. The temptation is to carry out only automated checks, as Makoushina found in her survey of tool use (2007: 38): 'the most popular QA approach to date is to perform any checks that are easily automated and not too time-consuming while neglecting rather important, but more complicated ones due to time constraints.' Translations can pass automatic QA with flying colours but nonetheless be of poor quality (e.g. in terms of clarity). Equally, automated QA tools rely on the quality and size of databases to pick up errors such as inappropriate register, so may well miss such significant problems.

Like PM and planning tools, QA tools have also been criticized for their 'out of the box' approach or applying a single standard model. Although tools can be configured to match specific project requirements, those applying them agreed they rarely changed settings. For example, the tools' weighting of critical, major and minor errors is designed to be flexible, so that specific parameters can be agreed with clients for project needs. PMs explained in interviews that clients were often unwilling or unable to engage with such processes, preferring to 'leave all that to the experts'. Another unintended negative effect of the tools was that some PMs felt that their use cut down on time which could more usefully be spent on translation. Although they are quick to apply, time has to be built in to the project for translators to check errors found by the tools. This was particularly frustrating when QA tools detected large numbers of false errors (e.g. different ST and TT punctuation rules). For some language pairs, the high number of false positives meant that applying the tools then checking results was a frustrating exercise, but it was sometimes imposed nonetheless because clients valued a standard, consistent approach, or because agency certification imposed certain processes for all certified jobs.

3.3.5 *Consistency/efficiency and the translation product*

Manufacturers claim tools improve efficiency (productivity) and consistency in the translation product (Drugan, 2007b: 81–3). Turnaround speed is essential for obvious reasons. Consistency is important in most professional contexts because:

- Clients demand consistent use of terminology and house style for branding;

- Many text types (e.g. user guides) rely on consistent terminology and style for simplicity, cross-referencing and ease of navigation (e.g. software users find synonyms such as 'Trash'/'Recycle Bin' for the same concept frustrating, particularly when searching documentation to resolve a problem);

- Users find variety in expression confusing (e.g. in technical domains).

Terminology, TM and localization tools enhance consistency; QA tools and features check for it. They do so across individual translators' work (e.g. prompting the same target term for the same source term whenever it appears in a file or in future translations); across teams of translators sharing resources (e.g. when Translator A first translates a segment, it is added to the shared TM and suggested to Translator B when he arrives at identical or similar segments; QA tools verify that Translator B complied); and over time (e.g. years after a segment was first translated, the original translator's TT is proposed for identical or similar segments). Recent developments (e.g. 'live' databases which are updated in real time) further enhance consistency. When client glossaries and TMs are sent out at the beginning of a project, entries added during the project are not available to all suppliers, or are available with a delay. The onus is also on translators to update databases regularly and check completed translations complied with updates. 'Live' databases remove such inconsistency.

Translators interviewed for this book raised concerns about data quality in such live databases, as QC processes are rarely imposed before updating. One had changed her preferred working method: she liked to draft a 'rough and ready' version then revise the entire text, but did not feel she could do this when her draft segments were added to the shared TM for all to see. Some systems allow translators to work offline in draft mode, uploading only final translations to the TM, but this defeats the purpose of real-time resource sharing. Users also found it confusing when multiple target versions appeared in databases; it was then unclear which to adopt (the most recent? The one previously approved by the client? The one which complies best with project guidelines?). Mossop (2001: 24) offers the illustration of the English term hot line/hot-line/hotline – each might be correct, depending on client preference. Such multiple variants are common, particularly when using tools: the user or client glossary, TM and MT might each propose a different solution.

The tools can have perverse effects. Their use sometimes *reduces* consistency. Claims that STs can be split across teams of translators without losing consistency in style met with scepticism in the industry. Some small groups of familiar collaborators felt they could achieve a similar style (e.g. a small group of in-house and freelance colleagues working on a long-term contract for a familiar client), but most LSPs felt this approach required more attention post-translation, ideally one reader reviewing the entire text. This was rarely feasible, and undermined the point of splitting the translation in the first place (improved speed); the 'bottleneck' was simply moved to the revision stage.

Another unintended effect for quality of working in such teams was that translators pre-empted their colleagues and aimed for a neutral style. One translator carefully respected the lead translator's known preferences, rather than producing her best work, to avoid unnecessary revision (she viewed this negatively, as 'pollution' of her style). Many interviewees disliked using TMs containing matches authored by other translators. They either felt the quality or style was lower than their own, or spent more time editing matches than translating would have taken, because matches were so different in style (e.g. extensive use of passives). Translators particularly disliked being forced to integrate poor quality matches into their own work. Interviewees expressed concern about how to approach such poor matches: should they adapt the style of the remainder of the translation to 'fit' with the poor translation, or produce a high-quality TT for the untranslated segments, leading to a 'jarring' experience for users, who would then find poor quality segments seeded through a generally decent text? Translators were also frustrated that poor quality content kept being confirmed and stored for future use.[8]

One of the key drivers of the tools, consistency, may not even be desirable: 'one person's improved consistency is evidently another person's perpetuation of poor models' (Chesterman & Wagner, 2002: 128). Reusing past translations means 'errors or awkward phrasings' may recur, and QA tools will not identify these as such: as long as the ST and TT segments or terms are in client databases, they will be approved, perpetuating the problem. Even high-quality matches may not be appropriate in new contexts (e.g. some years later when technical jargon has evolved). One final complaint made by translators was that, where the ST contained evident errors (e.g. Cannon for Canon), they were penalized by QA tools when they corrected it. Consistently *bad* translations are clearly not the aim, but can result from real-world use of the tools.

3.3.6 Translators' attention to quality issues

Users volunteered in interviews and during workshadowing that they used some tools precisely because they encouraged attention to translation quality. This was particularly true of voice recognition tools. As one user explained, 'dictating means I focus more on reading the ST and think[ing] about how to structure the TT rather than seeing multiple possibilities on screen or getting distracted by typing'. Confirmed users mentioned that, when they typed, translation was delayed when they were sidelined by typos or errors in inputting the TT, interrupting their train of thought. Under observation, many translators read the ST segment then dictated with their eyes closed, and focusing on the TT alone. Users were also convinced they spotted more errors when self-revising, as it was 'like seeing the translation for the first time, you haven't typed the mistake so it leaps out at you'. Some translators also volunteered that their reason for using TM and terminology tools was precisely for quality improvements. Many translators always worked in the TM interface, even for very short, one-off jobs, because they were familiar with the environment and relied on the quality checks bundled with the tool.

3.3.7 *Respect for client requirements and QA procedures*

Clients often impose certain tools because they force LSPs to comply with some quality requirements. For example, active terminology recognition in TM tools allows clients to check translators have used approved terms even when clients have no linguistic competence in their language. As Clark (1994: 306) and Bowker (2002: 87) stress, such compliance is significant to clients. There is little point in compiling extensive termbases if translators can ignore them. If QA tools return significantly higher error scores for one target language, clients can apply further (human) QA to investigate. Negative effects on quality were observed for such tools and features, however. Translators, unsurprisingly, found certain client-imposed methodologies short-sighted. Increasingly, LSPs in technical fields were sent TMs or pre-translated files containing a lot of MT output and found this frustrating, especially where MT content was not flagged as such. Translators working with localization tools highlighted another negative impact on quality. Such tools automatically generate a list of 'known' quality issues, which translators must check and approve or change before being able to generate the target file. Interviewees mentioned that these lists could run into dozens, even hundreds, of supposed 'errors', the vast majority of which were actually appropriate in the target language. One translator described this as 'crying wolf', the risk being that translators would click mechanically through multiple false positives, missing a real quality issue buried among the non-errors. More worrying was the temptation noted by several translators to pre-empt tools. Where translators knew that automated QC would be applied, it made sense to focus on elements checked by the tools at the expense of other aspects of translation quality which would not be checked, but which might, ironically, matter more to the client.

3.3.8 *Access to resources*

Translators who have worked in the industry for over a decade invariably comment on the wealth of tools and resources available today, and how much easier it is to access information and produce a high-quality translation. Translators in technical fields appreciated recent innovations enabling clients to embed images or videos in termbases. Large, frequent consumers of translation agreed that a significant advantage of tools was that they 'unlocked' expensive resources built up over time. Several international organizations also volunteered this as the main reason for their use. In technical subjects, a crucial aspect for translation quality was sharing expertise, particularly by leveraging and passing on the domain knowledge built up over decades by senior colleagues.

Corpora – including the Internet – were also recognized as offering important benefits for quality:

> A specialised monolingual target-language corpus can be of great help to the translator in confirming intuitive decisions, in verifying or rejecting decisions based on other tools such as dictionaries, in obtaining information about collocates, and in reinforcing knowledge of normal target language patterns. (Wilkinson, 2007: 111)

Corpora also allow 'unpredictable, incidental learning: the user may notice unfamiliar uses in a concordance and follow them up by exploratory browsing' (ibid.: 108). There are known problems in unlocking such resources effectively, however. Users require additional skills in research and critical evaluation of information for data to be useful. Few have been trained in this. Information scientists and other specialists previously provided support, but translators are increasingly required to develop these skills independently (Olvera Lobo et al., 2007: 518). Access to information is no longer problematic in many fields, but evaluating huge amounts of data requires different skills and time. Peer support resources have developed (e.g. online forums), but the most active users are some of the least experienced members of the profession, leading to concerns as to the quality of advice (Durban, 2010: 74–5). The sheer quantity of data available can now cause quality problems. Much online content is authored by non-native or non-expert speakers so is of limited helpfulness to professional linguists. 'The time that is often required for separating the wheat from the chaff resulting from the numerous "unreliable hits" that are generated' (Wilkinson, 2007: 112–3) makes its use problematic.

3.3.9 *Tool design*

Tool design was one of the most recurrent topics volunteered by users as having an effect on quality. Some commented positively, but in retrospect a substantial number of translators were still using an outdated and unsupported version of Trados because it allowed them to work in the MS Word interface, while others had switched to Wordfast for TM support for the same reason. Lagoudaki (2009: n.p.) found that some translators continued to work in MS Word, despite its limitations (no TM, few compatible file formats); they attributed this choice to quality features available in Word, notably autotext and simple macros. Overwhelmingly though, users believed tool design had a negative impact on quality. Terminology tools attracted particular criticism: too many did not support straightforward addition of new terms while translating, imposing a complicated key sequence or use of the mouse. Many translators ignored terminology features and relied on concordance searches of the TM. When they were subsequently unable to find a term they had translated previously (e.g. because it was inflected differently), this resulted in frustration and quality issues for the new TT.

TM tools were the most widely criticized for design flaws, notably:

- File conversion makes TM tools inefficient for some jobs, so translators worked in the native file format instead. If they wanted to benefit from future matches, they had to spend time on alignment afterwards. Translators emphasized it was often impossible to know when starting a job whether content would be useful in future;

- The absence or unreliability of WYSIWYG/preview features had effects on quality. Sometimes text was not identified as translatable so source language text was left in the localized version, but was not visible in the TM interface. Text might need to be altered depending on context (e.g. different capitalization rules for header and body text), but editing environments did not display the information;

- TM editing environments caused other quality problems: impossibility of navigating within the text while a segment is open for translation; unwieldiness (e.g. in modifying tags); technical issues with display/entry of character-based scripts; poor support for popular shortcuts (cut and paste, copy); lack of user customization (macros). Users were frustrated that standard shortcuts varied (e.g. Ctrl+S often saves not the whole file but the active segment alone, which had led to translators losing work, or not being able to export completed translations);

- Mark-up, codes, hidden text, headers and footers and images were often difficult to spot and required careful checking post-translation;

- Some TM tools (e.g. STAR Transit) make it difficult or impossible to export a draft translation for review then reimport for corrections. This risks TM resources not being updated effectively post-QC;

● Users expressed frustration that such known issues were ignored in repeated updates. Lack of clarity in the user interface also impeded effective use. Lagoudaki (2009: n.p.) cites one translator's frustration with a leading TM tool that prompts: 'Do you not wish to save the TM? Yes/No'. Over-technical terminology also made it difficult to understand certain features.

Tools were criticized for disparity in support for certain languages or scripts, notably CJK, Cyrillic and Arabic. Nor do most QA tools support character-based scripts effectively (Makoushina, 2007: 21). LSPs for certain language pairs felt they missed out on basic quality features (e.g. active term recognition) because of poor design.

3.3.10 Cost

An aspect of tool use affecting translation quality, raised in interviews by clients and LSPs alike, was the cost. Investment in tools has to come from the translation budget, so less of the overall spend is directed at translation itself. ROI was felt to justify the most obvious direct costs of acquiring the tools and associated training (plus ongoing upgrades and CPD training), but interviewees repeatedly raised a series of secondary costs as having a less easily measured impact on eventual translation quality. The spread of productivity tools has resulted in the rise of MLVs managing much more complex multilingual projects. Additional costs are then diverted to project management rather than linguistic aspects. Where PM costs were divulged, they were estimated at between 5–10 per cent of total project costs, but few LSPs were willing to share this information. MLV dominance was felt to have mixed effects for translation quality. Freelance translators who worked both for agencies and direct clients invariably believed that direct clients received a higher quality end-product, because translators could resolve any queries or concerns directly with the client, and were paid more for such work, meaning there was less pressure to work quickly. Some clients and most MLVs argued the opposite, stressing that consistency across languages and guarantees of quality checks offered benefits.

Increasing outsourcing of translation, rather than maintaining costly in-house divisions, was raised as having implications for quality. Translators who remained in-house stressed the benefits for quality of a team building up significant domain expertise. Unit heads and managers acknowledged this. Most organizations using a combination of in-house and freelance staff confirmed critical jobs were kept in-house, while gisting or rough jobs were those they outsourced. External suppliers' translations were usually subject to additional quality checks, and were often not integrated in termbases or TMs due to quality concerns. Freelance translators themselves raised a risk for translation quality, that of perceived downward pressure on rates, linked to tool use. Fuzzy match rates were typically reduced, yet translators argued they often spent as much time amending these as they would have spent translating from scratch. Established translators often refused to accept lower rates for matches for this reason.

3.3.11 *Cumulative impact*

Translators use multiple tools and resources, as the concept of the translator's workbench implies. Professional translators indicated or suspected complex effects for quality of the tools when used in combination. This is difficult to replicate in the lab, and thus represents a significant gap in research. Experiments on tools and translation quality have, with one exception, focused on the use of a single tool type in isolation. Equally, it is impossible to measure scientifically how multiple tools interact with one another in real life, as there are too many variables to control conditions (e.g. potential number of combinations of tools, user skill levels, resources in databases, language pairs). Where multiple tools and workflows are in use simultaneously, it is, however, unlikely they would not interact or have mutual effects, some of which were repeatedly suggested in research for this book.

Chief among concerns raised by translators was the impact of increasing integration of MT with TM tools. Poor quality TM matches are likely to be accepted in certain conditions (Bowker, 2005: 18). It is thus likely that, where MT output is suggested to translators working in similar conditions, it might be accepted without sufficient checking. Some TM tools do not flag MT output clearly (e.g. by use of colour coding). If the translator mistakenly confirms the segment, adding it to the TM, it will then be proposed to future users as a confirmed translation without being flagged as MT output at all. Translators were concerned at the long-term corruption of TM resources. Adequate TM maintenance or QC measures can of course address this, but the scenarios in which MT output was being integrated in TM use were typically high-pressured and unlikely to benefit from stringent review measures.

Manufacturers invariably stress that the tools make translation resources more valuable over time, through increased leveraging and database size. Many imply or claim that quality will also therefore be improved over time. Real-world experience was that the cumulative effect of a range of tools and large numbers of users actually had the opposite effect. The longer a database of terminology or TM matches was in use, the more 'pollution' or corruption of resources was found. This was linked to:

- The number of different suppliers. Databases might now be decades old, with thousands of suppliers contributing to resources, leading to inconsistent style and quality;

- Errors passing into databases. Even if errors are picked up during QC, corrections are frequently not fed back to the database. Clients in particular found it frustrating to have to keep correcting identical errors in repeat jobs;

- Impact of poor management. LSPs adopted various approaches to controlling who could approve/enter/update entries in the databases. Where anyone can add entries, there are clear quality implications, as drafts or unchecked material are easily imported. Imposing quality 'gatekeepers' to vet data prior to addition caused other issues. Translators complained that specialist terminologists entered excessive irrelevant data (part of speech, gender) when what they needed was the facility to enter a term in all possible forms and combinations (plural, tense) with a single key stroke. They were frustrated that segments or terms they had translated were not updated sufficiently quickly due to bottlenecks at the QC stage, meaning they had to repeat work or risked inconsistency;

- 'Unclean' data. Most TM resources include tagged text and other formatting, which affects match rates and can impede matches being found;

- Multiple entries with no weighting. It was common for multiple different matches to be returned, but translators commented that it was rare to be given advice as to which was preferable.

The concurrent use of PM, TM, terminology, localization and corpora/ bi-text tools over time has meant increasing database size and variety of content. Across the industry, different approaches to database management were being tested to try to identify the most efficient way to manage growing resources, but no standard model exists. LSPs were found to organize and separate TMs and termbases by language pair, client, domain, date of entry or level of quality checks applied. Many simply have one huge database from which subsets are extracted through filters according to individual job requirements, but this then raises questions about the most appropriate data every time a new job starts. Each of these solutions was seen as imperfect and presenting challenges for the quality of future translations produced with the support of the tools.

The one limited experimental finding in this area is also negative. Researchers examining translation editing environments drew a tentative conclusion that 'hybrid translation environments (word processor with TM functionalities) interfere to a greater extent in a translator's output' than working in either environment alone (Torres-Hostench et al., 2010: 269). Finally, participants in research for this book frequently indicated that using multiple tools, while increasingly necessary to work in the industry, meant they spent less time on translation due to non-linguistic tasks imposed by the tools. Database maintenance, alignment, conversion, importing, exporting and resolving technical issues (e.g. system crashes, 'interference' between different tools) reduced the time spent on producing translations, yet such work was rarely if ever remunerated. Frustration is frequently voiced at having to devote time to 'fiddling with formatting' rather than focusing on the quality of the linguistic content (Chesterman & Wagner, 2002: 109–10), and almost all freelance translators had horror stories of technical problems affecting delivery.

3.4 Conclusion: Tools, workflow and professional models of translation quality

The multiple approaches to TQA in the industry make it impossible to provide a detailed critique of every real-world translation quality model, as could more easily be done for the dominant theoretical models. As Larose explains, 'it would be impossible to provide a detailed analysis of all the translation quality assessment systems in use around the world, or even just in North America' (1998: 166; my translation). Larose's solution is to pick one system (SICAL) for consideration in detail. But access to a wide range of approaches, models and systems across many language pairs, industries and regions is of value, as patterns emerge. This is particularly true when combined with an understanding of how electronic tools are actually used in the industry.

In researching how quality was measured and compared, two main paradigms became apparent: one based on traditional industry approaches, and the second on emerging strategies adopted by new kinds of suppliers, including Google and Facebook. These companies, known for their emphasis on ease of use and international/intercultural communication, notably rejected established translation tools and implied workflows when they decided to translate their own resources. They instead invented new models and their own tools for MT, TM and translation management, largely bypassing the translation profession. They harnessed linguistic and product expertise rather than translation skills, then relied on user feedback to improve output quality. García (2009a: 199) has speculated that this combination of increasingly specialized tools and different approaches to workflow and management will mean that 'topic-proficient bilinguals' can take over from professional translators, working 'via simplified translation management processes and crowdsourcing approaches'.

These two different models are effectively opposites: one takes a top-down approach to translation quality, aiming to control and manage this. The second starts from the bottom up, then uses a variety of feedback mechanisms to build up quality. In Chapters Four and Five, each of these paradigms is now considered in turn, beginning with traditional industry top-down models.

CHAPTER FOUR

Top-down translation quality models

4.0 Introduction: Top-down models: Definitions and rationale

The death of hierarchical organizations and approaches has been widely predicted for nearly a century (Leavitt, 2005: 4–10). Management theorists forecast their demise, as egalitarian principles, democracy, efficiency drives and technological advances rendered them out of step with modern societies. In their place, 'orchestra', 'community' or 'network' models of organization were envisaged. Traditional hierarchical approaches to managing professional translation have similarly been portrayed as moribund, for similar reasons. It is claimed that better use of technology (e.g. higher quality MT systems) or greater democracy (e.g. harnessing the 'wisdom of crowds') will revolutionize top-down approaches to translation. For instance, TAUS and van der Meer (2009) have issued calls to 'let a thousand MT systems bloom', rejecting the industry's sceptical reaction as a 'battle between self-interest and the Zeitgeist. And the Zeitgeist is destined to win.'

Yet despite predictions of their demise, hierarchies continue to dominate all successful large organizations and industries. In many ways, technological advances have actually made hierarchies *more* deep-rooted. In summary, 'hierarchy may be the worst form of organization – except for all the others' (Leavitt, 2005: 40).

Top-down approaches have direct links to quality. Hierarchies rely on quality evaluation because they need to select and reward. Metrics to do this are always imperfect and measurements questionable, but the alternatives (selection and reward based on favouritism, nepotism, discrimination or random criteria) are worse. Hence, 'the one thing that may well generate even more fury than an existing evaluation procedure would be to have no evaluation procedure at all' (ibid.: 38). Agreed QA methods are at least open, uniformly applicable, and can be complied with, challenged and refined. Top-down approaches dominate for a reason, particularly in sectors where evaluating service quality is important.

Leavitt's overview of industrial and business sectors does not address translation, but his themes remain relevant. Top-down approaches to translation quality are the most appropriate in many scenarios, despite criticisms. Some of these criticisms affect all top-down approaches:

- They are relatively inflexible, often applying a single 'one size fits all' model

- Inefficiencies can be identified in their application and management

- They are costly and remove funding from the core activity (translation) to that of managing processes

- They may be slow to respond to technological advances

- The QE processes they adopt are imperfect.

Each translation quality model involves different weaknesses or combinations of criticisms. However, considering the strengths and weaknesses of each approach allows for the most appropriate to be chosen for typical translation scenarios found in the industry.

Rejecting top-down models in favour of apparently more radical bottom-up approaches can seem tempting, particularly when their relative costs are considered. Value-laden terms may also colour views. Associations with top-down approaches are conservative/traditional, paternalistic and authoritarian, in contrast to emerging liberal/radical, egalitarian, democratic ones. However, when illustrations of real-world translation contexts are considered, it becomes clear that both top-down and bottom-up models have their place. Van der Meer (2009) argues that the profession is therefore wrong to see new models as a threat. There is substantial unmet demand, hence the need for new models to fill the gap; but where existing models are more appropriate or can add value in terms of quality, they will thrive.

A range of top-down approaches to translation quality exists in the industry. Each section in this chapter outlines one broad top-down model, beginning with a sample case study to illustrate how each operates in practice. As for the theoretical models in Chapter Two, strengths and weaknesses of each approach are examined critically, along with the typical scenarios in which they are applied. Unlike theoretical models of translation quality, professional ones involve not just the translation product but also the process. Where stages in the process contribute to translation quality or its evaluation, these are also outlined.

It is not possible to publish detailed weightings and checklists used in professional TQA for each model, for reasons of space and confidentiality. LSPs visited in research for this book did share metrics and TQA documentation, but few were willing to make these public (or allowed to, where clients owned them). For professional models, this is not really problematic, as solely product-based approaches to quality are rare and samples of professional documentation are available elsewhere, if detailed illustration is required.[1] During professional QA processes, the goal is that *all* translations be approved for use, and many other factors are included in judgements on overall translation quality, not simply TQA of (part of) the TT. Equally, it is impossible to present a sample analysis of a translated text for each model. In professional contexts, TQA is performed not on short extracts but on samples of much longer texts, even entire texts, and in more complex formats. Texts themselves are owned by clients, so not usually available for reproduction. A summary of the process is instead given for each case, under the same headings to allow comparison.

4.1 Maximalist model

An international organization coordinating scientific collaboration has an in-house translation division of about 20 staff, mainly working from English into two official languages and two working languages; English unit staff translate six source languages. A full-time terminologist supports their work. Translators work in small language units, where colleagues share a mother tongue and report to a unit head. Source materials are commercially sensitive and critical for safety so translation quality is a priority. Freelance suppliers cover languages not supported in-house due to insufficient or fluctuating demand. Translators work only into the mother tongue.

Supplier recruitment	In-house: • relevant degree + at least two years' full-time experience • competitive entry exams • challenging recruitment process lasting several months • two-year probation period, working on a limited range of STs, with support from a mentor and regular feedback Freelance: • same stringent translation tests before acceptance onto the roster • must live locally

Supplier selection for jobs	• In-house prioritized • Translators allocated according to domain expertise
Pretranslation	• English is the shared language for scientists working in the organization, but most are not native speakers. A native English translator pre-edits STs drafted by multilingual teams of scientists and engineers in English. 'Client' checks revised ST • Project lead selected to communicate with internal 'client' • Terminologist and translators receive approved ST in electronic and hard copies, meet to identify terminology and research needs • Terminologist updates official termbase with approved terms in all project languages • Pre-edit ST; QA of ST; Preprocessing (may include pseudo-translation, sample translation); Test (sample product, e.g. software in pseudo-translated format; workflow as well as translation); QA of process and sample product; review planned processes and agree QA plan
Tools/resources	• Networked version of SDL MultiTerm • SDL Trados, networked TM for each language • One senior translator dictates (Dragon), views TM matches on-screen, post-edits in Word
Project processes, interim QC	• If new terms found in ST during project, translator proposes target language term to terminologist (only terminologist is authorized to update termbase). Terminologist verifies and adds to termbase, alerts all translators to new entries
Post-translation checks	• 100% of all translations • Translator performs pre-set range of automated checks in Trados (including term and TM verification, spelling), makes corrections, prints hard copies of entire TT, books meeting with translator-reviser colleague in same language pair • Translator reads TT aloud, sentence by sentence, reviser follows ST on paper • After each sentence, translator pauses; reviser either approves translation or suggests changes • Translator notes changes on printed TT • Particular attention paid to figures, acronyms, equations, in-house checklist of common error types • Stylistic changes rare, as translators highly familiar with house style • Freelance work checked in same way by in-house reviser, unless language pair not available in-house; then, similar external co-revision arrangements in place

	• Translator updates changed segments in Trados, generates revised target file, sends in native file format to original reviser • If substantial changes were necessary, further read-through meeting is held; if minor changes were made, reviser proofreads new TT, emails further suggestions to translator • Translator agrees changes, updates TM • On particularly sensitive projects, TT sent to sample users for review
Return	• Final target file generated, signed off by translator and reviser, forwarded to client
Post-return QC	• TM lead for target language confirms approved segments • Modifications discussed with translator/terminologist, databases updated
Post-project	• Automated email prompts clients to return anonymous comments online, whether critical or positive (e.g. noting effective aspects which should be maintained) • Terminologist post-aligns dictated translation, imports into TM for future use
Ongoing/Quality planning	• TM leads for each language meet terminologist monthly to review database content, maintenance and storage issues • CPD requirement: agreed at annual staff review (freelance and in-house) • Unit heads meet monthly to agree cross-language priorities and planning

The above case study was chosen because it encapsulates most features found in maximalist approaches, but no case study includes all possible features for the relevant model. Other common features of maximalist approaches are:

• Top-down project management. Standard workflow and project management stages are adequate in this organization, as translators rarely work on projects involving multiple files or complex file types (most STs are in Word, Excel or HTML) and the few external suppliers are unusually well-integrated in standard in-house processes. In more complex settings, the maximalist approach involves automated management tools and strict workflow (e.g. requiring participants to sign off project stages).

• Automated QA processes. The restricted translation needs of this organization, dominance of in-house staff and mandated revision stages lessen the need for such tools and processes. For more varied translation requirements, the maximalist approach integrates tools and metrics to stipulate QA steps at different project stages. In the examples observed for this study, these were calibrated to reflect in-house or client-agreed error checklists, with critical/major/minor error types, pass marks and associated scores agreed in advance.

● ICR. In commercial variants of the maximalist model, local specialists commonly test translations. For example, a photocopier installation guide translated from Japanese>English (pivot)>Portuguese would be sent to pre-selected Portuguese support staff employed by the manufacturer. They use the translation to install the new model, checking for accuracy, user-friendliness, appropriateness for the local market, and consistency of company terminology, branding and style.

Disadvantages of the maximalist approach are evident. The resources devoted to every job amount to overkill. Laborious QA, particularly during preparation and revision stages, is rarely financially viable. Time is a significant factor – often the crucial one – in most professional contexts so delays inherent in this level of checking are usually unacceptable. Nor does it guarantee quality: 'spending a lot of time on revision [does] not necessarily produce a high quality text' (Mossop, 2007: 9). Human error and tiredness can have detrimental effects. Investment of time in recruitment, initial training and mentoring, then ongoing CPD is also elevated. Closely related to time implications is cost. Maintaining in-house translation divisions of this nature is more expensive than relying on external suppliers, as office space, IT infrastructure and support, pensions, social security, annual leave and other costs must be met by the employer. Reliance on highly trained freelance staff for some needs also makes employers vulnerable, where they may not be available when needed. The high standard of training required for all suppliers makes stopgap agency staff unsuitable replacements, particularly because of the unpredictable effects for quality. A fixed supply of translators also makes it hard to scale projects up or down, something which is necessary in most of the industry. If a project requires substantial translation input for one or more languages, it is difficult to respond to demand while maintaining quality. Conversely, if work for a particular language pair is in short supply at a certain time, perhaps because the organization's strategic priorities move to a different region, in-house linguists cannot be assigned to alternative activities. Inefficiency is thus a strong criticism which can be levelled at this model.

In interviews with staff working within this model, certain criticisms were repeatedly voiced. Motivation suffered when QE processes were perceived as systematic, repetitive and boring. Most revisers found carrying out full read-throughs of colleagues' work frustrating at times, and argued that the model was not suitable for all jobs: 'it would be better to save this level of QC only for the jobs where it really matters, then we would be more focused'. Although QA *stages* are never omitted in this model, the QE of the actual *text* can also be seen as flawed. Reliance on human checking, beyond basic automated TM and terminology checks, means human error cannot be avoided. In observations of read-throughs, both translator and reviser failed to spot missed words, incorrect figures/conversions and other such errors, particularly in long texts which might take hours to revise 'live'. This happened even while they knew they were being observed and recorded for research. During training, this issue was flagged and frequent breaks were recommended to address the problem, but revisers acknowledged that these might be skipped, particularly when a deadline was imminent. Revisers stated they sometimes went too quickly or lost attention and therefore missed errors. Künzli (2007a: 115) has demonstrated that revising in such conditions can actually *harm* quality, with (albeit less experienced) revisers sometimes introducing more errors than they addressed. Translators and revisers both identified a temptation to anticipate the reviser's or house style rather than producing the best possible translation (though some viewed such increased standardization as a benefit). Inbuilt hierarchy in QE processes was frustrating for junior colleagues, who felt translations were inappropriately rejected in a 'dismissive' manner. The question of what constitutes an error also remains open to interpretation. The house style guide and checklist of common errors were useful reference material, but disagreements between translator and reviser were difficult to resolve. This was particularly apparent in the case of one in-house translator whose mother tongue was US English, whereas all revisers used UK English. No scoring system or overall mark was awarded for translations: the aim of QE processes was to produce an approved translation of acceptable quality, not to rank individual performance on a given text. If performance was at issue, the translator's probation would not be confirmed or freelance translators would undergo a review process, then be dropped from the roster.

Problems for quality were associated with support and safeguards in place in this model. When revisers, the terminologist and TM leads were overworked, bottlenecks quickly developed. Generous leave entitlement caused similar backlogs: as one translator complained, there was no point trying to work in August. The need for suggestions to be approved before being added to databases was frustrating for translators. When they reached material they knew they had already translated, but the match had not yet been added to the TM, they either had to waste time performing local searches or retranslate the segment, undermining consistency.

Its expense and inherent delays mean this model would be quickly rejected if it did not bring strong quality benefits. Its emphasis on translators, not just the translation process or translated product, is something recognized widely as key to quality in the industry: 'the bottom line is that good quality human resources are vital if good quality output is to be achieved' (Samuelsson-Brown, 1996: 107). Stringent recruitment criteria are combined with anonymous competitive exams, with a high proportion of applicants rejected.[2] Contracts are not confirmed until consistent satisfactory performance is demonstrated over an extended probation. Post-appointment monitoring leads to support then sanctions if performance deteriorates (e.g. where a translator living in the source language culture loses mother tongue fluency). The emphasis on translators is associated with quality in various ways. Domain expertise is built up over many years, usually encouraged via ongoing training, and opportunities to carry out research on the organization's core activities or call on in-house technical experts. Job security, employee benefits and the opportunity for career development (e.g. from probationer to translator, reviser, mentor, language lead, unit head, head of translation section) promote staff retention and resulting high levels of expertise in translation types common in the organization. Those adopting maximalist models often pointed to security benefits to justify its use. In certain contexts (e.g. national security, localization of sensitive products), confidentiality, staff vetting, NDAs and exclusivity were critical.

Workflow also benefits. All suppliers become very familiar with QA processes, adopt standard tools and workflow and receive training to use them appropriately. Frequent team meetings and other contact promote clarity of objectives and sharing of best practice. The opportunity for specialist linguists to improve ST quality prior to translation, relatively rare in the industry, can prevent errors before they arise. ST authors and clients appreciated relationships with translators developed over time, frequently commenting in interviews that sending a text for translation resulted in an improved source language version too, as translators highlighted ambiguities or flaws in the original. The model views translators working into the mother tongue, and revision performed by subject specialist mother tongue speakers, as critical for quality.

QA processes are critical in the maximalist model, as indicated by the time devoted to these in the production cycle. Revising 100% of all texts means that no error is missed simply because it appears in part of the text not selected for QC, as happens with any sampling system. Thoroughness of revision was mentioned by translators as a motivating factor in producing high-quality output, as they knew everything would be scrutinized. Revisers and translators all commented on the strong 'house style' developed by the process, with benefits for domain expertise, knowledge of the organization and awareness of colleagues' approaches. Variety in workloads was appreciated, as most staff performed a range of activities (revision, liaison with authors, regular meetings, mentoring). This allows staff to juggle activities depending on energy and concentration levels. Translators recognized the impossibility of producing high-quality output at all times, so avoided errors by switching to other activities when tired or at a challenging point in a text. Peer support through frequent revision and team meetings was also valued for its effects on quality: colleagues established trusting relationships and knew whom to consult on particular points, being familiar with their expertise. Freelance translators felt both valued and of value to the organization, as they built unusually long-term relationships with such clients. The regular positive feedback available through this approach is rare in the industry, but translators recognized its value for motivation, setting benchmarks and understanding what was appropriate for future work.

There is evidence that the maximalist approach picks up more errors. Brunette et al. (2005: 29) demonstrated in experimental conditions that bilingual revision (i.e. full comparison of ST and TT) was more than twice as effective as monolingual revision (i.e. simply proofreading or revising the TT without reference to the ST). The frequency and repetition of revision in this model also means revisers' skills are honed. Staff mentioned they knew 'exactly what to look for', were primed to spot common errors in their specialist domains, and also got to know individual colleagues' strengths and weaknesses (e.g. 'you know who is a stickler for detail and whose work you need to check more carefully'). Frequent client feedback supports QA and revision processes. In another real-world example of the maximalist model observed during research, product designers indicated that in-house linguists established strong relationships with staff involved in ICR, ensuring new products met local standards in a technical domain. Translators therefore contributed not only to translation quality but also to enhanced *product* quality.

Despite the associated costs and time, versions of the maximalist model were found relatively widely, particularly in high-risk domains (e.g. hi-tech, legal, pharmaceutical), and for sensitive projects (e.g. where rivals might steal industrial prototypes). It was observed in both public and commercial contexts (e.g. public examinations bodies, automotive translation). In-house staff dominated overwhelmingly and freelance suppliers were generally retained on medium-term contracts or booked in advance for extended periods. All instances of this model observed in research involved the translation of relatively 'fixed' final versions of STs, though it could be adapted to evolving texts where time was not a critical factor. Conversely, it is clearly not suited to urgent deadlines, conditions where cost is imperative, or general domains where adequate quality is available at much lower rates.

4.2 Client-driven model

One of the world's largest agencies provides services in over 40 languages to a huge range of clients, from one-off short jobs for individuals, to long-term contracts for informed consumers of translation, localization and transcreation, awarded after competitive tender. Hundreds of in-house linguists in regional offices support Chinese, English, FIGS and Japanese, but most work is outsourced to freelance providers. All domains are covered, including specialist sectors. Permanent software engineers, terminologists, IT staff and resource managers in the headquarters and regional offices support multiple electronic tools and resources. A sizeable division of PMs allocates work and manages projects once contracts are signed. It was claimed suppliers worked only into the mother tongue, but during research visits, this was not always the case (e.g. for under-resourced target languages).

Supplier recruitment	• Relevant degree + three years' full-time experience to join supplier database • Timed tests in controlled conditions. Tests graded using a single process/scale for all languages; those who pass provisionally approved for jobs • After satisfactory translation of 100,000 source words (or equivalent), confirmed as suppliers • Exceptions: rare languages; when sudden demand makes additional recruitment necessary
Supplier selection for jobs	• Work allocated through online supplier database based on language pair, availability, rate, ability to use tools, previous experience. Client stipulates any supplier requirements (e.g. domain experience) • Suppliers may work for single client on ongoing contracts
Pre-translation	• Variable • Sales/PM staff liaise with client to agree workflow, supplier criteria, QA processes, tools, resources, added-value services, final deliverables • Clients may opt out, use default PM approaches • In-house support staff prepare reference materials, including file conversion • Reference materials, source files, job details (contact for queries, deadlines, deliverables) sent to all translators
Tools/resources	• Variable • MT sometimes used, post-edited by suppliers at lower rates than translation
Project lifetime checks	• Variable • Clients in certain sectors, notably localization, stipulate exacting QA/management processes • Company is certified to comply with several quality standards • Two dedicated QA tools available in combination with company or client-agreed metrics where desired

Post-translation checks	• Variable • Most jobs: standard TPE process, TT sampling for monolingual revision (usually 5–10% of ST, selected at random) • If clients prefer not to pay for QC, jobs go unchecked
Return	• Variable: client-stipulated formats
Post-return QC	• Variable • Suppliers are not remunerated until client receives final deliverables and project is signed off as complete • Where quality issues affect client satisfaction, suppliers must correct at no cost. If not, payment withheld and/or removed from supplier database
Post-project	• PM seeks client feedback informally after every stand-alone job, or at agreed intervals for long-term contracts • Variable update/review of resources
Ongoing/Quality planning	• Variable

Other common features of client-driven approaches are:

- Clients adapting pre-translation processes to sidestep quality problems. Some regular clients limit scope for problems in outsourced translation by adapting their production strategy, so content can more easily be adapted to suit target markets rather than translated in the traditional way, that is, 'transcreation'. This means the TT should 'give [readers] the exact same experience as the source text gave to readers in the original language' (Humphrey et al., 2011: n.p.), with the emphasis on effect in the TL rather than translation of content. Increased reliance on images and minimal use of text are common features of this approach. This can lead to challenges for agencies, however, where a small number of critical source words, often containing product names, idioms, puns or brand-critical slogans, must be rendered effectively in dozens of languages, taking account of local cultural norms.

- Ongoing agency–client relations. Regular clients build long-term relationships with the larger LSPs able to support their needs (multiple/rare languages, complex file formats). Such relationships can enhance efficiency and tailored QA, as standard client-approved processes can be developed.

- Bypassing agencies. Regular clients may recruit translators directly. This approach was only found where clients needed translation into a limited number of languages. Those who chose it all indicated that their motivation was enhanced quality and improved control. Freelance translators interviewed for this study preferred this relationship, because it was better remunerated and they could be confident that the client was satisfied with quality, as objectives were clear on both sides, feedback was provided and queries were addressed directly.

The defining features of this model are variability and scalability. Various disadvantages are associated with the client-led approach, but its flexibility means weaknesses differ from case to case. The most significant problem for quality inherent in the general approach is its reliance on clients. In a study of the Danish market, Rasmussen and Schjoldager identified 'customers' general lack of understanding of the translation process' (2011: 87) as a significant barrier to quality and this clearly applies more broadly. Most clients are not informed consumers of translation, so relying on them to identify translation needs accurately or help design systems to ensure quality is risky. They may not understand agencies' or translators' questions, or make unfounded assumptions about what translation involves. PMs repeatedly volunteered naïve client comments (e.g. 'it's a straightforward text, not much legal content', where it transpired the ST was a detailed contract for use under a different legal system, entailing specialist sworn translation and adaptation to target jurisdiction requirements). Clients rejected QC processes, including basic revision, on the grounds that 'we've already done the QC on the original so you can just translate it'. Clients were also surprised to realize their interpretation of common terms and processes such as 'revision' did not reflect reality (e.g. clients were unlikely to realize that agencies only provide unilingual, not comparative, revision unless this is specified). Some clients rejected offers to collaborate in identifying project aims and quality levels, preferring to 'leave it to the experts'. Substantial client education was therefore highlighted as essential to achieve satisfactory results. The size and relative importance of the client was also a factor in translation quality. Long-term clients or large contracts were favoured over one-off or smaller jobs, especially where finding suitable resources was an issue (e.g. translators were reallocated from other jobs to meet a looming deadline for an important client, leaving untested suppliers to complete less 'important' work). Where clients worked directly with translators, QC was invariably left to translators. Most had longstanding arrangements with a colleague in the same language pair to check work. Some freelance translators working in unusual language pairs or specialist domains struggled to find competent colleagues to revise work, and instead self-revised and then sent the TT to a non-specialist target language speaker for proofreading.

Relying on agencies as middle-men had some negative implications for quality. Additional costs devoted to project management and value-added services such as engineering, testing or DTP meant that the overall budget for translation was reduced. Time available for translation was also cut by management processes (e.g. planning, but also hold-ups caused by PMs centralizing translator queries). The agency approach added an 'extra layer', risking translator queries not being understood or taken seriously. PMs' power in this model was criticized by some translators, who were left unaware of what QE (if any) would be done by the agency or client. Some argued that, where PMs understood neither SL nor TL, they might fail to realize the critical nature of the text/intended use. This might mean important QA was omitted. Others were alarmed, when carrying out later work for the same client, to receive the updated TM and discover their carefully crafted translations had been post-edited by the agency or client and errors introduced.

General claims made by agencies working in this model hid great variation in standards. Staff frequently admitted that, in practice, it was not always possible to impose policies or quality requirements. At the recruitment stage, busy times or rush jobs led to untried providers being recruited (e.g. the three-year experience requirement was waived for many suppliers). Translators with two or more source languages indicated that they felt the admission tests were not of equal standard across languages. For reasons of confidentiality, little information was provided by agencies visited in research for this book as to how such tests were assessed. Some agencies made their marking schemes or TQA grids available, but these left interpretation of error gravity to individual assessors for each language pair, implying that this could differ from one language (or marker) to another. All PMs interviewed for this book were asked to volunteer the main criteria by which they select suppliers for particular jobs. Where more than one supplier is suitable in terms of language pair and tool use, the response in virtually all cases was that the lowest cost supplier would be chosen, not the translator with the highest quality ranking. A few PMs did assert that, for certain clients or job types, they would emphasize quality. Uneven provision is another weakness of this model. Agencies invariably present their services as uniform across languages, but there was evident variability (e.g. in resources available). There was no in-house provision for most languages, meaning less support for QC. Very limited availability of suppliers for some languages meant it could be impossible to carry out QC for some jobs, and even automated checks were more likely to be dropped (e.g. there was less reference material to check for compliance with client preferences).

QA processes, particularly post-translation, were also varied, misunderstood and likely to affect quality. The most common version of QA offered was proofreading of the TT alone, or comparative revision of a sample of the text. Agencies explained that clients were unlikely to pay for entire jobs to be revised comparatively. This inevitably means errors will be missed. Guarantees (e.g. 'revision' or 'checking') commonly implied only *self*-revision by translators. Revision and QA processes were most often the ones to be dropped or cut (e.g. sampling less of the text) where delivery on schedule was at risk. The lack of experienced revisers for some language pairs meant that QC might mean different things for different languages in a project, and revision was sometimes done by non-experts (e.g. PMs/editors who understood only the target language). Revisers were generally other translators and little or no training was offered in what was expected. The details of revision (e.g. what to assess, how to rate colleagues' work) were often left to revisers themselves to decide and there was evidence of very different levels of understanding, skill and experience across those involved. Rasmussen and Schjoldager (2011: 108) found this to be true in the Danish context, with agencies assigning the responsibility in this area to clients: 'It all depends on the text type and the wishes of the customer. Customers sometimes give us sort of a style sheet, but we don't need our *own* checklist!' A final issue highlighted by translators was that they felt they were working in a 'void', with insufficient information on what was expected from them. Suppliers working for the agency described in the case study were unsure what QC was performed after they submitted work, so did not know if performing TM compliance checks was duplicating effort. The temptation was to omit the checks, but if the agency or client was not performing those later, quality might be harmed.

As with its flaws, advantages of the client-driven model vary from one case to another, due to its flexibility. Its flexibility and scalability are themselves advantages for quality. Unlike the maximalist model, excessive resources are unlikely to be routinely allocated. If exhaustive QC processes are adopted for a project, it thus provides a clear signal that quality has particular significance. Services can be provided 24 hours a day, 365 days a year, as suppliers are dispersed around the globe. Particularly at holiday times in certain locales, this allowed urgent jobs to be resourced. The scalability of the model in response to client needs was also important for quality: resources could be allocated to the most significant aspects of clients' projects. Clients valued having suppliers who charged different rates, as sometimes a 'quick and dirty' translation is sufficient so it makes no sense to pay more or wait longer for higher quality. The lack of ongoing costs or commitments to suppliers (e.g. holiday entitlement) also means that translation overheads are lower, though this was mitigated by costs for PMs and support staff.

The large size of most LSPs in this model brings quality benefits. They can offer a higher number of tools and value-added services, which are then available for particular jobs without additional expense. Economies of scale mean greater investment and customization are feasible, and the availability of technical support in-house allows problems to be addressed where they might delay delivery from other suppliers. Agencies visited for this study stressed they could 'throw people at the problem' where an unforeseen issue might otherwise cause delays. Large MLVs can support a far greater range of languages, with potential benefits for standardized quality of service provision and efficiency, where this is well managed.

Teams of PMs can also have positive effects for quality. When project management is central to a large LSP's business, there are dedicated training programmes, established workflows, support and regular review of quality processes. PMs share agreed processes and tools, so illness, leave or staff moving on cause fewer problems. Large LSPs invest in specialist QA and PM tools to support the role, bringing additional quality checks and processes to most or all jobs. Agreed quality processes are unlikely to be skipped or missed where a PM is responsible for confirming that these have been performed. Clients appreciated a single point of contact, acting as a 'filter' for queries on multilingual projects, rather than multiple instances of the same query arriving over several weeks. Freelance translators also appreciated agency support, notably in pre-processing and providing technical assistance where tools caused problems. Close monitoring of project progress means fewer problems meeting delivery deadlines. PMs built up strong ongoing relations with some clients. This allowed attention to quality issues over time and fine-tuning where necessary.

In the client-driven model, problems with supplier quality can be more easily addressed. The use of trial periods mirrors probation in the maximalist model, but clients and agencies have much greater scope to drop suppliers immediately. If suppliers do not deliver acceptable quality on one occasion, they are typically asked to redo the work for free. If further problems arise, they are simply removed from the supplier database.

Strong client input has some general benefits for quality. Informed, regular clients can have a 'trickle-down' impact on the service available to others. For instance, if a client insists on the use of a given tool to perform automated checks, the agency must invest in it. This is then available for use on subsequent jobs, even for clients who could not themselves afford the investment. Occasional clients can benefit from working practices established on behalf of experienced customers. LSPs are accustomed to managing client-specific QA processes, such as checks for compliance with client resources. Strong client input where freelance translators work directly with the client has quality benefits. Ongoing relationships are often in place, so the supplier gets to know the customer's preferences and typical content, just as in-house providers do in the maximalist model.

This model is probably now most widespread in the industry, witnessed by the recent growth of large MLVs and increase in freelance numbers. It is found at both ends of the scale. It makes sense to call on expert support for one-off or irregular jobs (so clients do not have to become experts themselves), but equally for substantial multilingual projects which are too complex for non-specialists to manage (e.g. software localization). Large LSPs, who can prepare complex tenders for multiple languages, dominate in certain sectors (e.g. outsourced EU contracts). They also dominate in domains where multiple tools are needed: SLVs cannot match their investment, technical support and customization. MLVs are better able to support the rising need for complex value-added services (DTP, testing, focus groups). The direct client model is also widespread. The most common direct client scenario found in research was where occasional recurring projects needed high-quality translation, often re-using client resources (e.g. annual company reports, website updates).

This model can easily be adapted to any project type, from Agile localization to short texts in basic formats. It is suited to urgent deadlines, as suppliers can share work, slotting into established workflows and using tools efficiently. The range of suppliers available through large MLVs, and increasing provision of post-edited MT output, also make it suitable whenever low rates and speedy delivery are important factors.

4.3 Experience-dependent model

An international organization working on a diverse range of STs and file formats has about 100 in-house translators working across six languages, with most texts needed in all languages. Translators are based in several regional units. Full-time terminologists and a technical helpdesk support their work remotely. Freelance suppliers and interns are used for certain projects or at times of high demand, but most translation is done in-house. Translators work only into the mother tongue, excepting one language pair where insufficient translators are available. QC processes depend on translators' experience. In-house staff are promoted to 'senior translator/ reviser' status on satisfactory completion of several years' work and a training course on how to provide feedback using the organization's checklists and rating scheme. Freelance suppliers always retain 'translator' status.

Supplier recruitment	In-house: • Relevant degree + competitive entry exams • 12-month probation period, mentored by senior colleague Freelance: • Recruited in various ways, including via agencies • Test translation, marked in-house Interns: • Competitive anonymous entry tests

Supplier selection for jobs	• Automatic alert to all in-house translators with brief details (reference code; timeframe) • First in-house translator to accept job becomes project lead, assumes coordination (e.g. making sure all language pairs are allocated to suppliers) • If external suppliers needed, unit head and terminologist liaise to recruit, inform lead translator • For revision, automatic alert to all senior colleagues in language pair; first to click on link 'locks' job
Pre-translation	• Terminologists process source material against TM and terminology databases, collate relevant reference material (using codes which automatically identify analogous texts) • Reference materials/source files posted on intranet
Tools/resources	• Translators use SDL Trados/MultiTerm with local TM and termbase. Updated resources are not shared during translation
Project lifetime checks	• None
Post-translation checks	All staff: • Automated QC steps (spelling, formatting, TM compliance) must be confirmed on job sheet Translators: • Senior translator from same language pair revises 100% of work comparatively • Revision performed in TM editor or Word (using Track Changes/Comment Functions); reviser chooses • Revisers use in-house style guide, prompt sheet, electronic feedback sheet with tick boxes for QA • Comments, corrections, feedback sheet returned to translator with reviser's contact details via intranet • Translator contacts reviser in case of queries or disagreement, makes necessary changes in TM editor Senior translators: • Decide whether to send work for QC on job-by-job basis; can send entire translation, sample, or no text for revision or proofreading by a senior colleague • Generally self-revised, sending sections for comparative revision if unsure about content or expression; mainly for technical texts
Return	• Translator generates target file(s), posts updated TM, termbase and TTs to intranet

Post-return QC	• Support staff in relevant units perform formatting/QC for complex file formats (e.g. dedicated website unit checks HTML and XML files). Support staff are non-linguists so such checks are purely functional/formatting • Lead translator informed automatically when final files are uploaded, checks materials complete for each language pair, notifies commissioning unit (client) that job is complete
Post-project	• Automatic alert to terminologist who created original reference materials; imports new content into relevant databases
Ongoing/Quality planning	• Unit heads monitor performance, including regular freelance suppliers • Client/lead translator/terminologist feedback prompted automatically after each project, used in annual staff review cycle • Internal staff required to attend regular CPD courses (e.g. TM use, reviser training) • Subsidized membership of professional association

Other common features of experience-dependent approaches are:

- Various methods of selection for QE. The above case is a common in-house solution, but other methods exist, particularly where agencies apply experience-dependent QE to freelance work. Suppliers may be ranked by the length of service, number of words translated, scores in TQA evaluations or other means.

- Top-down project management. The above case represents an in-house setting with fairly standard workflow, mostly automated, for familiar 'clients'. In more complex settings, the experience-driven approach involves stricter controls on workflow stages (e.g. requiring inexperienced providers to check off deliverables according to a pre-agreed schedule).

- Stronger QA processes. The relatively fixed translation needs of this organization and dominance of in-house staff lessen the need for QA tools and processes. For LSPs with more varied requirements, the experience-driven approach may integrate tools and metrics to stipulate QA steps at different project stages, based on supplier experience of working for the client or the job type.

- Opt-in freelance networks. Some freelance translators organize themselves in groups to provide QE support based on relative experience. Professional organizations run peer mentoring schemes (e.g. that offered by the UK's ITI, where experienced providers offer QE and support to new members). Online forums allow translators to find more experienced suppliers in the same language pair or specialization, to arrange mentoring and QE. Some national standards require QC steps to be performed by a more experienced colleague. Independent translators working in these contexts used informal networks to provide this.

Experience-dependent approaches imply numerous disadvantages. The combination of 100% revision/strong QA processes for junior translators with only opt-in QA for senior colleagues can result in the worst of both worlds, with translators resenting inevitability of QA (where this is unwarranted), while senior colleagues' errors are missed. Time and cost for QA for junior/external staff cause similar problems to those found in the maximalist model. Many 'new' colleagues in the case study were actually highly experienced, having moved to in-house positions after extended freelance careers. Time and cost associated with recruitment, training, mentoring and support processes are lower than in the maximalist model, but remain significant. Once deemed senior, self-referral for QE involves risks for quality. The self-referral approach relies on translators' self-awareness and recognition of their weak points. Translators working in this model noted the temptation not to refer work for QE when a deadline loomed. Relying on humans for QA makes errors inevitable. Some language pairs suffered a lack of sufficient senior colleagues. Those who could carry out QA then spent most of their time checking others' work rather than translating themselves, something many found frustrating. One senior translator mentioned that increasing time spent on others' work sometimes led to premature 'burnout'. Those subject to 100% revision and QE raised the same issues as translators working in the maximalist model, that is, it was necessarily hierarchical and often demotivating.

Greater dependence on freelance translators in this model implies vulnerability at times of peak demand. Suppliers may not be available when needed, meaning less able or untested providers are used with greater in-house QE and 'repair'. Allowing translation out of the mother tongue also requires more checks, so senior staff waste time on basic corrections. The model only works efficiently when there is a steady flow of new staff and progression to senior status, or a stable cohort of senior staff. If a new language pair is introduced or several senior colleagues leave, quality challenges take time to address, given stringent recruitment and training requirements.

All final translations and terms are added to databases for future re-use. Where errors are missed, they are therefore perpetuated. Some variants of this model only add senior colleagues' work to databases, but this too involves drawbacks for quality: senior colleagues' work will still contain errors; and high-quality translations by 'junior' staff are omitted. Effective maintenance is vital in this approach, but this was often neglected or shared across multiple staff, none of whom saw it as a priority.

Experience-based approaches nonetheless offer advantages. The balance of in-house and freelance suppliers improves scalability and flexibility, but maintains advantages associated with strong recruitment/probation arrangements, quality of resources/tools, staff retention and domain expertise. Robust support and development for staff through lead translators, revisers and annual review were welcomed. One recent recruit felt that she was 'not left to figure it out on her own'. Clear career progression for in-house staff (translator, lead translator, mentor, reviser) again enhanced responsibility, remuneration, variety in workload and retention. Most language pairs had a highly experienced pool of senior translators/revisers. Their experience led to the knowledge of institutional structures and working methods being passed on effectively. Senior translators demonstrated solid awareness of the style guide and other resources, and shared understanding of what QE processes involved. Indeed, this was evident across all staff, because all underwent regular QC on all jobs for extended periods. In interviews, senior translators noted the need for sensitivity in managing QE, having undergone the processes themselves (e.g. they were less likely to direct colleagues to make changes but would offer 'suggestions').

Many working in this model felt that it offered the best of both worlds. It is more flexible than the maximalist model and takes account of the circumstances of production (e.g. in cases where translation was done out of the mother tongue, all jobs were subject to full QC, even those by senior staff). Interviewees commented that, because QC was kept for jobs where it was essential or the translator had himself recognized the need, checks were taken more seriously: 'if a very experienced colleague asks me to look at a text, I do so with extra attention and care'. Bilingual revision has been recognized as the most effective, but requires substantial resources and time. Self-selected sampling once experience is gained means that overkill is avoided while the benefits of comparative revision are enhanced. Confidence in QC processes also maximizes resources. All suppliers' contributions are added to databases, including those produced by freelance suppliers. Translators work locally in the TM tool, so they see their own internal repetitions. Their final approved translations are not added to the archive until QC has taken place, enhancing overall quality of shared resources. Knowing that their approved segments would be stored for future use was motivating for translators, particularly freelance staff who often worked for the organization over many years. Regular feedback through the annual review and agreed targets (e.g. for productivity, domains to develop) were also motivating, and staff were clear as to how they could progress within the organization.

The experience-led model is again widespread, as it is scalable and useful in different contexts. It is popular with both agencies and freelance translators, subject to certain safeguards (e.g. how 'senior' colleagues are identified and trained), as it is perceived as fair and a rational use of resources. It allows for support to new colleagues and capitalizes on expertise. However, it depends on ongoing relationships. Where turnover is high, there is no opportunity to develop the required cadre of senior staff. A balance of experienced and new staff is needed if senior translators are not to spend too much time checking others' work rather than producing high-quality translations. It can lead to patchy provision (e.g. where clients introduce new languages without any trained senior colleagues to perform QC at the same level as for established languages).

4.4 Content-dependent model

A small company has four in-house translator-revisers working from two source languages into one Nordic language. Two PMs, who speak the three languages concerned, coordinate their work and that of freelance suppliers, all based in-country. Originally an automotive translation specialist, it has expanded to other domains, notably legal, general and limited pharmaceutical/medical. Some source materials are critical for safety and QA processes are strictly controlled. At the other end of the scale, jobs are general, for quick turnaround with basic quality requirements. The company is ISO-certified. The in-house translator-revisers were all co-founders of the company, have equal stakes in the business and long experience in the relevant domains. Experienced freelance suppliers are employed for most projects. All work into the mother tongue.

In this model, various levels of QA and management are tailored to jobs depending on content. The two extremes are outlined below.

Supplier recruitment	In-house: • N/A (co-founders) Freelance: • Recommendation by in-house staff or existing freelance suppliers • Domain-specific test translation(s), marked in-house; variable probation period
Supplier selection for jobs	Sensitive content (e.g. automotive shop manuals, engine specifications): • Translators selected according to industry-specific knowledge, experience • Suppliers assigned long-term to core clients' jobs to enhance consistency General content: • PM identifies available suppliers according to availability/rate

Pre-translation	Sensitive content: • PM liaises with client to agree requirements (resources, style guides, tools, QC) • PM checks source materials, corrects layout and potential translation issues; reviews STs for terminology, checks unapproved terms not in glossary with client, updates termbase; checks client TMs, reference material • PM converts source files, sends to translators with termbase/TM, expected workflow (e.g. import steps, instructions for tool use), deadlines, QA expectations. General content: • PM agrees rate/deadline, sends source files and any reference materials supplied by client
Tools/resources	Sensitive content: • TM tools always used; SDL Trados/MultiTerm and STAR Transit/TermStar fully supported (customized in-house); other tools if client-stipulated General content • Translators choose which tool to use, use local TM and termbase if wished
Project lifetime checks	Sensitive content: • Document tracking system prompts QA stages throughout project • Client-stipulated checks integrated General content: • None
Post-translation checks	Sensitive content: • Translator performs specified QC processes, returns draft to PM, in TM format • PM applies automated QA features in translation tools and dedicated QA tool (designed in-house) • Other tools and metrics at clients' request • Approved in-house translator-reviser revises 100% of text comparatively in TM editor. ST issues raised with client. TT issues and summary of automated QA report sent to translator for review General content: • Translators self-revise
Return	Sensitive content: • Translator returns updated TM, termbase using agreed method General content: • Translator returns TT in native file format by email or agreed method

Post-return QC	Sensitive content: • Further proofing stage performed by second reader, checking TT for stylistic issues • PM runs further automated QA checks, exports final files to native formats, checks layout and content • PM updates and returns client TM, termbase, translated files, by FTP or client-stipulated alternative General content: • PM reads TT sample in native file format. • If satisfactory, files returned to client • If sample contains significant errors, file returned to translator for checking. PM then proofreads 100% of revised TT
Post-project	• If for regular client, new TM/term resources imported into company-maintained client databases
Ongoing/Quality planning	• Formal annual review of quality management, including all client feedback • Ongoing clients meet assigned PM twice yearly to review processes • Subsidized attendance at external CPD events for all staff (including freelance)

Other common features of content-dependent approaches are:

● File *format* determining QC. 'Content' may refer not only to the text but also to the way it is stored. For some complex formats (e.g. games localization), suppliers are selected for their ability to use particular tools or perform certain types of QC (e.g. testing).

● Selecting translation methods based on content (e.g. jobs suited to MT + post-editing). Content also influences what QC steps are used in some settings.

● Imposed QC based on content. Where translation is for certain regulated industries, client expectations regarding text production must be respected.

● Allocating translators to different job types. The above case relies on experienced technical translators, but larger LSPs allocate work based on file content. In interviews, PMs stated that they kept some high-paid suppliers on the database solely to work on challenging content. A similar system often operates in large in-house divisions, with senior staff assigned to critical content (e.g. controversial or commercially sensitive texts). One in-house department had an 'isolation chamber', where exceptionally sensitive texts were translated using a stand-alone desktop. The translator had no contact with those outside the room and worked without access to online resources or recording materials (including paper or pencils). Only trained senior colleagues with security clearance worked on such content.

Content-dependent approaches pose problems for quality. The manner in which content is identified for different levels of QA is crucial. In the above case, the restricted range of languages and familiarity with niche sectors allow PMs with many years' experience reliably to do this. In other contexts, LSPs may need to judge which checks to use without sufficient understanding of the context. Where file format alone determines QA, this might lead to overkill for basic textual content. Conversely, important errors can be missed where basic file formats or apparently general content obscure the presence of challenging text, perhaps only in sections of the ST.

The necessary emphasis on project management in most instances of this model means that when PMs are busy, bottlenecks can arise. In the above case, this was insignificant as other in-house staff were competent to step in, but elsewhere, it can mean delays or QC processes being rushed or skipped. In content-dependent models, more standard processes are used; this can lead to overkill, both in management and QA (particularly where ISO or other compliance imposes unnecessary stages). PMs working in this model found performing repeated checks on the same unchanged text at several project stages demotivating. Because content is central in this model, linguistic QC was sometimes performed in isolation from other checks (e.g. layout, formatting). This sometimes led to issues with text presentation, necessitating an extra layer of QC.

The wide range of possible content poses further problems for quality. Less challenging texts are usually translated by less experienced colleagues and receive fewer checks, but these may be ones of critical importance to a company's image. The need to provide the highest quality for certain texts also means that expert translators are required. However, if no complex jobs are live, these translators may be assigned to basic content, an inefficient use of resources. Alternatively, expert translators may grow frustrated and fatigued when they always work on challenging content. The above case works smoothly in a locale with long traditions of translation in the domains concerned and a decent cohort of expert linguists for the relevant languages; in other locales, where word of mouth or small markets do not permit easy recruitment of the best staff (e.g. the PRC), it is less viable. Some features (e.g. systematic translation into the mother tongue) are not feasible in certain markets or specializations.

The reliance on human input for high quality also involves challenges. In the case study, the four co-founders were due to retire within a few years of one another and other staff had concerns about the company's future once their expertise was lost. A danger of associating quality with content is that suppliers are encouraged to become ever more specialized. This has clear advantages where the sector is expanding and expertise will be increasingly useful but makes their eventual replacement challenging, though tools and resources can preserve their expertise to some extent. Reliance on human translators to perform their own QC is also problematic, as explained in previous models.

Content-based approaches nonetheless confer some obvious quality advantages. Like maximalist and experience-dependent models, they focus strongly on the quality of human resources, with attendant benefits (e.g. translation exclusively into the mother tongue for given content types, an emphasis on in-country staff to maintain fluency). Expert suppliers are more likely to be identified for relevant sectors. The model is scalable at peak times due to its typical reliance on a mixture of in-house and external suppliers, but because suppliers work long-term on each client's jobs, there is improved consistency and awareness of QA requirements. Translators working in this model found it motivating to know that their approved segments would be stored for future use, particularly where they worked regularly for the same clients and were able to benefit from their own and others' high-quality matches. The variety in workload (e.g. different workflows for different content types) was appreciated.

Content-led approaches rely on strong management, both pre-translation (when someone has to identify the best workflow, suppliers and QC processes for the particular case) and during the project, where QA steps must be efficiently monitored. The strong role for PMs also confers quality advantages. Many in this model had unusually long experience in the industry, where the norm is for PMs to move on to other roles after a few years. Unusually, they were often involved in linguistic aspects (e.g. proofreading). Because content determines workflow and QA processes, there is increased variety and flexibility in this model so overkill is less likely. PM and support staff were also linked to translator satisfaction, with suppliers commenting positively that efficient pre- or post-processing meant they could focus on linguistic aspects.

The relationship between content and QA has evident benefits for quality. Because suppliers and PMs know only critical content is subject to the highest level of QA, it is taken seriously. The emphasis on effective recruitment of top quality staff also allowed informed peer support and a collegial approach to revision and other checks. Client feedback was more regular in this model than most others observed, due to the controlled sectors in which this approach was often found and the required review provisions of certification. Those working in this model typically had longstanding relationships with core clients and had thus been able to fine-tune their approach to quality over the long term.

Selecting quality procedures based on content is more common in high-risk sectors, where cost is less important than the potential impact of low-quality provision (e.g. where translation amounts to a tiny percentage of overall production budgets). This can be because the industry is a controlled one (e.g. medical equipment manufacturing), or because low-quality translation would be fatal to the brand or product (e.g. high-end games localization). Frequent commissioners of translation dominated in this model, no doubt because they are more likely to be aware which aspects of content are critical.

4.5 Purpose-dependent model

The European Commission DGT employed a purpose-based approach from the 1990s until the 2004 enlargement, when the model was adapted. When this model was observed, translators and revisers worked in units for each official target language. Approved working practice was to translate only into the mother tongue, but pressures linked to the looming enlargement meant that translators might be asked to work from their C into their B language (e.g. a Dutch translator translating German texts into English). Some jobs were outsourced to MLVs who had won ongoing contracts to supply the institutions through competitive tender. Diverse text types are translated in the institutions, from constituents' handwritten letters to constitutional texts. Jobs may be required into one target language, the three working languages, or all 23 official languages. Most STs were in MS Word; hard copy STs remained common.

Supplier recruitment	In-house: • Degree, mastery of at least two EU source languages + mother tongue • Competitive system of closed examinations, interviews assess translation and other aspects (e.g. knowledge of EU history) • Intensive initial training, including appropriate tool use, workflow • Probation period with mentoring, feedback Freelance: • Recruited via MLVs; variable
Supplier selection for jobs	In-house: • Standard allocation/document tracking system in place in each unit • Available in-house translators choose 'fiche de travail', with job specification, ST in hard copy Freelance: • Selected by MLVs • Jobs sent to MLVs based on content type/purpose. Only non-critical STs outsourced, only when insufficient provision in-house

Pre-translation	• Automated support services prepare TM, terminology, provided through intranet via job code
Tools/resources	In-house: • Translators choose whether to use tools • Substantial in-house reference materials available, including documentalist/resource centre for each language unit • All translators can access customized versions of SDL Trados/MultiTerm • Available language pairs have MT (Systran), voice recognition (Dragon Dictate) • 'Clients' commissioning translation can be contacted with queries • Helpdesk, TM lead for each language for technical support Freelance: • Limited access to terminology resources, reference materials • No tool imposed; translator/agency decides • Internal contact for queries
Project lifetime checks	In-house: • None Freelance: • Variable; dependent on MLV
Post-translation checks	• Dependent on 'translation quality type' (i.e. eventual purpose) of ST. In descending order of importance: • Legal (e.g. legally binding treaties). Fully revised (comparatively with ST); special attention paid to factual accuracy (names, dates, etc) • Image (e.g. official website content). Fully revised (comparatively with ST); special attention paid to 'clear and elegant style' • Official (e.g. letters for Commissioners). Checked (i.e. proofread) or revised • For information (e.g. reports for committees). Checked or revised if necessary • Basic comprehension (e.g. meeting minutes requested in a new language). Unchecked, unrevised. Might include MT output • All freelance work subject to additional revision by senior in-house staff • Revisers expected to attend to range of text features, including stylistic, using language-specific style guide • Most revisers worked on hard copies, met translator to agree changes • Translator made changes in TM or native file format

Return	In-House
	• Via intranet + hard copy
	Freelance
	• TT to target language unit, variable methods
Post-return QC	• None
Post-project	• In-house STs + TTs aligned for storage and future use, whether or not translator used TM
	• New terminology verified by super-user; terminologist added terms to institutional termbase
Ongoing/Quality planning	• Unit head received regular 'client' feedback, informed annual performance reviews
	• Each translator agreed annual targets, areas for development, supported by training plan (e.g. half-day per week to learn new language)
	• Regular in-house training for all units (e.g. TM use)
	• Dedicated technical support units plan future tool use, customize tools, manage resources (e.g. database structure, maintenance)

Other common features of the purpose-dependent model are:

● Use in commercial contexts. Commercially sensitive translations (e.g. patents) may require additional security and QA measures. The intended purpose of the translation may also indicate the use of certain tools or resources to achieve required quality levels (e.g. client glossaries where a translation's purpose is building brand identity).

● Use in varied markets. Large agencies which accept a wide variety of job types use the purpose-based approach to identify those which require high levels of QC and to allocate appropriate resources to different projects.

● User considerations. Translations intended for certain user-groups (e.g. children, gamers) may be allocated different kinds and levels of QC.

● Budget considerations. Where budgets are tight, identifying translation purpose allows LSPs to allocate resources effectively within projects, with critical content attracting stronger QC and a higher proportion of the budget than background materials.

Purpose-dependent approaches involve challenges for quality. As with the content-driven model, it is critical that purpose is correctly identified, yet it is often unknown. Clients may also specify a clear intended purpose, but this later evolves: a translation may originally be requested for informal gisting purposes, then be discussed in a committee, used to inform a decision and eventually selected for publication online to explain a policy. If the initial translation is not subject to enhanced QC measures for the later purposes, the image of the institution can suffer.

Translations are subject to the full range of QC procedures in this model (including no QC at all), so serious errors are inevitably missed. This has effects for subsequent reliability of tools and database content. Where unchecked segments are added, they should be tagged in some way so translators treat them with caution if proposed as future matches for documents with different purposes. Low-quality matches should be picked up in QC for future jobs with more sensitive purposes, but reliability of the databases is nonetheless damaged. The policy not to incorporate matches produced by freelance suppliers in databases meant that potentially valuable resources were not available for re-use.

There are implications for staff development and quality levels in this model. These include the risk that those who need it most get less feedback on their work (e.g. junior translators not allocated to sensitive quality types). This can be avoided in in-house settings with strong career development paths and mentoring provision, such as the EC, but in commercial contexts or less controlled conditions, translators may not be given sufficient opportunities to learn from mistakes and improve quality. Conversely, work by highly experienced translators may be constantly checked where this is not necessary, as they tend to be the ones working on the most sensitive texts. Experienced senior translators spent progressively more time revising others' weaker translations rather than producing polished work of their own, something they found frustrating. Bottlenecks were again identified where senior staff were busy, particularly whenever more work was outsourced and had to be checked more carefully. A further complication was that translators disliked having to offer different quality levels. QC measures can be varied according to translation purpose, and work can be allocated to translators with different skill levels, but almost all those interviewed objected to producing lower quality translations.

The increased need to use English as a pivot language as new member states joined the EU led to substantial increases in the English unit's workload. This created logjams, as other language units waited for the English pivot before they could begin work, and led to some dissatisfaction and potential impact for quality, where translators in other language pairs found themselves working out of their mother tongue or translating from their third or fourth language rather than their preferred source. A final problem with the purpose-driven model is that budgetary considerations can outweigh purpose. An obvious example is where NGOs or underfunded organizations cannot afford to support high-quality levels even for jobs with critical purposes, whereas content for use in some highly trivial purposes may have ample funding for QA.

Purpose-based approaches do bring clear advantages for quality. Chief among these is their flexibility, something appreciated by both suppliers and clients. Where the purpose suggests specific tools, workflow or QA, these can be imposed, but otherwise translators have unusual freedom to work as they prefer. Clients expressed frustration that they often did *not* want high quality, just a very fast basic translation (still of human quality, not simply MT output); but this was not an option. The purpose-driven approach allows for the use of post-edited MT or translation out of the mother tongue in such circumstances, at a lower cost.

Because a relatively rapid cost/benefit analysis can be performed for each job, this approach is among the most efficient and scalable. Clients appreciate control over sensitive projects where these might affect their image or involve legal risks to the organization and efficient allocation of limited resources (linguistic and financial). The concept of 'fit for purpose' translation is linked to such efficient allocation of resources and has been increasingly important in the context of rising translation demand. Those responsible for QC commented positively on motivation levels, as they know that QC is performed for a specified purpose. Awareness of the purpose of each translation must of course be communicated to translators and those carrying out QC for this to be valid. In the above case, impressive in-house training supported this, with staff appreciating the different end-purposes of various job types and understanding what QC measures would be applied to their work, but this was less well understood externally and in some commercial contexts.

This model was again widespread in the industry, with particular adherents among clients in industries where brand reputation was critical (e.g. luxury goods, marketing) and in contexts where high quantities of translation were needed, but with a range of final purposes. Regular consumers of translation services were most likely to be aware of different quality levels and to prefer to pay less for jobs where high quality was not necessary. The model was less well-suited to contexts where the purpose or end-use of texts evolved over time. It is also evidently inappropriate in industries where all translated materials are needed at a consistently high- or low-quality level.

4.6 Conclusion: Top-down models and quality

The above case studies were selected because they represent relatively 'pure' forms of each distinct top-down approach to translation quality. In the majority of cases observed in research for this book, however, models were not as fixed or rigid as the illustrative outline of each type might imply. LSPs often adopted some combination of types in a hybrid approach. Some models explicitly recognize the combination of two or more considerations in allocating resources to QA, notably that in use at the OECD. Faced with a combination of growing demand, the effects of computerization, pressure to keep costs down and increasingly tight deadlines for translation of complex content, the translation division recognized that 'no translator can claim to achieve perfect quality and at the same time keep scrupulously to deadlines' (Prioux and Rochard, 2007: 21). They therefore implemented a combination model to allocate resources and identify appropriate levels of QC, notably by selecting suppliers and tailored levels of revision. Their model combines three of the above approaches: it is content-, experience- and purpose-dependent.

The OECD classes content in a hierarchical system of three types, illustrating each with a number of examples (ibid.: 25). The top level includes legal texts and press releases, while documents for internal discussion are classed in the lowest level. Translators are similarly ranked in four levels, according to experience and reliability, with illustrations of the typical qualities for each level and an indication of the corresponding internal employee grade (ibid.: 26). The top level includes senior revisers and top-level freelance translators with extensive experience, while the lowest level includes suppliers whose reliability is in question or the quality of whose work has yet to be confirmed. Finally, the translation's purpose is assessed, with a ranking from one to three stars depending on its importance and potential impact.

The OECD approach involves consulting a table listing all potential combinations of content, experience and purpose to identify automatically whether the match for each job is very good, good, poor, very poor or represents an over-allocation of resources (overkill). The aim is to match supply and demand as efficiently as possible, then to allocate the most appropriate combination of QC measures to achieve the required quality level. Further tables indicate the QC measures indicated for each potential combination of content, experience and purpose.

Such hybrid models, where a combination of features determines QA levels, are the most obvious exception to the singular top-down cases outlined above. Other frequent exceptions were also found. No provider was found to have a single invariable approach to QA used for all clients/jobs/ suppliers in practice. This could be for positive reasons (e.g. responsiveness to evolving needs and scenarios) or negative ones (e.g. when appropriate suppliers could not be found for a particular language pair, corners were cut or aspects of mandated QA processes dropped). Clients were not always aware of these changes.

When the approaches found in the real world are considered as a group, it is apparent that top-down models share core features:

● An emphasis on resources. Human and technological resources have a strong impact on quality, so achieving the optimum balance of these is a central concern. This is done for suppliers through such methods as entry qualifications (both formal, e.g. degrees and grades; and informal, e.g. amount of relevant prior experience); tests (including TQA of their translations, often using similar strategies to those proposed by theorists); probation periods or ongoing review, with clearly signalled consequences where targets are not met; and ongoing feedback. For tools and automated checks, LSPs either identified the most suitable combination for their sector, or adopted various combinations, tailored to the job, client or other significant factors.

- An emphasis on structures, workflow and processes. Real-world providers focus on the optimum conditions for the production of translations of the requisite quality, building on experience to pre-empt problems and errors in future projects.

- An emphasis on addressing quality problems and errors without overkill or waste of resources. At the heart of real-world models is the concern to obtain value for money. Providing higher quality levels than those needed by the client represents an undesirable misuse of limited resources.

- A corresponding emphasis on different quality levels. The industry is not concerned solely or principally by how to achieve the highest quality levels, but by how to balance various levels of quality with other core requirements (e.g. quick turnaround).

Case studies of real-world practice also highlight contrasts with existing academic research. Real-world providers aim to recruit either the best translators or suppliers of different abilities, to address the need for different quality levels. All experiments on translation quality carried out thus far have instead used either student subjects or, occasionally, untested freelance volunteers working in dictated conditions. The research on quality thus fails to include the highest quality providers, as used exclusively in many top-down models, especially in-house. Findings regarding error types or translators' weak points may be skewed by the failure to include the best real-world providers. In the industry, translators also build up long-term relationships with clients and expertise in their chosen domains. They become familiar with expected workflow(s) and QA processes, habitually use certain tools and resources in the same setup, and are clear how to raise queries or concerns during a project. In research contexts, even when they are unaware that they are taking part in an experiment, subjects are observed in highly artificial conditions which are likely to have a negative impact on quality. Findings from research on quality relate to either the text alone, ignoring the significant impact of production conditions; or to naïve or atypical suppliers. Researchers are looking for where errors arise and whether they are noticed in controlled conditions, or at how tools are used in limited circumstances. In contrast, the emphasis in the profession is on identifying how to allocate limited resources efficiently and in compliance with client preferences. Finally, the real-world context is constantly evolving: LSPs cannot establish one TQA method or approach that works and stick to it. Translation quality remains a core concern because there must be ongoing review of approaches and adaptability, responding to changing client needs and expectations, new file types, increased demand, new tools and capabilities or different language combinations.

There is concern that some translation quality needs remain unaddressed. Samuelsson-Brown refers to significant 'quality gaps' between client, agency and translator expectations and awareness, for example (1996: 109–112). There is widespread recognition in the industry that some aspects of translation quality and demand for services are not being addressed in current models. As O'Brien argues in a TAUS report, 'quality measurement in the translation industry is not always linked to customer satisfaction, but rather is managed by quality gatekeepers on the supply and demand side'.[3] Recent years have hence seen the emergence of distinct bottom-up approaches to respond to these gaps; these are outlined in the next chapter.

CHAPTER FIVE

Bottom-up translation quality models

5.0 Introduction: Bottom-up models: Definitions and rationale

As in other industries (e.g. publishing), a combination of downward pressure on costs and technological advances has resulted in different translation approaches. Simultaneously, new kinds of demand have arisen, which the industry is not fit, able or willing to meet. Examples are user-generated material, constantly changing dynamic texts, texts with a short shelf-life but high interest to many language communities, or new types of 'clients'. End-users increasingly demand translation or do it themselves (the 'pull' model), rather than established clients and producers deciding what to translate and delivering it to consumers (the 'push' model).

This new paradigm is associated with different conceptual models and vocabulary. Some are relatively established (e.g. 'orchestra', 'community' or 'network' models (Leavitt, 2005: 4–10)). Others, though, particularly many common in translation today, are recent developments. Activist, crowdsourced, fan, hive and volunteer translation[1] have gained importance and recognition over a short period, provoking traditional providers' interest and concern. These new approaches overturn core industry tenets (e.g. that translation should be into the mother tongue, domain experts are needed in technical translation, quality should be measured and controlled). Technological advances (e.g. free MT in a wider range of languages) have both enabled and shaped the emerging models.

Bottom-up approaches can be seen as standing in philosophical or political opposition to top-down models. In this view, such translation approaches are valuable because they extend access (e.g. to those who cannot afford to pay, or who speak languages where there is an insufficient high-earning critical mass to justify commercial translation).[2] Users drive supply, so there is less waste: material is only translated when needed. Bottom-up models share a libertarian/trusting assumption that user input and reactions will lead to appropriate quality. Top-down emphasis on standards and measuring quality may thus be actively harmful: what *can be* easily measured or controlled determines what *is* measured or controlled, and the focus on quality is deformed.

Some of these innovations have in fact come from the industry, particularly clients and LSPs frustrated at increasing time and money spent on QA with lessening returns (Bourland, 2010: 50), or hoping to achieve higher or similar levels of quality faster:

> In some cases, human translation does not make business sense – in most cases, because it takes too long. When a community is being built by its users and content is being created every second, a translate-edit-proof process simply does not work. By the time it reaches the editing stage, the source text has expanded or changed (Kelly, 2009: 62).

Bottom-up models question basic assumptions about necessary or desirable levels of translation quality and adopt new strategies to providing it. There is predictable industry interest in how these might be adapted and adopted.

Like top-down models, bottom-up approaches vary but can be grouped in three broad classes. These are now outlined with a case study illustrating each type.

5.1 Minimalist model

Founded in 1999, ProZ.com had 536,671 registered users in 2011, of whom over 300,000 were freelance suppliers. It is thus 'the world's largest community of translators' and 'most popular portal in the translation industry'.[3] Over 4,000 discrete translation, proofreading and editing jobs are posted monthly, in any combination of languages. Translators pay a subscription to register and bid for jobs, but many jobs are open to casual users without registration, as demonstrated by the actual number of paying members ('over 20,000', that is, around one in 15 in 2011[4]). Many users offer translation in both directions (into/out of the mother tongue), or bid for jobs working from their C to their B language (e.g. a native Spanish speaker may translate from English to Portuguese). ProZ advises potential clients how to select for quality in advance of jobs, in very general terms and without advising post-translation QC. It suggests two quality levels:[5]

- 'human translation of unspecified quality', from suppliers who 'offer translation services without offering concrete guarantees or assurances concerning the quality of their work';

● 'high-quality human translation', recommended when 'it is important that a translation read well and be free of errors (because it is intended for publication, use with customers, involves safety, health, significant financial or legal risk, etc.)'. To achieve this quality level, ProZ simply recommends working with 'professional, accredited translators (or translation companies who can demonstrate that they only use such translators)' who offer 'some level of guarantee or assurance concerning the quality of their service (for example in contracted terms and conditions, services agreements [sic], or other ways)'.

The ProZ approach to quality thus depends entirely on selecting appropriate suppliers. Even in this, however, their recommendation is far from that required in traditional top-down approaches. Clients are advised only that it is 'preferable' the translator be 'a native speaker or part of a team where all work is checked by native speakers before delivery'.

Supplier recruitment	• Anyone can register, no checks • Option to become 'Certified PRO' member, after submitting work sample, references and other materials. Sample translations evaluated by reviewers 'using an interface and process that involves the SAE J2450 Translation Quality Metric' (http://www.proz.com/pro-tag/info/faq); 'PRO' status conveys no extra rights but clients can search for members who have passed test
Supplier selection for jobs	• Client posts job, translators indicate interest and quote by deadline • Clients can stipulate supplier conditions, but for most jobs, details provided are: language pair, content type (e.g. 'medical/technical validation reports'), file format, deadline, number of source words/characters. Clients occasionally request sample translation of short ST extract (typically < 50 words) • Bidder meeting client-specified conditions at lowest rate usually wins contract • 'Over half' of job postings only open to paying members for first 12 hours[6]
Pre-translation	• None
Tools/resources	• Client can stipulate tool in job post; most do not
Project lifetime checks	• None
Post-translation checks	• Standard approach: none • Suppliers bidding for jobs may volunteer QC (e.g. proofreading by colleague), but rare

	• Proofreading/revision jobs listed separately but assumption is that supplier bidding for work will do this effectively; no details of style guides, tools. Site monitored over several months in 2009–10, no QA tool/ mandated checks in CAT tools specified in hundreds of jobs consulted
Return	• Client-stipulated
Post-return QC	• Left to client
Post-project	• Rating system allows suppliers to rate clients, rather than clients rating translation quality or translators
Ongoing/Quality planning	• Terms of service indicate suppliers failing to 'respect site etiquette' can be barred

This case figures many common features found in minimalist approaches; others include:

- 'Free market' approaches. Some providers market services on low cost/quick turnaround alone, with no quality guarantees.

- Self-referral by translators. A few in-house translation divisions allow staff to decide whether they are competent to take on jobs and what QC, if any, ought to be performed.

Disadvantages of the minimalist approach are evident. Anyone can bid for jobs, leading to the proliferation of 'bottom feeders', novice language learners and others with no understanding of professional translation quality. Clients cannot know if stipulated tools or processes were used, nor can they rely on translators' stated credentials (e.g. mother tongue). The combination of uninformed clients and inadequate suppliers can lead to dangerously poor quality in contexts where the impact might be significant. ProZ does flag the absence of safeguards, stressing that:

> We are not involved in the actual transaction between outsourcers and freelancers. As a result, we have no control over the quality or legality of the services, the truth or accuracy of information posted, the ability of service providers to perform services as represented or of service consumers to properly evaluate finished services. We cannot and do not control whether or not the parties to a transaction will perform as agreed.[7]

The lack of revision or other QC measures presents further challenges for quality. The model relies on translators' awareness of their weaknesses, and willingness to admit these in a context where suppliers compete against one another. Serious errors are likely to be missed (and perpetuated, if client resources are updated with such unchecked content). Where translators are unpaid for QC, working to tight deadlines, or required to undercut competitors to gain contracts, the temptation is to offer low-quality output and omit checks, particularly since there is little comeback for affected clients, beyond not using the supplier in future. ProZ is often presented as a gateway into the industry for new translators, allowing them to start practising when most LSPs require minimum experience before offering work. This means that the very translators who would most benefit from regular feedback on quality are least likely to receive it.

Languages less often needed in translation are well represented on the site, but this poses some challenges for quality. Where LSPs or clients rarely need a particular language, they are unlikely to have tested, qualified suppliers ready to work at short notice; ProZ makes it simple to identify translators in the relevant pair. This means that some less-translated languages are integrated in multilingual projects with fewer quality controls than those for the major language pairs (sourced through traditional top-down means), with a resulting imbalance in quality for different language communities.

Clients without target language competence may be entirely unaware of quality issues with translations until legal or other serious consequences become apparent. Unless they pre-empt problems in advance contracts, little redress is available. Even then, they have little opportunity for compensation, particularly as they may not know the translator's identity or location. As ProZ Terms of Service warn, 'there are risks of dealing with foreign nationals who may not fall under the laws of your area, minors, and people acting under false pretense'.[8] The impersonal nature of the arrangement and need to bid on a job-by-job basis makes ongoing relationships rare, with potential problems of isolation and suppliers being unable to monitor their development and improve through feedback, unlike top-down direct client approaches. Few agreements on ProZ thus meet usual industry quality standards.

Nonetheless, the model would not have become so quickly established and grown consistently for over a decade without clear benefits and strengths. A major factor in professional concepts of quality, as we have seen, is availability of a fit-for-purpose translation in time and at an affordable cost. This approach allows previously unmet demand to be addressed, with clients able quickly to access 'live' suppliers online for urgent tasks. Jobs are often listed with tight deadlines in relatively unusual language combinations (e.g. 21 words from Lithuanian to English in two hours). In interviews, MLV staff mentioned speedy access to suppliers with rare language combinations as a useful feature of the site. PMs had found ProZ suppliers whom they then tested and added to the database for future jobs, applying standard QA arrangements. MLVs post a high proportion of jobs, indicating the site's usefulness. For translators, ProZ takes no percentage of income, so apart from registration,[9] there is no further impact on earnings, no matter how many jobs are taken. The site offers increased autonomy (e.g. working when it suits translators rather than LSP/client timetables, deciding what QC to perform).

Some site innovations offer potential benefits for quality, particularly sharing information (e.g. forums, advice on linguistic, technical or business issues), financial benefits (e.g. substantial tool discounts through group purchase) and community support (e.g. 'powwows', where members meet to discuss translation, usually at no cost, in contrast to CPD events run by professional organizations). Free or low-cost training and other support are accessible online. There is clear potential for such support to improve quality (e.g. reaching isolated freelance translators or new providers whose languages, location or personal circumstances make it impossible for them to access traditional training). A danger is that under-qualified members may spread bad practice, of course. ProZ relies, like other bottom-up approaches, on members' ability to rate information and support in a critical, informed manner. Weak or inexperienced suppliers may be misled, but intelligent use of the site's resources can contribute to quality (e.g. in accessing fixes to technical problems in widely used CAT tools).

Overall, ProZ is supplier-driven. Where users urge change, the site has a record of responding. For instance, ProZ translators protested in 2010 about the incentive to undercut other members to win jobs, as this lowered overall rates and expectations and discouraged decent providers. This resulted in changes to guidelines on quoting and client budget setting.[10] Although established professional translators interviewed in research were dismissive of the site, citing its low rates and minimal attention to quality, they recognized its potential if certain weaknesses could be addressed. They appreciated its focus on putting translators and clients in direct contact to achieve mutually agreed quality levels. ProZ presents itself as a community and shares with other bottom-up approaches a positive emphasis on collaboration to improve working conditions and address problems (not least relating to quality). Its 'cornerstones' emphasize 'camaraderie', 'shared objectives' and ongoing improvements:

> The ProZ.com community has already redefined what it means to be a translator – the profession is more collaborative, more efficient and more fun than it was before this site existed. But we believe there is much more we can do together in the future. (http://www.proz.com/about/cornerstones/)

The minimalist approach is widespread in other translation contexts:

- One-off jobs for clients unfamiliar with the industry. Wizards prompt new clients through the job-posting process. Such clients are unlikely to be aware of top-down approaches to quality or able to source these easily.

- Agencies (SLVs/MLVs) subcontracting larger projects which their registered suppliers cannot take on. Top-down quality expectations and approaches are thus sometimes integrated within this model.

- Projects for markets or locales with sporadic translation needs. Providers are available when need arises, even if there is insufficient ongoing demand to sustain permanent provision.

- Established markets with insufficient linguists. Clients may be unable to recruit suppliers using traditional top-down methods (e.g. for particular language pairs). If the alternative is no translation, the minimalist model can be the 'least worst' option.

5.2 Crowdsourced model

Free and Open Source Software (FOSS) is licensed differently than commercial applications so users can 'study, change and improve its design through the availability of its source code' (DiBona et al., 1999: 2). Almost all software is produced in English. Commercial localization is only financially viable where producers can recoup costs through license fees for translated versions. FOSS localization extends ICT access to communities who cannot access commercial tools (as they do not speak English and operating systems or software are not translated into their language), or cannot afford localized versions, particularly for contexts where access is most useful (e.g. education, government). Various strategies have been adopted for FOSS localization, but the crowdsourcing model is most widespread. FOSS localization 'has maintained a volunteer approach to translation matters since its inception – it did not have a choice' (García, 2010: 4).

One of the most successful and long-running crowdsourced FOSS localization projects is that of Internet browser Mozilla Firefox. On the basis of revised source code to Netscape Communicator, by 2011 Firefox was fully localized into over 70 languages; 11 more are underway.[11] The non-profit Mozilla Foundation manages the development of OS software, designed to be 'internationalization-ready'. Firefox localization is 'one of the largest l10n communities on the face of the Earth',[12] with a huge number of volunteers supported by a small paid staff. Localization arrangements for each language version have varied dramatically (e.g. in scope, duration, recent 'rapid release' process[13]) but workflow and QA strategies in the case presented here are relatively consistent.

The bottom-up approach is evident from the outset, in the option to initiate localization into a new language. A clear infrastructure and ample guidance are provided, developed and refined over two decades and now managed and supported by the paid staff. If a localization 'effort' and corresponding team does not yet exist for a given locale, anyone can set one up by clicking on a web link and following simple step-by-step instructions.[14] A wiki explains how localization typically works and provides a common workspace in English for all localizing Mozilla. The localization effort and team are approved, then translation begins. At least one 'admin' (voluntary or paid) is appointed for each team. No assumptions are made regarding ability or prior experience. Each community can customize its own model (e.g. the French-France team organize live 'à la carte' translation sessions, where professionals and experienced contributors help less experienced volunteers).

Supplier recruitment	• Anyone can register, no qualifications needed (e.g. mother tongue speaker, prior experience of localization)
Supplier selection for jobs	• None. Volunteers reserve 'task' (i.e. pre-set section of text for translation, revision or proofreading) and alert other contributors, usually via community mailing list
Pre-translation	• Webpages explain localization process, existing communities, standard workflow management features (e.g. dashboards, project trackers, blogs); homepage for each locale provides information in target language
Tools/resources	• Online checklists take new suppliers through required local set-up, notably four possible translation environments/tools (Narro, Verbatim, Koala, Plain Text); all users must select one • Getting Started guides explain how to download ST for translation, provide information on file types, formats, support materials • 'Rules for translation', Glossaries (how to use, why term consistency matters), advice on project stages, what to translate, quality (basic style guide for each language; text presentation recommendations, e.g. accented characters) with basic illustrations for novice contributors
Project lifetime checks	• Links to signal bugs, technical problems available throughout • Contributors contact other volunteers to discuss problems; unresolved issues flagged to admins or designated representative • Localizers struggling with technical/linguistic problems encouraged to admit weaknesses and access peer support during process
Post-translation checks	• Versions consulted by the author recommended that all translations be revised comparatively and then proofread by two further contributors to ensure quality[15]

	• Revision/proofreading volunteers referred to existing resources, links for target language (e.g. state-sponsored technical glossaries, online termbanks). Errors/suggestions flagged to original translator who reviews, decides whether or not to accept • Toolbox, discussion lists suggest appropriate responses in case of dispute, archived in searchable format for future occurrences of similar issues
Return	• After translation and linguistic QC, translator sends localized text for code review and approval by 'l10n-drivers'; translator checks work back into Mozilla repositories • When entire tool, supporting materials (e.g. user guides, target language website) are localized and approved, version is released
Post-return QC	• Ongoing feedback from users of localized product encouraged • Wiki, blog and mailing list keep contributors updated on user feedback post-release
Post-project	• Updates continue to be localized
Ongoing/Quality planning	• By paid staff in conjunction with admins and volunteers • Experienced volunteers advise those working into new target languages

Common features of other crowdsourced translation models include:

● Official support. Infrastructure is sometimes supported by government (e.g. the PRC backs some Chinese projects), developers (e.g. Sun), NGOs or users.

● 'Content that is constantly being edited collaboratively by a large, loosely coordinated community of authors' (Désilets, 2007: n.p.). Many crowdsourced initiatives (e.g. Wikipedia) pose greater challenges than FOSS localization, where the ST is relatively stable and subject to QC before localization.

● 'Chaotic' workflow (ibid.). In FOSS localization, there is only one source language, almost invariably English. In other contexts, source content may originate in dozens of languages, with thousands of contributors translating material in multiple combinations. For instance, if an English Wikipedia entry is translated into multiple target languages, an author may then amend one of the translated entries. His update can then be translated back into English and also into multiple other languages. An even more likely scenario is continually evolving diverse content with no real 'original'; that is, authors in multiple languages simultaneously edit translated versions.

- Dedicated resources and tools. Developers have created translation environments to support crowdsourced projects, including some in the commercial sector (e.g. Lingotek). Shared resources are also being released (e.g. Wordfast's Very Large Translation Memory (VLTM), or the MyMemory project, which claims to be the world's largest TM[16]);

- 'Micro'-crowdsourcing, when huge numbers of contributors make tiny contributions to large projects. This model requires greater coordination and planning, particularly for reasons of quality, but can boost speed of completion.

- Support systems to mitigate quality problems related to unqualified volunteers. Large teams offer support (e.g. 'buddy'/mentoring schemes, online discussion boards for technical and comprehension queries, shared lexicons with clear definitions). In professional top-down approaches, translators are often discouraged from 'bothering' clients or fellow translators, but crowdsourced volunteers are encouraged to question ST sense or workflow, share information and tips, and flag concerns regarding others' contributions via report features. Voting mechanisms are common to identify best solutions or highlight problems.

- Positive feedback. To maintain volunteers' enthusiasm and commitment, various positive feedback mechanisms are common (e.g. 'badges', points).

Because crowdsourced translation approaches are diverse, disadvantages vary, and are addressed more or less effectively in different initiatives. One challenge shared by all, however, is the need for some top-down direction. Although crowdsourced initiatives rely on bottom-up participation and are moulded by participants, 'communities need community leaders' (Howe, 2008: 285). For complex localization and translation projects, substantial input in planning, workflow preparation and creating appropriate tools and resources is needed to ensure that projects run smoothly, are completed without volunteers becoming frustrated and produce reasonable quality. Managing these projects can actually be more complicated than top-down equivalents, where professional PMs are trained and rewarded. For example, it is often difficult or impossible to predict deadlines (and hence workflow) because there are few or no precedents, and because dependence on volunteers' goodwill makes imposing fixed targets unrealistic. Monitoring and proscribing certain behaviours notoriously linked to MOC contexts (trolls, spamming, harassment) is essential. If robust responses to abuse are not in place, high-quality contributors may leave.

Exacerbated challenges make achieving adequate levels of translation quality difficult for many crowdsourced approaches. Contributors may have no prior experience and limited linguistic ability. There are usually no bars on minors participating, for example. Target languages often have little tradition of translation in the domains or file formats required, and complex scripts may pose real problems. It is harder to translate between English and many crowdsourced target languages than between English and more similar languages/scripts with well-established resources and tools: 'the grammar, spelling conventions, word length, collation, and other factors are not similar at all' (Souphavanh and Karoonboonyanan, 2005: 29). Some projects require additional pre-translation processing than in commercial contexts. For example, when localizing FOSS software into Lao scripts, no technical bilingual glossary existed and the written script presented acute challenges (e.g. there are no spaces between words; vowels may appear before/after/under/above consonants) (ibid.: 18). This 'severely hampers efforts to translate software' (ibid.: 20). A further threat is that some languages benefit from official support for translation or can draw on sufficient linguistically competent contributors to create high-quality resources, while others, with fewer technically competent volunteers or poor infrastructure, are left even further behind.

QC processes also involve problems for translation quality in this model. Disagreements among contributors and users are more difficult to resolve than in top-down models, where expert revisers or bilingual subject specialists can judge. When views differ, it can be impossible to know who is correct, given the democratic structures, range of abilities and deliberately malicious behaviour from some participants. Crowdsourced initiatives rely on feedback mechanisms and the so-called wisdom of crowds to adjudicate in such instances (e.g. by voting) (Surowiecki, 2004: xi–xiv). However, this relies on the existence of a crowd in the first place, which is unlikely for translation in some specialized contexts and language pairs.

Crowdsourcing offers positive benefits for translation quality too. It permits translation which would otherwise be impossible or unaffordable, and the content thus translated often has the power to transform lives. The model is highly adaptable: contributors can translate a few words or substantial amounts of text, or take responsibility for complex processes (e.g. project management), often learning on the job. Even if final product quality does not match that of professionally sourced translation (and this is unclear, as it has not been tested), FOSS already has a significant impact on communication, education and infrastructure in certain locales. The mix of novices and experts, perhaps with product knowledge rather than translation experience, was also cited in interviews as contributing to quality. Several interviewees had extensive experience in more traditional top-down translation/localization contexts but were impressed by quality levels in FOSS equivalents, believing motivation and shared values compensated for deficiencies. 'A million willing developers' are an important resource in supporting high-quality output (Souphavanh and Karoonboonyanan, 2005: 5). Because geographically distributed volunteers can work remotely, these projects can also call on such expertise wherever in the world it is based.

Involving motivated users in translation is likely to have a positive impact on quality (García, 2010: 3–4). They may have a stronger understanding of the product or source material than professional translators, be familiar with relevant jargon and understand what parts of STs are essential or less useful, so can focus energy and QC on critical content. Novel approaches in crowdsourced models might bear fruit for traditional translation methods. For example, beta glossaries are usually developed early in FOSS projects and instantly uploaded to 'an official "portal" detailing the prescribed terminology and standards' for immediate use (Souphavanh and Karoonboonyanan, 2005: 26). Once glossaries are finalized, it is simple to update all terms consistently for later translation versions using standard tools. New QC methods also benefit quality in this model. Large groups can improve quality by reviewing/rating translations, thanks to collective intelligence. Using voting mechanisms and embedding QC throughout the project lifespan means ongoing user feedback can contribute to continuous quality improvements, even after translation is complete.

This relatively new model is attracting increasing attention in professional contexts. As Howe stresses, it is not a single strategy, but 'an umbrella term for a highly varied group of approaches that share one obvious attribute in common: they all depend on some contribution from the crowd. But the nature of those contributions can differ tremendously' (2008: 280). LSPs and tool developers (e.g. Lingotek, SDL) are attempting to harness aspects of crowdsourcing to more traditional top-down approaches. A sector with some success in this combination is translation for NGOs and charities. Organizations such as Médecins du Monde draw on a combination of volunteers and professionals to provide translation in critical contexts. They blend top-down workflow, management and resources (e.g. official glossaries) with motivated volunteers and feedback from in-country specialists to achieve high-quality translation at low cost, even in critical/ technical domains.

5.3 User-driven model[17]

The most common user-driven translation scenario is when someone wants to access information in a foreign language and generates unedited automatic translation into his mother tongue or another language he does understand. This is a major recent shift for the industry. Such users are most likely to access SMT through Google Translate, the most widely used free tool. They can either cut and paste text directly into the interface (http://translate.google.com/#), or upload files or entire websites. Users may not even realize this is how they are accessing translations, if a website translation is proposed automatically. Output is entirely unedited, though some free MT engines link to advertisements for professional post-editing or translation services, so users can access higher quality if needed.

Apart from such 'DIY' translation, other user-driven approaches include:

- Fan translation. Fans of popular culture resources and products (e.g. video games) often create translations rather than waiting for official versions, as these may only be released sometime after the original. They use MT to produce a gist translation then post-edit this using specialized domain knowledge and context (e.g. by playing the source language version of the game to elucidate the sense of unclear text), or work in teams or crowdsourced initiatives to share expertise and increase productivity. Notorious examples include speedy fan efforts to translate each new instalment of the Harry Potter series and 'scanlation' of translated comics, especially manga. Fansubbing refers to amateur subtitling of Japanese anime, and more broadly to any fan subtitles of foreign language films (O'Hagan, 2008: 161).

- Unprompted MT via 'hover' features. MT features present users with suggestions in their default target language whenever they hover over terms or short segments of text using the mouse. Google Translate supports this feature, proposing alternative suggestions for any translation. Facebook enables similar auto-translation of foreign language text into the user's default language, allowing them to view friends' status updates, for example.

- Businesses using free MT to translate websites. Naïve use is often encouraged by MT providers (e.g. 'add Google's website translator to your webpages, and offer instant access to automatic translation of the pages. Adding the website translator is quick and easy'[18]). Eventual quality is unlikely to be adequate for commercial use, but some such users' motivation is not to increase sales but to improve results through SEO.

- Integration of MT/TM, human and user-driven translation. Some 'virtually instant' human-assisted translation solutions[19] use APIs (Application Programming Interfaces) to provide translation quickly when users need it. New translatable content on client sites is detected automatically and sent for either human translation (integrating client TMs) or post-edited MT.

- 'Filling in the gaps' of partial website translation. In professionally localized websites, some content may remain untranslated. This is true even of established providers such as Apple, whose website

is apparently fully localized (e.g. http://www.apple.com/fi/mac/)
until users click to make a purchase and can access only English
language content (http://store.apple.com/fi/). In these circumstances,
'self-service' MT can be useful.

Scope for translation quality problems is most evident in this approach.
Free MT is restricted to a tiny proportion of languages. MT systems require
substantial bilingual text resources to make a language pair even vaguely
useful, so this is unlikely to change soon for many languages, increasing
the digital divide. For languages that are supported, much important
material remains frustratingly unavailable as certain content types are not
translatable (e.g. secure websites (https), text contained in images). Some
language pairs achieve far better results than others. A danger in this is
that uninformed users assume that all pairs offer similar quality (e.g. after
testing a small sample of French>English, they assume French>Chinese will
be as good). Free MT systems such as Google tend to use English as a pivot
language. For instance, a German speaker accessing a Japanese ST is actually
sending the text from Japanese>English>German, multiplying the risk of
errors. Studies have identified translation quality as the 'main weakness'
of unedited user-generated MT (e.g. 'wrong translation of pronouns and
verbs that were frequently dropped, incorrect word order, mistranslated
compounds and limited lexical coverage') (Gaspari et al., 2011: 19–20).
Most users, especially monolinguals, are unlikely to understand such
limitations.

A final quality-related issue is that users are unlikely to read the terms
and conditions, under which they effectively sign over rights to any text
entered in free MT engines to the provider. In professional contexts where
confidentiality is critical or NDAs have been signed, uninformed use of
this approach may have consequences (Drugan and Babych, 2010: 6).
Similarly, where fans use MT to generate amateur translations, they are
'on shaky ground in terms of copyright law' (O'Hagan, 2008: 162). These
effects are also important for quality because, once raw MT is available,
it may be ranked in future matches above or with professionally produced
human-quality translation released later.

There are some benefits for translation quality in this approach,
though. Above all, it allows communication and understanding which
would otherwise not take place. Most users of free MT would not pay
for human translation, even if sufficient capacity were available. Sheer
availability of translation virtually instantly can be critical in many
contexts. Despite the caveats regarding naïve expectations, in many
contexts, users are best-placed to judge whether the quality is sufficient for
their needs. 'Assessment is tempered by fitness for use: if users are satisfied
with results, anything more is a waste of resources' (García, 2009a:
206). García found that user satisfaction ratings, even with free MT,
were as high as for human translation for some purposes and languages

(ibid.: 205). Users generating MT or fan translations can also prompt a high-quality human translation. This might be user-commissioned (e.g. on seeing 'gist' MT output, understanding that content is sufficiently important to merit paid human translation). Publishers may realize that a substantial market exists for a game or product in a locale which they had not considered for translation. Ongoing improvements also suggest that user-generated output might become more valuable in future. For example, human users can rate MT output quality on Google Translate, feeding back into the system and raising quality levels for future queries. Integration of MT with voice recognition and dictation technologies for mobile use is now available in limited languages and further extends access to translation/interpreting which was previously too expensive or protracted to be useful.

Some theorists suggest that this approach may ultimately improve levels of professional translation quality. García predicts a future where translation returns to the realm of 'topic-proficient bilinguals' rather than linguists, supported by translation technologies. In his live 'hive' translation model, users would communicate needs to translators rather than relying on client-driven provision (2009a: 208–9). This would not only cut waste but also potentially improve quality, as users better understand which content is critical. Similarly, fan translation can produce higher quality output than professional linguists, who may not have the required genre expertise. Strong familiarity with a product or service, combined with technological support and robust ongoing QC through review processes and user voting, may ultimately achieve superior quality to that available via current professional models (O'Hagan, 2008: 163–4; 180).

This approach was rarely observed in professional contexts, though this may be attributed in part to understandable reluctance to admit use of free MT systems, given confidentiality issues. Clients occasionally commissioned freelance translators to produce a full human translation after generating a 'gist' through MT to ascertain whether the content merited translation, and some sent the relevant MT output along with the ST. Most Wordfast and some SDL Trados users were aware that they could access Google Translate output in the TM editing environment, though none said they found it useful or referred to it often. MT use in industry relies more on custom engines than free online systems. One interviewee suggested that free online MT was only useful where she knew or suspected a text had previously been officially translated. She gave the illustration of an official UN document or treaty amendment. If asked to translate the title or a reference to the document, it might take some time to find the recognized translation, but entering the text in Google Translate provided the relevant link instantly. She would then double-check the target language version to ensure that the hit was accurate.

5.4 Conclusion: Bottom-up models and quality

As for top-down models, the above cases represent relatively 'pure' forms of each distinct bottom-up approach to translation quality. Again, however, real-world approaches are often not as rigid as the illustrative outline of each type might imply, but combine features of different types in some hybrid. One example is the localization by Facebook of its site into 75 languages in less than two years, using a combination of crowdsourcing, paid professional translators, tools developed in-house and top-down design and management of processes. By 2010, more than half of all Facebook users were non-English speakers and 400,000 volunteer translators had contributed to its localization (van der Meer, 2010: n.p.). Twenty language versions were supported by professionals and the remainder provided by crowdsourced site users. As García points out (2010: n.p.), these users knew the site better than professional localizers could. This, along with faster translation, was the motivation for involving them, rather than a desire to cut costs. In fact:

> Creating the platform to enter the contributions of volunteers where users could vote on them, and then implementing the changes must not have been cheap. However, it worked well as a community building exercise, and a perusal of the Spanish (Spain) version indicates to me, that it could not have improved much, had Facebook used professionals. Criticisms by translators (initial occurrences of *aser* instead of *hacer* in Spanish) did not hold weight and errors were corrected. A new strategy for quality assurance emerged, based not on the opinion of the expert, but on votes, on the wisdom of crowds.

Wooten (2011: n.p.) also stresses the costs involved in 'building a collaborative translation capability into the product [Facebook] itself', managing the process and providing QC, concluding 'translation crowdsourcing regularly costs as much as, if not more than, traditional professional translation'. Critics often assume that volunteer Facebook translations are not subject to QC, but the standard workflow does in fact integrate substantial checks, in addition to user voting. Wooten indicates further advantages besides speed of translation and informed input: participating in sharing the platform with one's linguistic community enhances 'brand loyalty' and led to increased usage. A kind of virtuous circle then results, with frequent users continuing to contribute to ongoing localization of ever-increasing quantities of dynamic content.

Bottom-up models share core features, as top-down ones did:

- An emphasis on resources. Unlike top-down models, however, bottom-up approaches focus on technology, but pay little or no attention to the background, qualifications or skills of human contributors. The one exception is top-down selection, recruitment, training and support for managers and technicians working behind the scenes to support the tools and infrastructure the models need to function.

- An emphasis on structures and processes. Unlike the top-down focus on carefully designing and dictating workflow, with QC steps integrated and imposed throughout the process, the bottom-up model emphasizes getting tools right, providing resources and encouraging community support to address problems as they arise. In this model, users' ability to judge for themselves is respected. This may seem counter-intuitive: in top-down models, high-quality professionals are carefully recruited, trained and rewarded, while in bottom-up models, anyone can participate. Surely the second group would need more, not less, direction and guidance? Instead, the bottom-up model is apparently more trusting.

- Addressing quality problems and errors before/after translation. Volunteers and users are trusted partly because, when they make mistakes, these are addressed after translation. Scope for errors is limited, sometimes by addressing these pre-translation (e.g. through official glossaries and instructions on their use). Alternatively, errors can be allowed to happen, then picked up through stronger user input post-translation.

- Flexibility. These models survive where they adapt to contributors. Members strongly influence the form and community atmosphere of each different language effort in crowdsourced models, for example, and multiple user strategies and settings are provided in free MT tools.

- Different strengths. Participants in bottom-up approaches compensate for any comparative lack of linguistic competence, training or professional awareness (e.g. low or no cost, willingness to learn, strong motivation, commitment to project ideals, technical knowledge).

- An emphasis on ongoing feedback. This keeps contributors motivated (e.g. through kudos in the community), but is also critical to translation quality, as blogs, user forums and so on permit continual improvements.

- An emphasis on recognizing one's limitations. Unlike traditional professional contexts, where admitting weaknesses or doubts regarding performance is likely to undermine client confidence or provide competitors with an advantage, those working in bottom-up models are encouraged to be self-critical and flag difficulties to others in the community so they might work together to resolve them. Evidence on discussion boards of linguistic and technical issues being resolved demonstrates benefits of this approach for quality, particularly since solutions are archived and easily searched for future reuse.

Bottom-up approaches emerged to meet the needs and demands of today's translation contexts, STs and users, neglected or overlooked by the industry. When he considered one of these new phenomena, Massive Online Collaboration (MOC), and its potential impact on translation, Désilets concluded that 'many of the traditional top-down, command and control translation paradigms we use today fall apart' (2007: n.p.). This is true not only for MOC. New translation demand and approaches involve questions, challenges and potential lessons for traditional top-down industry models, which are now summarized.

Ongoing massive increases in source content are likely as more users come online, and use different platforms. While the arrival of ubiquitous computing may be overstated or some way off, even today users are continuously creating and amending content on platforms such as phones. Given the industry's inability to translate even 1990s content levels, how can it keep up? Even bottom-up approaches drawing on thousands of contributors are unlikely to be sufficient. Significant changes for translation workflows are likely: they will be 'much more open and chaotic [...] than in a traditional environment' (ibid.). This has clear implications for quality as currently managed in the profession. How can automated top-down QC processes be integrated where workflow is radically altered in this way? Expectations (e.g. that simship is desirable) become unviable when there are far greater numbers of languages, no single source, and content is evolving.

The changing translation context also has implications for today's standard tools and resources. TM and localization tools face evident challenges where there is no longer a single source language. Terminology tools are less affected: most tools allow any term to be linked to its equivalents in multiple target languages, and the source can be switched to any language in the database. Capacity may be an issue for significant numbers of languages, as termbases typically support fewer than ten. TM tools are not so flexible. Most do not allow users to reverse direction of aligned content, and hardly any allow alignment of multiple languages. There are good, quality-related reasons for this. 'Products of translation' differ from natural (non-translated) STs in two principal ways, which have been demonstrated in research: 'interference from the source language spilling over into translation in a source-language-specific way' and 'general effects of the process of translation that are independent of source language' (Koppel and Ordan, 2011: 1318). This phenomenon, known as 'translationese', means that reversing the direction of TMs, or matching two aligned target languages translated from the same source content, would be less likely to result in matches for new natural language texts. No experiments were found where an ST written in Language A was translated into multiple target languages (B, C, D and so on), then Language C aligned with Language D to create a TM. Would such database content ever be useful, particularly where content from different languages is edited and modified at different rates and in different permutations?

Two further factors suggest that new tools will be needed to respond to the new paradigm: first, such tools and approaches are already emerging; and second, most bottom-up providers offering translation for the first time have designed their own platforms, rather than relying on existing tools. The most striking example of this is Google's revolutionizing of MT provision, but many bottom-up approaches have quietly redesigned TM, localization and terminology tools to make them more user-friendly, and indeed to remove the need for users to realize they are using such technologies at all.

An increasing trend towards 'unlocking' data and resources complements such new approaches and presents both practical and philosophical challenges to top-down models. The OS movement has demonstrated potential benefits of greater openness. Organizations such as TAUS have made some progress in sharing translation resources and putting pressure on leading players to contribute. Some strongly top-down providers (e.g. the EU) have released terminological and TM resources for others' use. This tendency is likely to intensify. Even if providers do not themselves unlock data, once material is online, it can be automatically aligned or mined for bitexts and other purposes. Désilets argues that the next logical step in this trend is increased trust, allowing users to edit and add to shared resources (2007: n.p.). Editing could be restricted to a larger community of translators (perhaps ranked by experience level) or simply open to anyone. In his view, enhanced database quality might result, particularly if greater openness is coupled with rating systems, so users can rank content quality. Advantages would be additional matches, increasing buy-in to the use of resources, and extending to freelance translators economies of scale that are now only available to in-house staff in large organizations. Désilets suggests ProZ might host such resources in future. This of course poses a significant philosophical challenge to the standard top-down model of large organizations owning content, but may be more likely if they perceive clear benefits (e.g. adding further languages cheaply and quickly). Désilets' optimism regarding the benefits of increased database size is also untested: while it seems logical that greater text quantities will increase TM usefulness, there may be unintended drawbacks for quality (e.g. increased difficulty of effective maintenance, making the resources less useful beyond a certain point; user difficulty in choosing between multiple matches).

The individuals who use and contribute to bottom-up approaches involve challenges for quality and top-down models too. Bottom-up approaches embrace locales and providers with little experience of professional translation. Outsourcing of some TQA aspects to low-cost countries (e.g. post-production processes) means that important stages may be divorced from linguistic expertise, with resulting risks to quality (as already observed in the subtitling industry, where separation of linguistic and technical QA is common). An unintended effect of bottom-up attempts to address divisions and inequalities might therefore be to exacerbate them in some ways. For instance, FOSS localization can be seen to have resulted in three quality 'tiers':

1　Traditional top-down localization and translation, with high levels of QA as standard, for markets with sufficient customers and income levels.

2　OS/bottom-up solutions for locales with sufficient technically and linguistically competent contributors and/or official backing. Quality levels vary depending on contributors and processes.

3　Vast regions with no or very low-quality access, due to lack of support, insufficient numbers of educated bilinguals to translate, absence of standard written scripts.

Quality may be seen as a privilege. Evidently this is already true of most industries, products and services: those who can pay are able to access high quality unthinkingly, while many must make do with lower quality than they would choose. Extending translation quality or attempting to raise levels through new means can therefore be political, and might, for example, target linguistic minorities or language communities with the lowest resource levels.

Sceptics have criticized the expectation that crowdsourced volunteers can be relied on:

> A prominent strain of enthusiasm for wikis, long tails, hive minds, and so on incorporates the presumption that one profession after another will be demonetized. Digitally connected mobs will perform more and more services on a collective volunteer basis, from medicine to solving crimes, until all jobs are done that way. (Lanier, 2010: 71)

Lanier and others raise the obvious question of how such volunteers pay the rent, and query whether the model can work long-term. Is there a tipping point when time or goodwill evaporate? Because the crowdsourced model is new and emerging, it is easy to get wrong, particularly in professional contexts. The clumsy approach to bottom-up translation at LinkedIn is notoriously cited as an example[20]. Where users and contributors find them offensive, bottom-up approaches are also vulnerable to targeted abuse or deliberately inflammatory translations. As traditional clients explore how to integrate or benefit from bottom-up models, there are clear risks to quality and motivation of both paid and unpaid contributors. Gneezy and Rustichini (2000) have demonstrated the counterintuitive ill-effects on motivation and quality of financial rewards for contributors in some contexts. The sheer scale of professional translation also raises questions about how far bottom-up models can spread beyond their current scope. If paid professionals cannot meet current demand, it is unlikely that collectives of volunteers could do so, nor that their motivation would stretch to the text types traditionally commissioned from paid translators. Even if large cohorts of sufficiently 'bilingual' motivated volunteers could be identified (e.g. language learners), the scope for negative impact on quality is evident.

Advocates of bottom-up approaches nonetheless point to this stage being 'just a prelude to a far more pervasive transformation', with a 'crowdsourcing generation', wider Internet access and online communities supplanting the 'conventional corporation' (Howe, 2008: 261–2). There is ample corroboration of the model's success in some contexts: Wikipedia is 'proof by construction that people are able to collaborate very efficiently and create high quality content in that way' (Désilets, 2007: n.p.). In all this, though, quality is the unknown quantity. While Wikipedia does contain high-quality content, it does not do so uniformly and reliably; is rejected in many contexts as a result (e.g. citations for academic purposes); and itself poses further challenges for translation (e.g. localizing its dynamic content). Because the model is untested, particularly in professional contexts, negative potential consequences for quality are feared (e.g. amateur translators driving down rates in mature markets or leading to a general deskilling of the profession).

Despite the remaining uncertainties, bottom-up models already hold some lessons for traditional approaches. They see translation and quality as ongoing processes, rather than discrete jobs, which can be signed off and archived; post-translation feedback, user voting mechanisms and other such features are standard. The current professional paradigm is 'active translation agents and passive or unknowable translation recipients', but if 'translation consumers' increasingly become 'translation producers' (Cronin, 2010: n.p.), informed reactions and subject expertise might be co-opted to improve professional translations post-release. The potential for top-down models to integrate such expectations and improve quality is clear. Nor is the leap to such integration a large one. There are evident parallels, for instance, between ongoing user feedback to improve translation and philosophical building blocks of professional translation quality such as Kaizen and Six Sigma, with their emphasis on ongoing incremental improvement. This model also makes sense in terms of today's text production approaches: if texts constantly evolve, translation must follow.

Another feature of bottom-up approaches from which the industry might learn is their encouragement of openness and self-criticism regarding limitations and weaknesses, coupled with strong community support to address resulting issues. This again has evident potential advantages for quality, but involves a greater shift in professional mindsets, particularly in freelance contexts where suppliers are conscious of competitors and persuading clients their work is of high quality. ProZ seems an obvious site to host such translator interaction, but its failure to attract many high-quality providers and combination of job offers/marketing with support would be likely to limit translators' confidence in admitting weaknesses. Separating the forum elements, or limiting access to translator-to-translator advice, might address such concerns. In larger in-house conditions, they might also be addressed relatively easily, for example through 'representatives' who collated anonymous queries and translation problems for language unit discussion, perhaps via a wiki or blog.

A final feature of bottom-up models which the industry might adopt more widely is the acceptance that it is better to provide some translation with available resources than none, even if quality is lower. This might seem standard practice in the industry already, but in research, translators recognized they struggled to produce different, particularly lower, quality levels. Those who accepted occasional jobs out of the mother tongue or agreed to post-edit MT output for less than their standard rate found such work 'really frustrating', even impossible: 'I ended up doing it to my usual standard. It took so long I was being paid less than the minimum wage. I told [the agency] I wasn't available for those jobs in future, it's not worth it'.[21] Providing different (particularly lower) quality levels therefore requires a significant shift. Involving different types of provider, making greater use of technology, or integrating unedited MT output with professional translation might provide solutions, but all have implications for quality. It would be relatively straightforward, for example, to supplement professionally translated website content with unedited MT output. Where a user hovered the mouse over untranslated sections, the site could flag any alternative languages available through MT (or human translations in other target languages) so users might access information, even if its quality were not as high as surrounding text. The approach might even improve translation quality by more efficient allocation of resources to the content that matters most. In interviews, translators frequently wondered how far their work was ever read. Internet studies indeed show that reading patterns have changed: users typically browse for brief periods (< 30 seconds) before moving on to the next page (Cronin, 2010: n.p.). If the above approach were adopted for websites, it would be possible to track user-generated requests for MT content, and therefore measure what is actually needed in translation and what can safely be omitted. Returning to the Apple illustration above (Section 5.3), instead of translating all but one (important) page, translation effort could be focused on the sections actually read by most users, and professional resources spread more evenly. Users who accessed MT output could also rate and/or edit suggestions to improve quality.

Discussing MOC contexts, Désilets underlined that 'our intuitions about what can and cannot happen are often wrong' (2007: n.p.). This applies equally to bottom-up models of translation quality. Predictions must be cautious, given the models' little-tested and evolving nature. More concrete conclusions can be drawn on other implications, however, notably those of industry approaches for translator training, ethics and the future of translation quality. These questions are now considered in Chapter Six.

CHAPTER SIX

Conclusion: Lessons from industry

6.0 Introduction

The translation industry has experienced great change in the past two decades and remains in a state of flux. Massive increases in content, different kinds of texts, unmet demand and improved technology and resources have entailed imaginative new ways of translating. Some effects of these changes for quality are already apparent, and are likely to become more profound in future. Translation theorists' focus on quality in the text alone means we risk failing to notice or account for these developments. The translation process has a significant impact on quality, and long-established processes are currently undergoing dramatic change. Translation is increasingly continuous, rather than a fixed stage in the text production cycle, and plays a more important role in more people's lives than ever before. Ongoing study of real-world approaches as they evolve in response to client and user needs is therefore essential to understand which models are most helpful in different contexts.

There are positive signs this is beginning to happen, with emerging bottom-up approaches in particular attracting the attention of theorists (O'Hagan, 2011) and many in the industry. However, it is important that traditional top-down approaches are not neglected in the turn to newer models. It remains essential to observe and learn from real-world strategies, and to study the industry closely as it reacts to emerging models, particularly because this has been a significant research gap until very recently. There is also a risk that bottom-up models are perceived as threats rather than opportunities. Both top-down and bottom-up approaches have much to learn from each other. Bottom-up approaches have been able to do this naturally to some extent, coming after (and in reaction to insufficiencies in) the top-down tradition. They were able to integrate best practices from top-down models (e.g. borrowing effective management strategies for certain aspects where volunteers would struggle to fulfil functions effectively). For top-down models similarly to benefit from bottom-up ones will require willingness to reassess long-established ways of working, and sufficient time, energy and investment to investigate how new models might make a useful contribution. Yet this is needed at a point when those working in traditional models are under more pressure than ever. The impetus may come from clients and users, perhaps bringing new assumptions from their experience of other models (e.g. expecting to be able to feed back on quality post-publication). Translation tools and resources also have a role to play, as they become ever-more integral to translation processes for an increasing number of language pairs and as some automated QC steps become standard. A threat here is potentially patchy development, if uptake remains expensive and requires infrastructure, training and support.

Examining and comparing theoretical and real-world approaches to quality in this book points to some lessons for clients, users and different translation scenarios. First, all approaches benefit when client and user expectations are effectively communicated to those producing the translations. Professional associations have long emphasized this point and supply client guidance (e.g. Durban, 2006). Equally, however, LSPs have a responsibility to communicate what they will provide. In interviews with clients and LSPs, they regularly had strikingly different expectations, even on basic points (e.g. what key terms such as 'revision' or 'proofreading' meant the LSP would do; many clients were unaware that sampling was standard practice). Second, the existence of multiple approaches to translation quality in both theory and the profession underlines that different translation scenarios and needs benefit from different strategies. It is hoped that the sample case studies outlined in Chapters Four and Five, and the summary of scenarios in which each model is typically applied, will help clients identify the most suitable approach for their own needs. Hybrid approaches can also be drawn out, including some which bring together aspects of top-down and bottom-up models. By considering positive and negative effects for quality of each model, LSPs can adopt the combination most suited to particular jobs.

The industry has reacted warily to bottom-up approaches, citing quality concerns to explain its scepticism. However, the practical examples outlined in Chapter Five suggest some positive contributions the models could make, including potential quality improvements. Other established industries have experienced benefits from the emergence of bottom-up approaches. In the software industry, the Open Source movement was initially viewed as a clear threat to proprietary models and established providers. In reality, both benefitted (Désilets, 2007: n.p.). Microsoft, Google and other providers of tools and resources assimilated successful strategies developed in the OS community (e.g. workflow, communication methods). Software vendors fund OS efforts, because the symbiotic relationship bears fruit for traditional providers too. The translation industry is similarly unlikely to be undermined by new models, given demand levels; but the industry, clients and users could gain much from examining emerging practice where this might offer new ways to address common concerns and challenges.

There are thus lessons from, and for, the translation industry in relation to quality. Further implications of this study are for training, ethics and future research. These are now outlined.

6.1 Training implications

Quality has always been central to training, not least because trainers must assess learners' work and justify their ratings. What trainees learn about quality and TQA is also important because it 'sets the standards for what (future generations of) translators, translation-users and clients will understand by a "good" translation' (Hönig, 1998: 15). Given the industry focus on different quality levels and processes, particularly in the face of rising demand, translator education could valuably extend to a range of other challenging quality-related issues, however. Many training providers recognize the need for applied training, engaging students in 'authentic' tasks, and 'studying workflow scenarios [which] involves not only considering how tasks can be handled but also being able to explain and discuss the relative merits of possible alternatives' (Somers, 2003b: 324). However, rapid and substantial changes affecting the industry and emerging new approaches to quality pose real challenges for those training tomorrow's translators. Lambert (1996: 272) suggested universities are not 'flexible enough to account for systematic and rapid changes', concluding that 'in our contemporary world, we need new models for observation, analysis, action – and teaching' (ibid.: 275).

Industry approaches to quality have particular implications for training in:

- Workflow and processes. These affect quality significantly, but are often neglected in favour of a focus on assessing students' translation products. Few programmes offer students training in different kinds of workflow, or essential industry pre- and post-translation processes (Drugan & Rothwell, 2011), such as technical ST authoring skills (Kingscott, 1996b: 295) or MT post-editing (O'Brien, 2002: 99);

- Tools and resources. While many providers now train students to use standard terminology, TM, localization and MT tools, the focus is typically on how to use the tools and critical evaluation of their functions. Little attention is paid to their impact on quality (MT being a possible exception), how they are integrated in a range of industry workflows and processes, their contribution to

TQA or how they are evolving to meet new industry demands (e.g. collaborative 'cloud' platforms). Many providers offer training in only one tool for each type, so students are unaware of different approaches and ill-prepared for the industry, where they may be expected to use multiple tools and be confident in adapting to substantially different and more complex new tools as these come on-stream. Increasing industry integration of post-edited MT output means students might benefit from training in this distinct skill (O'Brien, 2002);

- QA processes. Providers may offer training in some aspects of quality and its assessment (e.g. revision/editing, theoretical approaches to TQA), but as in translation theory, there is little attention to how processes affect quality. This is true both for standard top-down approaches (e.g. few students learn how test translations for agencies will be assessed) and for emerging approaches such as crowdsourcing. Hague et al. (2011: 260) claim trainers are beginning to respond to industry needs by stressing 'the skill of following a variety of specifications', and requiring their use for exit examinations. Professional QA tools, automated processes and training in how QA is integrated in different workflows nonetheless remain conspicuously absent from training;

- Industry expectations. Given the scale of the industry and increasing range of roles available, careers guidance is essential. Rapid change makes this challenging for providers. The switch from the traditional translator's 'monastic' isolation (Cronin, 2010: n.p.) to different industry expectations about collaboration, openness and sharing also mean 'teamwork and project management should become parts of our training in technical translation and translation technologies' (Pym, 2006: n.p.). Adaptability when faced with change is also key in the current (and likely future) professional context, 'avoiding any illusion that there is only one eternal kind of professional translator' (ibid.);

- Range of languages. Demand for translators in many languages is unsupported by existing training, because there is no local provision, or because established providers' fees place their courses out of reach of the vast majority, even if entry qualifications could be met by sufficient numbers of students to justify running a group. Perhaps another established industry can learn from bottom-up approaches here. If traditional training in certain language pairs is unaffordable or unsupported, the bottom-up model of online provision, new kinds of 'trainer' and support for community learning may be one way to address clear need.

If training providers are to offer courses which keep up with the pace of change in the real world, the relationship must be two-way, with strong ongoing input from professionals. However, Pym (ibid.) indicates that 'for sociological reasons, relations between the localization industry and the academy are bound to be difficult'. Similarly, whether for 'sociological', financial or institutional reasons, achieving regular input from the broader translation industry is complicated. For bottom-up approaches, merely identifying contributors poses challenges, and they may be based anywhere around the globe. This, and the approaches' comparative novelty, makes it unlikely that they are playing a significant part in training. Pym recognizes that tension in industry–academy relations can have benefits too, though: it allows trainers to act as critical friends, scrutinizing industry assumptions and offering insights from theory.

Translation ethics is one important area in which academics can contribute such insights, one in which the industry is less well-placed to be self-reliant. Strong academic traditions in ethics training and increasing turn to applied ethics in many countries can benefit the industry. Translation can learn from the experience of other professions who have longer traditions of training in ethics (e.g. law, medicine), at a moment when ethical issues are assuming growing importance (Drugan & Megone, 2011: 183), not least due to their links to quality.

6.2 Quality and ethics

Academics have debated ethical issues relating to translation,[1] but only rarely in connection with professional practice (Drugan, 2011; Künzli, 2007b; McDonough Dolmaya, 2011). Professionals seem implicitly to believe that ethical issues such as loyalty or integrity, and more specific concerns (e.g. feminist translation approaches) are less problematic in the real world than in theory. Many ethical decisions are not 'left to the individual translator', but dictated in company policy, client specifications, etc.: 'acceptability and house style must take precedence over the translator's personal beliefs' (Chesterman & Wagner, 2002: 103). While freelance translators have debated some ethical issues around ownership, copyright and signing work (e.g. Durban, 2006; 2010), these discussions remain rare in the 'corporate environment' or other collective translation models (Chesterman & Wagner, 2002: 107). Yet a consideration of translation quality in practice, particularly in today's context, does invoke broader questions of ethics and ethical behaviour.

Quality is directly linked to ethics because clients and users expect to be able to rely on certain quality levels when using professional translation. The profession's standing is closely linked to this expectation. This is particularly true for critical domains such as medical translation. Translator competence is thus a core professional responsibility in all leading Codes of Conduct/Practice. Translators should only take on work they are qualified to perform. Under the British Code of Professional Conduct (shared by the ITI and CIoL), for example:[2]

> 3.8 Practitioners shall only accept work which they believe they have the competence both linguistically and in terms of specialist knowledge or skill to carry out to the standard required by the client, unless they are to sub-contract the work under the terms of 4.6 or they are informed that their work will be revised by a person with the competence required to ensure that the work will satisfy the standards set out in this Code.
>
> 3.9 The competence to carry out a particular assignment shall include: a sufficiently advanced and idiomatic command of the languages concerned, with awareness of dialects and other linguistic variations that may be relevant to a particular commission of work; the particular specialist skills required; and, where appropriate, an adequate level of awareness of relevant cultural and political realities in relation to the country or countries concerned.

As in most countries, though, the United Kingdom is an unregulated translation marketplace. Members may sign up to the above Code and respect its requirements, but many practising translators are not members. Bottom-up models also have entirely different expectations regarding translation competence. How is translation quality to be understood by clients and users under such models? Might new approaches undermine professional ethical codes?

New approaches to translation raise other issues related to ethics and quality. They highlight ethical gaps in translation provision, by attending to needs that would otherwise go unmet. Drawing attention to underserved linguistic communities and beginning to offer access to translated materials has the potential to change what is routinely translated and to enhance lives through access to information and communication. A related issue is the idea of quality 'tiers', however, with differential provision and quality levels for different communities. New models may address the digital divide and other translation gaps, but an unfortunate side-effect may be to entrench inequalities and undermine translation professionals. Downward pressure on rates predicted or observed by many professionals has implications for both quality and ethics. Undercutting, notably by suppliers in low-cost countries or with no experience, threatens quality, particularly for some language pairs.

New uses of tools and resources raise ethical issues relating to quality. Sharing translated content, particularly without the client or translator's awareness or consent, contravenes ethical and professional expectations about confidentiality, ownership, attribution and quality of future translations. For instance, some new tools (e.g. the VLTM or MyMemory) allow users to store aligned content 'in the cloud', with user-defined restrictions on access. However, many questions remain regarding ownership, liability in case of breaches and potential future uses of data stored in such ways. While no professional translators interviewed for this study admitted use of free MT, most translation contracts seen by the author imposed no restrictions. Bottom-up approaches make no recommendations regarding the use of free MT tools. Yet sending texts to such engines (especially sensitive ones such as medical records, pre-embargo press releases), or using translators' forums such as ProZ to enquire about potentially sensitive terminology or text, contravenes standard professional expectations about client confidentiality and trust. Many in the industry were unaware of the implications of using such tools. If standard bottom-up expectations about greater collaboration and sharing spread, there are risks to both quality (e.g. import into databases of translated material which has been subject to little or no QC) and ethical standards. Even in top-down models, basic issues such as ownership of TM content are far from resolved: informed clients and providers stipulate this in contracts, but for a surprisingly large proportion of jobs observed in research, lack of clarity prevailed. Translators, agencies and clients sometimes simultaneously believed that in future they alone had the right to use content created during the job, including for different clients.

Changing translation contexts raise broader issues of rights, whether for translators (e.g. the right to earn a reasonable income in return for their investment in training and effort), clients (e.g. the right to have NDAs respected by suppliers) or users (e.g. the right to suffer no harm through use of a translation, where the ST would have caused no harm). Changes affecting the industry threaten client-translator relations in some ways, but there are potentially positive effects for quality and ethical progress in this (e.g. less passive end-users, ongoing review of translated content and a broader choice of approaches for clients). Potential ethical benefits include enhanced ongoing communication, greater openness and increased cooperation between translation users, producers and clients.

6.3 Conclusion: Next steps

Discussing MOC contexts, Désilets argued (2007: n.p.) they might:

> change the rules of the game for translation, by sometimes introducing new problems, sometimes enabling new and better solutions to existing problems, and sometimes introducing exciting new opportunities that simply were not on our minds before.

Comparing different approaches to translation quality spotlights just such new problems, potential solutions and further opportunities for exploration.

First, bottom-up models pose challenges and questions for both researchers and the industry. How will the influx of volunteers in a traditionally top-down sector affect quality expectations (among users, clients, LSPs)? Research could contribute to understanding here, for instance by comparing crowdsourced translation quality with translations sourced through traditional models (e.g. consistency, accuracy, etc. might be compared across standard software and FOSS localization products). In addition to comparing the two products, though, it would be constructive to examine how translation processes, workflow and management contributed to any quality difference. Substantial challenges for such research include cost, access (particularly where monitoring disjointed translation processes across multiple locations and providers), comparability of different text types, different motivation levels, effects of different language pairs (e.g. resource availability, technical challenges). Controlling or intervening in workflow would allow testing of different tools' or processes' impact on end products (e.g. how far do automated QA tools improve overall product quality compared to no QA or post-release review by users?). Translation theorists also have a role to play in examining new models critically and drawing out their theoretical underpinnings. Even if academic TQA models are impractical in the real world, traditional top-down professional approaches demonstrate some clear links with the underlying ideas. This seems less true of emerging bottom-up models, however. How can translation theory describe, account for and contribute to this new paradigm? There is scope for exciting interdisciplinary approaches here. For example, translation studies and ethics might jointly contribute to understanding of new models of cooperation in bottom-up approaches, or of the challenges in their integration with top-down models.

The meeting of the two sets of approaches to quality raises further questions. How are bottom-up approaches best integrated with top-down models if the aim is to improve quality? What sectors are most likely to benefit from such hybrids? What lessons can be drawn from others' experience of similar evolutions (e.g. journalism)? Other sectors are far ahead of translation in areas such as user feedback. How might ongoing user input improve translations post-delivery? Where quality improvements take place, how can resources benefit? For example, if users improve a translation, might updated content be automatically flagged so relevant TMs and TBs are updated and raise future quality levels? Other new challenges to traditional use of translation tools and resources have implications for quality. How will massive increases in content affect databases, whether in top-down and bottom-up models? Should TM content be separated as in traditional models (e.g. by thematic content, client, date, LSP, project, language pair) or do other ways of organizing content enhance future reuse?

More imaginative uses of existing tools have quality implications which might be tested in experiments. For example, the creation of huge TM databases across multiple languages offers scope to align material in new ways (e.g. pairing two or more target languages, without reference to the source) and check its potential for useful matches. As already demonstrated for MT, do certain language pairs result in more matches, even if TM direction is switched or two target languages paired in a new TM? Existing tools are likely to be integrated in more imaginative hybrid solutions to address translation problems in future. Integration of corpora and MT output in TM tools is already being tested, but there is clearly scope for other such innovations. Might bilingual or multilingual thesauri, perhaps with ongoing links to dynamic online resources, be used more efficiently to update TBs without laborious user conversion and maintenance? Would such content be useful in highly technical fields if data sources were controlled? What effects would such resources have on database quality? Which sectors would be most affected? Are there related training needs, or might lessons be learned from bottom-up models so that such resources could be used intuitively with little understanding on users' behalf as to backroom processes? Is it possible to assuage confidentiality and quality concerns yet still access benefits of large corpora such as the Internet?

Users exploit emerging technologies in unpredictable ways and this is also likely to affect the industry. For example, smartphones' portability and enhanced features (e.g. apps for dictation, text recognition, MT) might be combined with feedback on translated content in context (e.g. by scanning text and autotranslating). This could feasibly contribute in contexts where professional translations are unavailable or unlikely to be commissioned (e.g. tourists commenting to improve menu quality). Especially for some language pairs, such changes could offer accessible, cheap and rapid improvements to quality.

There are new opportunities, and substantial challenges, for training. The absence of bars to entry in bottom-up approaches affords trainees opportunities to participate in real-world projects, for example. This raises questions as to their usefulness for the industry more broadly, though, as quality expectations remain quite different. Assessing such participation would present clear challenges, given the collaborative, voluntary and changeable nature of the work. How are trainers to reflect rapid substantial change in the industry when preparing students for their eventual roles? What kind of training is most effective in preparing graduates for careers in the industry? Little research has tracked which linguists succeed in building long-term careers in translation and related occupations, and how their training equipped them to do so; as the industry continues to evolve and diversify, it will become ever more challenging to assess this.

Theorists and practitioners have long recognized that '[scholars] should spend more time studying real translators in real action' (Chesterman & Wagner, 2002: 136). At a time of drastic change for the industry, this is truer than ever. Happily, bottom-up models emphasize openness and sharing. There are encouraging signs that these strategies, and their participants' enthusiasm, are infecting the industry more broadly, with the EU, TAUS and other large organizations taking previously unthinkable steps to enhance access to data and understanding. Observing real translators in real action is becoming increasingly possible, and increasingly rewarding.

NOTES

Introduction

1 Howe, who coined the term (2008: 300), defines crowdsourcing as 'taking a job traditionally performed by employees and outsourcing it to an undefined, generally large group of people in the form of an open call'.

2 The access necessary for studies by Cao and Zhao (2008) for the United Nations, and Drugan (2004, 2007) and Koskinen (2008) for the European Union remains exceptional (see the general absence of publications on large translation companies and organizations).

3 I refer to the most widely available version, reproduced in Venuti's *Translation Studies Reader* (2000: 180–92).

4 Chesterman (2009) examines such reactions and adds significantly to Holmes' original categorization.

5 Kussmaul and Tirkkonen-Condit (1995) give a critical account of TAPs' relevance and limits for translation research.

6 China reports complete lack of translators, interpreters, *People's Daily*, 21 February 2006 [online] http://english.peopledaily.com.cn/200602/21/ eng20060221_244409.html.

Chapter 1

1 British Parliamentary Office of Science and Technology, 'ICT in developing countries', *Postnote*, No. 261, March 2006, 1.

2 *ITU World Telecommunication/ICT Indicators Database* [online] www.itu.int/ ITU-D/ict/statistics/ict/index.html.

3 Google Translate supported 63 languages by August 2011, Microsoft's Bing Translator supported 36 and Yahoo! Babel Fish supported 13. It is estimated there are nearly 7,000 living languages (Lewis: 2009) so the vast majority remain unserved even by automatic translation.

4 eMpTy Pages blog [online] http://kv-emptypages.blogspot.com, 27 April 2010, 'Falling translation prices and implications for translation professionals'.

5 Simultaneous shipping in multiple languages.

6 Gouadec summarizes arguments for and against such regulation (2007: 252–5).

7 There is little consensus on the term's meaning, but most definitions stress 'speed and time (accelerating, rapidly developing, etc.), processes and flows, space (encompassing ever greater amounts of it) and increasing integration and interconnectivity' (Ritzer (2007: 1), whether they hail from the 'globophilia' or 'globophobia' camps, from developing countries or more privileged societies. Robertson et al. outline why defining globalization remains contentious (2007: 54–66).

8 www.tausdata.org/blog/about-taus-data/.

9 Sprung defines internationalization as 'designing a product (e.g. software) so that it supports usages around the world (e.g. number, date and currency formats) and can be easily adapted and translated for individual local markets' (2000b: x). Localization is 'taking a product (ideally, one that has been internationalized well) and tailoring it to an individual local market (e.g. Germany, Japan). "Localization" often refers to translating and adapting software products to local markets' (ibid.).

10 Cronin cites compelling figures from Goldblatt: in 1909, the world had 37 intergovernmental and 176 nongovernmental international organizations; by 1989, there were 300 and 4,200 respectively (2003: 109).

11 Council of the European Union, *Directive 2010/. . ./EU of the European Parliament and of the Council on the right to interpretation and translation in criminal proceedings*, [online] http://register.consilium.europa.eu/pdf/en/10/pe00/pe00027.en10.pdf.

12 J. P. Fried, 'Speaking in (many) tongues can be profitable', *New York Times*, 30 April 2006, [online] www.nytimes.com/2006/04/30/nyregion/30homefront.html?ex=1304049600&en=5ced97b426f03864&ei=5090&partner=rssuserland&emc=rss.

13 National Assembly for Wales, *Welsh Language Scheme 2007*, p. 3 [online] www.assemblywales.org/jds_welsh_language_scheme_english.pdf.

14 Esselink defines a locale as 'a specific combination of language, region, and character encoding. For example, the French spoken in Canada is a different locale to the French spoken in France' (2000: 1).

15 http://ec.europa.eu/education/languages/languages-of-europe/doc135_en.htm [online].

16 Bulgarian, Czech, Danish, Dutch, English, Estonian, Finnish, French, German, Greek, Hungarian, Irish, Italian, Latvian, Lithuanian, Maltese, Polish, Portuguese, Romanian, Slovak, Slovene, Spanish and Swedish.

17 Interview with the author, May 2004.

18 'The translation market in ten years' time – a forecast', *tcworld*, December 2008, 14–15, [online] www.tcworld.info/index.php?id=78.

19 National Commission on Terrorist Attacks upon the United States, 'Law enforcement, counterterrorism, and intelligence collection in the United States prior to 9/11', [online] www.9–11commission.gov/staff_statements/staff_statement_9.pdf.

20 World Travel and Tourism Council, March 2010; [online] www.wttc.org/.

21 Over 16 million MMOG subscriptions were recorded in 2008, almost certainly an underestimate: 'An analysis of MMOG subscription growth' [online] www.mmogchart.com.

22 For example, the BBC's coverage [online] http://news.bbc.co.uk/1/hi/6052800.stm.

23 Microsoft and others use Live Translation (www.livetranslation.com).

24 All quotes from interviews with the author.

25 Six, S., 'Summary of ATA's latest translation and interpreting compensation survey', *ATA Chronicle*, February 2008, 12–15.

26 www.iti.org.uk/uploadedFiles/surveys/ITI2001R&S.pdf.

27 www.proz.com/polls/9376

28 www.atanet.org/docs/compensation_survey_2007.pdf.

29 This survey is now dated (2001).

30 For illustration, imagine you are translating the English webpage relating to a recent international campaign into French. It contains a link to the latest annual UNICEF-UK conference. In your translation, should you keep the link to the English-language conference site; or change it to the equivalent French-language conference site, referring to the event held in France? What if the context is a reference to a debate or speaker only at the UK event?

31 A 1998 PhD study found that 45 per cent of STs received by freelance translators still arrived as hard copy (Webb, 1998, cited in Bowker, 2002: 22). The situation has since improved, but hard copy STs continue to constitute a significant proportion of translators' workloads in some fields (e.g. legal translation). Translators reported in interviews that scanned texts and text embedded in images had grown as a proportion of workloads.

32 The standard industry approach is: 'professional translators work only into their native language' (Durban, 2010: 11). There are few studies testing the validity of this belief or comparing relative quality of translation output by native and non-native speakers, perhaps because it is such a core tenet for the industry. Pokorn's work points to a more nuanced picture (2004: 113).

33 The UK's *Daily Express* and *Daily Mail* often highlight such spending, for example, 'Police spend £82m talking to migrants', *Daily Express*, 29 August 2011, [online] www.express.co.uk/ourcomments/view/265874. Similar campaigns have gathered momentum in the United States of America.

34 Author interview with freelance translator specializing in automotive translation.

35 Where an identical ST segment has previously been translated, its target language equivalent is a 100 per cent match. Where a highly similar ST segment has previously been translated, its target language equivalent is a 'fuzzy' match; a percentage figure indicates its similarity to the original segment. A match of below 70 per cent (the level may be user-defined) is normally a new segment, to be translated from scratch.

36 The possibility of greater consistency by sharing resources such as TMs was often seen as exaggerated, however. Translators stressed this was only achieved across small teams or by more intensive revision (Drugan, 2006: 82–3).

Chapter 2

1 Academic research tends to conflate translation quality with the more specific concept of TQA, as demonstrated in House's entry on 'Quality of translation' in the *Routledge Encyclopedia of Translation Studies* (1998/2001: 197–200), which, despite its title, considers TQA alone. This may explain academics' initial failure to engage with other aspects of translation quality which are important to the industry (QC, processes).

2 The last published version was LISA QA Model 3.1, outlined later in this chapter. The LISA website is no longer supported but the Model and other resources relating to standards developed by LISA are still used widely.

3 In interviews with the author.

4 Many further questions apply in relation to MT in particular, as this has been a significant focus for research. However, these are not directly relevant or applicable as yet to professional (human) translation quality. MT quality issues are also widely discussed in specialist literature, so are not included here.

5 The 2002 reference relates to a baseline survey of professional and academic approaches to assessment, carried out by Arango-Keeth and Koby (2003: 244). The survey found substantial differences between academia and the profession.

6 These categories are developed elsewhere by House (1997: 1–24) using slightly different terminology (e.g. the first group becomes 'Anecdotal, biographical and neo-hermeneutic').

7 For example, Gutt (1991: 13) and Lauscher (2000: 153–5).

8 Only extracts of longer texts are analysed, for example, ten pages of Goldhagen's book.

9 Reiss's work on this topic is mainly available in German. The overview presented here is based on translations or summaries of her ideas in English-language sources.

10 There are some exceptions, as noted above (e.g. attention to translation competence and norms).

11 Quote from an EC in-house translator/reviser, interview with the author.

12 www.iso.org/iso/survey2009.pdf.

13 Virtually all MLVs visited in research for this book recognized at least one standard. The larger MLVs recognized multiple standards, depending on their leading markets.

14 Quality management approaches are based on the concept that quality must first be measured to be better managed, an idea variously attributed to Galileo, Kelvin and numerous others. Total Quality Management (TQM) was originally devised by management theorist W. Edwards Deming as a way of applying statistical methods to improve quality; quality is 'fully satisfying agreed customer requirements'. It suggests techniques to benchmark, standardize and regulate business and production processes to achieve this ongoing goal (Deming, 2000).

15 Kaizen is the Japanese term for improvement. The philosophy is widely applied by leading translation clients, particularly in the automotive sector. The core concept is that improvement should be continuous, in an eternal cycle. Measurement, standardization, innovation/refinement, and quality assessment lead to change, then the whole cycle is repeated from the beginning. Kaizen advocates stress that 'quality improvement and cost reduction are compatible', and that 'quality is the responsibility of everyone in the organization and not exclusively of the quality department' (De Sutter, 2005: 25). When applied to translation, Kaizen means that 'everyone involved in a translation project monitors the quality at every stage of the process' (ibid.).

16 Developed at Motorola during the 1980s, Six Sigma is 'a business strategy that employs a disciplined approach to tackle process variability using the application of statistical and non-statistical tools and techniques in a rigorous manner' (Antony, 2004: 303). Drawing on TQM and Kaizen theories, it offers rigorous training and certification to practitioners, emphasizing the role of quality experts ('Green/Black Belts'), and again sees quality management as an ongoing process.

17 As previously noted, in this discussion, TQA means Translation Quality Assessment and QA means Quality Assurance.

18 Some use a more restrictive definition of QC. For Brunette (2000: 171), for example, QC 'is always performed on only part of a text, a sample. [. . . QC] may simply be a reading or a "formal language check" of the translated text, whereas quality assessment is essentially comparative.' Such restricted definitions are not how the terms are generally used in the industry, however.

19 These different processes are distinct but often confused; they are rarely, if ever, all applied. Brief definitions are thus provided here, drawing on those of Mossop (2001, 165–71) and Esselink (2000: 467–75). *Consistency checks* are making sure that terminology or style usage is consistent within a translation project. *Compliance with client resources* is checking that translators have respected client preferences (e.g. for terminology or translation memory matches). *Copyediting* is bringing a TT in line with house style or usage guidelines. *Editing* is checking a TT in the target language, without reference to the ST, for errors or to make the text more suitable for its intended use. *Functional testing* is checking that a translated product works (e.g. the tasks or commands performed by running localized software). *In-Country Review (ICR)* is sending a draft translation or translated product to local specialists (e.g. sales staff) for expert target-language review of both the content and linguistic elements. *Linguistic testing* is testing all language-related aspects of a localized product in context (e.g. checking menu content in context in the localized software application). *Product checking* is checking physical aspects of the translated product (DTP, formatting, presentation, layout). *Proofreading* refers both to the final comparison of a printer's proof with a manuscript, and a target-language rereading for final corrections. *Review* is performed by a subject-matter expert, to check TT content for conceptual or terminological errors, or to assess its contribution to the field, accuracy etc. *Revision* is checking a draft TT for errors, in comparison to the ST, including a consideration of the TT suitability for the intended use, and recommending

amendments where needed. *Sampling* is partial revision of a TT by checking only an agreed proportion of the text (e.g. the first 1,000 words, or 10%); it may be carried out during the translation stage, so feedback can be incorporated on a rolling basis. *Spot-checking* is partial revision of a TT by checking only randomly selected paragraphs or sections.

Chapter 3

1   There are some studies of productivity rates and other aspects of electronic tools (e.g. Yamada (2011) considers productivity for English-Japanese with TMs). There are also translation quality studies which consider different language pairs before modern tools were used (e.g. Carroll (1966) considers Russian-English). However, no published research on electronic tools and translation quality was found for other language pairs. Such research may, of course, have been published in other languages.

2   Interviewees were asked to list each tool they used, but also to detail workflow for sample job types, in order not to miss any which users did not class as 'translation tools' (otherwise, only terminology and TM tools tended to be volunteered). Almost all used the first six tools/functionalities. Smaller numbers utilized the remaining tools, with spikes in particular sectors (e.g. subtitling software was used by most translators specializing in audiovisual translation).

3   The diverse solutions found in the industry account for sometimes substantial differences in word counts. In large projects, this can mean a significant price difference, which must be explained and justified to understandably sceptical clients.

4   'A subset of a natural language with an artificially restricted vocabulary, grammar and style' (Kaji, 1999: 37).

5   A corpus is a body of natural language text in electronic format. Comparable or multilingual corpora are bodies of texts in two or more languages matched for similarity, for example, in 'size, domain, genre and topic' (Quah, 2006: 107). These help translators identify possible translations for specialist terms/ concepts, meta-language for technical fields or typical usage. Parallel corpora refer to STs linked with their TTs. These are most useful as they can be exploited to compile bilingual termbases or searched for previous translations, as in TM applications.

6   Somers (1998/2001: 137–49) gives a clear account of MT history and the various approaches.

7   Exceptions remain (e.g. text embedded in images); but these are not picked up in alternative working environments either. LSPs demonstrated high levels of awareness of such issues.

8   It might seem that translators should simply feed back to clients that content quality is poor and suggest changes, but in many circumstances this was unfeasible (e.g. agencies told translators that this was the approved version and it would not be changed).

Chapter 4

1 For example, Williams (2004: 3–5) outlines the SICAL model. The LISA QA Model is widely available online. Koo and Kinds (2000) give a detailed account of one application of the latter model.

2 When the EU held competitive translation examinations in 2004, 2,155 candidates sat the Polish test. 306 passed and 58 were appointed, a success rate of about 3 per cent. ('Translation in the Commission: where do we stand two years after Enlargement?', Press release, 27 April 2006, ref. MEMO/06/173, 2).

3 O'Brien, S. (2011): 'Translation quality evaluation is catching up with the times', [online] www.translationautomation.com/best-practices/translation-quality-evaluation-is-catching-up-with-the-times.html.

Chapter 5

1 These terms' recent appearance means they merit definition here. *Activist translation* refers to those working outside or against the standard view of translation as impartial. Activist translators 'ought to be involved, engaged, over and above [the] act of substituting one lexical item for another' (Barsky, 2005: 17–18). *Crowdsourced translation* refers to projects which are organized via an open call for self-selected volunteers, sometimes working alongside or under the direction of professionals. *Fan translation* refers to those translating products such as electronic games or comics, usually unofficially and without permission, often into languages which would otherwise not have translation provided. *Hive translation* draws on the image of the beehive, with workers each contributing small parts to complete a much larger overall task, for example, 'the outsourcing of web content translation to bilinguals within the community' (García, 2009b: 31). *Volunteer translation* is a broader term, which may embrace the above categories. It also refers to longstanding arrangements relying on unpaid volunteers such as translation for charities.

2 See the Rosetta Foundation's work to translate content for 'underserved customers'; www.therosettafoundation.org/.

3 Unless otherwise stated, data in this paragraph are all from www.proz.com/about/ and www.proz.com/about/ipetition/input. All sites were last checked in December 2011.

4 Source: personal communication from Member Services, December 2011.

5 http://wiki.proz.com/wiki/index.php/Translation:_Determining_what_service_you_need_and_what_it_will_cost.

6 www.proz.com/membership/campaign.

7 www.proz.com/?sp=user_agreement.

8 Ibid.

9 Annual registration in 2011 was $129; student members paid $39 (www.proz.com/membership/campaign).

10 www.proz.com/about/ipetition/.

11 Free downloads and a regularly updated list of all target language versions are available at www.mozilla.org/en-US/firefox/all.html.

12 https://wiki.mozilla.org/L10n:Contribute.

13 Since August 2011, the 'rapid release' process issues a new version every six weeks, mirroring (indeed outstripping) commercial localization approaches; http://blog.lizardwrangler.com/2011/08/25/rapid-release-process/.

14 https://wiki.mozilla.org/L10n.

15 For example, see www.frenchmozilla.fr/regles/.

16 http://mymemory.translated.net/doc/features.php.

17 As most features of other models do not apply here, only a summary of the approach is given.

18 http://translate.google.com/translate_tools?hl=en.

19 For example, myGengo (http://mygengo.com/), OneHourTranslation (http://onehourtranslation.com/).

20 Four European language versions of the site were translated using a traditional top-down approach and paid professional translators. Members were then invited to translate into further languages without financial recompense. The American Translators Association, among others, campaigned strongly against the move. See the LinkedIn internationalization PM's blog on the issue, including translators' responses http://blog.linkedin.com/2009/06/19/nico-posner-translating-linkedin-into-many-languages/.

21 Freelance translator, interview with the author.

Chapter 6

1 For a definition of ethics and its relationship to translation, see Drugan and Megone (2011: 188–9).

2 CIoL (2007: 3–4).

BIBLIOGRAPHY

Al-Qinai, J. (2000), 'Translation quality assessment: Strategies, parametres and procedures', *Meta*, XLV (3), 497–519.

Alves, F. (ed.) (2003), *Triangulating Translation: Perspectives in Process Oriented Research*. Amsterdam/Philadelphia: John Benjamins.

Alves, F. and Liparini Campos, T. (2009), 'Translation technology in time: Investigating the impact of translation memory systems and time pressure on types of internal and external support', in S. Göpferich, A. Lykke Jakobsen and I. M. Mees (eds), *Behind the Mind: Methods, Models and Results in Translation Process Research*. Copenhagen: Samfundslitteratur Press, pp. 191–218.

Ansaldi, M. (1999), 'Translation and the law: Observations of a law professor/translator', *Language International*, 11 (1), 12–17.

Antony, J. (2004), 'Some pros and cons of six sigma: An academic perspective', *TQM Magazine*, 16 (4), 303–6.

Austermühl, F. (2001), *Electronic Tools for Translators. Translation Practices Explained*. Manchester: St Jerome.

Baker, M. (1992), *In Other Words: A Coursebook on Translation*. London/New York: Routledge.

— (ed.) (1998/2001), *Routledge Encyclopedia of Translation Studies* (3rd edn). London/New York: Routledge.

Barsky, R. F. (2005), 'Activist translation in an era of fictional law', *TTR: Traduction, Terminologie, Rédaction*, 18 (2), 17–48.

Bédard, C. (2000), 'Mémoire de traduction cherche traducteur de phrases', *Traduire*, 186, 41–9.

Bell, R. T. (1991), *Translation and translating: Theory and practice*. London: Longman.

Beninatto, R. S. and De Palma, D. (2008), *Ranking of Top 25 Translation Companies*. Common Sense Advisory. [online] www.commonsenseadvisory.com/Research/All_Users/080528_QT_2008_top_25_lsps/tabid/1492/Default.aspx.

Bey, Y., Kageura, K. and Boitet, C. (2005), 'A framework for data management for the online volunteer translators' aid system QRLex', *Proceedings of PACLIC 19, the 19th Asia-Pacific Conference on Language, Information and Computation*. Taiwan: PACLIC, 51–60. [online] http://panflute.p.u-tokyo.ac.jp/~bey/pdf/PACLIC19_40-Bey-Kyo.pdf.

Boucau, F. (2005), *The European Translation Industry: Facing the Future*. [online] www.euatc.org/conferences/pdfs/boucau.pdf.

— (2006), *The European Translation Markets. Updated Facts and Figures, 2006–2010*. NP: European Union of Associations of Translation Companies.

Bourland, W. (2010), 'Who decides translation quality?' *Multilingual*, October/November 2010, 50–2.

Bowker, L. (2001), 'Towards a methodology for a corpus-based approach to
    translation evaluation', *Meta*, 46 (2), 345–64.
— (2002), *Computer-Aided Translation Technology: A Practical Introduction.*
    Ottawa: University of Ottawa Press.
— (2005), 'Productivity vs quality? A pilot study on the impact of translation
    memory systems', *Localisation Focus*, March 2005, 13–20.
— (2007), 'Translation memory and "text"', in L. Bowker (ed.), *Lexicography,
    Terminology, and Translation: Text-Based Studies in Honour of Ingrid
    Meyer.* Ottawa: University of Ottawa Press, pp. 175–88.
Brace, C. (2000), 'Language automation at the European Commission', in
    R. C. Sprung (ed.), *Translating into Success: Cutting-Edge Strategies
    for Going Multilingual in a Global Age.* Amsterdam/Philadelphia: John
    Benjamins, pp. 219–24.
Brunette, L. (2000), 'Towards a terminology for translation quality assessment: A
    comparison of TQA practices', *The Translator*, 6 (2), 169–82.
Brunette, L., Gagnon, C. and Hine, J. (2005), 'The GREVIS project: Revise or
    court calamity', *Across Languages and Cultures*, 6 (1), April 2005, 29–45.
Byrne, J. (1999), 'Translator, localiser or jack-of-all-trades? New challenges
    facing today's translator', *Translation Ireland*, 13 (1). [online] www.jodybyrne.
    com/804#more-804.
— (2006), *Technical Translation. Usability Strategies for Translating Technical
    Documentation.* Dordrecht: Springer.
— (2007), 'Caveat translator: Understanding the legal consequences of errors in
    professional translation', *The Journal of Specialised Translation*, 7, 2–24.
Caminade, M. and Pym, A. (1995), 'Annuaire mondiale des formations en
    traduction et en interprétation', Special Issue of *Traduire*. Paris: Société des
    Traducteurs.
Cao, D. and Zhao, X. (2008), 'Translation at the United Nations as specialized
    translation', *The Journal of Specialized Translation*, 9, 39–54.
Carroll, J. B. (1966), 'An experiment in evaluating the quality of translations',
    Mechanical Translation and Computational Linguistics, 9 (3/4), 55–66.
Carson-Berndsen, J., Harold Somers, C. V. and Way, A. (2010), 'Integrated
    language technology as a part of next generation localization'. *Localisation
    Focus*, 8(1), 53–66.
Chartered Institute of Linguists (CIoL) (2007), *Code of Professional Conduct.*
    [online] www.iol.org.uk/Charter/CLS/CodeofProfConductCouncil17Nov07.pdf.
Chesterman, A. (1997), *Memes of Translation: The Spread of Ideas in
    Translation Theory.* Amsterdam/Philadelphia: John Benjamins.
— (2007), *Memes of Translation: The Spread of Ideas in Translation Theory.*
    Amsterdam/Philadelphia: John Benjamins.
— (2009), 'The name and nature of translator studies', *Hermes: Journal of
    Language and Communication Studies*, 42, 13–22.
Chesterman, A. and Wagner, E. (2002), *Can Theory Help Translators?
    A Dialogue Between the Ivory Tower and the Wordface.* Manchester:
    St Jerome.
Choudhuri, I. N. (1997), 'The plurality of languages and literature in translation:
    The post-colonial context', *Meta*, XLII (2), 439–43.
Chriss, R. (2006), *Translation as a Profession.* N.p.: Lulu.

Clark, R. (1994), 'Computer-Assisted translation: The state of the art', in
    C. Dollerup and A. Lindegaard (eds), *Teaching Translation and Interpreting 2:
    Insights, Aims, Visions*. Amsterdam/Philadelphia: John Benjamins, pp. 301–8.
Cogan, M. L. (1953), 'Towards a definition of a profession', *Harvard Educational
    Review*, XXIII, 33–50.
Concise OED, 11th edn (2009), Oxford: OUP.
Cronin, M. (2003), *Translation and Globalization*. London/New York:
    Routledge.
— (2010), 'The translation crowd', *Revista Tradumàtica: Traducció i Tecnologies
    de la Informació i la Comunicació*, 8, December 2010. [online] www.fti.uab.
    es/tradumatica/revista/num8/articles/04/04central.htm.
Crystal, D. and Davy, D. (1969), *Investigating English Style*. London: Longman.
De Sutter, N. (2005), 'Automated translation quality control', *Communicator*.
    Institute of Scientific and Technical Communications, Summer 2005, 22–5.
Deming, W. E. (2000), *The New Economics for Industry, Government,
    Education* (2nd edn). Cambridge, MA: MIT Press.
DePalma, D., Sargent, B. B. and Beninatto, R. S. (2006), *Can't Read, Won't
    Buy: Why Language Matters on Global Websites. An International Survey
    of Global Consumer Buying Preferences*. Lowell, MA: Common Sense
    Advisory.
Désillets, A. (2007), 'Translation wikified: How will Massive Online
    Collaboration impact the world of translation?' *Translating and the Computer
    29*. London: Aslib, n.p.
DiBona, C., Ockman, S. and Stone, M. (eds) (1999), *Open Sources: Voices from
    the Open Source Revolution*. Sebastopol, CA: O'Reilly.
Directorate General for Translation at the European Commission (2005),
    Translation Tools and Workflow. [online] www.europa.eu.int.
Dollerup, C. (2001), 'The rainbow languages: The scene in South Africa',
    Language International, 13 (1), 34–9. [online] www.cay-dollerup.dk/
    publications.asp.
Dong, D.-H. and Lan, Y.-S. (2010), 'Textual competence and the use of cohesion
    devices in translating into a second language', *The Interpreter and Translator
    Trainer*, 4 (1), 47–88.
Dove, C. (2010), 'PayPal case study', *Localization World*, Seattle, 7 October 2010.
Drugan, J. (2004), 'Multilingual document management and workflow in the
    European institutions', *Translating and the Computer 26*. London: Aslib, n.p.
— (2007a), 'Intervention through computer-assisted translation: The case of
    the EU', in J. Munday (ed.), *Translation as Intervention*. London/New York:
    Continuum, pp. 118–37.
— (2007b), 'The effects of computer-assisted translation tools on translation
    quality', in I. Kemble (ed.), *Translation Technologies and Culture. Proceedings
    of the Conference held on 11 November 2006 in Portsmouth*. Portsmouth:
    University of Portsmouth, pp. 80–96.
— (2011), 'Translation ethics wikified: How far do professional codes of
    ethics and practice apply to non-professionally produced translation?' in
    M. O'Hagan (ed.), *Translation as a Social Activity*. Linguistica Antverpiensia
    New Series – Themes in Translation Studies 10. Antwerp: University Press
    Antwerp, pp. 111–30.

Drugan, J. and Babych, B. (2010), 'Shared resources, shared values? Ethical implications of sharing translation resources', in V. Zhechev (ed.), Proceedings of the Second Joint EM+/CNGL Workshop. *Bringing MT to the User: Research on Integrating MT in the Translation Industry.* American Machine Translation Association, Denver, Colorado, November 4 2010, pp. 3–9.

Drugan, J. and Martin, T. (2005), 'Revision management: Changes, chances and challenges'. Presentation to the UK Institute of Translation and Interpreting annual conference, Cardiff, September 2005.

Drugan, J. and Megone, C. (2011), 'Bringing ethics into translator training: An integrated, inter-disciplinary approach', *The Interpreter and Translator Trainer*, 5 (1), 189–211.

Drugan, J. and Rothwell, A. (2011), 'The rise of translation', in P. Lane (ed.), *French Studies in and for the Twenty-first Century.* Liverpool: Liverpool University Press, pp. 155–67.

Dunne, K. (2006), *Perspectives on Localization.* Amsterdam/Philadelphia: John Benjamins (American Translators Association Scholarly Monograph Series XIII).

Durban, C. (2006), *Translation: Getting it Right. A Guide to Buying Translations.* [online] www.iti.org.uk/pdfs/trans/GIR_english.pdf.

— (2010), *The Prosperous Translator. Advice from Fire Ant and Worker Bee.* N.p.: FA&WB Press.

Eckersley, H. (2002), *Achieving Objectivity in Measuring Translation Quality.* [online] presentation at the Association of Translation Companies annual conference, 11–12 September 2002 [online] www.atc.org.uk/ITR_ATC_2002A.ppt.

Esselink, B. (2000), *A Practical Guide to Localization.* Amsterdam/Philadelphia: John Benjamins.

— (2001), 'Web design: Going native', *Language International*, February 2001, 16–18.

Fiederer, R. and O'Brien, S. (2009), 'Quality and Machine Translation: A realistic objective?' *The Journal of Specialised Translation*, 11, 52–73.

Fiser, D. (2008), 'Recent trends in the translation industry in Slovenia', *Journal of Specialised Translation*, 10, 23–39.

Flanagan, M. (2009), 'Using example-based machine translation to translate DVD subtitles', in M. L Forcada and A. Way (eds), *Proceedings of the 3rd Workshop on Example Based Machine Translation.* Dublin, Ireland, November 2009, pp. 85–92.

Fraser, J. (1994), 'Translating practice into theory: A practical study of quality in translator training', in C. Picken (ed.), *Quality – Assurance, Management and Control.* ITI Conference 7 Proceedings. London: Institute of Translation and Interpreting, pp. 130–41.

— (2000), 'The broader view: How freelance translators define translation competence', in C. Shäffner and B. Adab (eds), *Developing Translation Competence.* Amsterdam/Philadelphia: John Benjamins, pp. 51–62.

Gaal, A. (2001), *ISO 9001:2000 for Small Business: Implementing Process-Approach Quality Management.* Boca Raton/New York: St Lucie Press.

García, I. (2009a), 'Beyond translation memory: Computers and the professional translator', *The Journal of Specialised Translation*, 12, 199–214.

— (2009b), 'Research on translation tools', in A. Pym and A. Perekrestenko (eds), *Translation Research Projects 2*, Tarragona Intercultural Studies Group, pp. 27–31.

— (2010), 'The proper place of professionals (and non-professionals and machines) in web translation', *Revista Tradumàtica: Traducció i Tecnologies de la Informació i la Comunicació*, 8, December 2010. [online] http://ddd.uab.cat/pub/tradumatica/15787559n8a2.pdf.

Gaspari, F., Toral, A. and Naskar, S. K. (2011), 'User-focused task-oriented MT evaluation for wikis: A case study', in V. Zhechev (ed.), *Proceedings of the Third Joint EM+/CNGL Workshop 'Bringing MT to the User: Reseach Meets Translators'*. Luxembourg, 14 October 2011, pp. 13–22.

Gerasimov, A. (2007), 'A comparison of translation QA products', *Multilingual*, January-February 2007, 22–5.

Gneezy, U. and Rustichini, A. (2000), 'Pay enough or don't pay at all', *Quarterly Journal of Economics*, 115 (3), 791–810.

Gouadec, D. (2007), *Translation as a Profession*. Amsterdam/Philadelphia: John Benjamins.

— (2009), *Profession Traducteur*. Paris: La Maison du Dictionnaire.

Groves, D. and Way, A. (2005), 'Hybrid example-based SMT: The best of both worlds?' in *Proceedings of the ACL Workshop on Building and Using Parallel Texts*. Ann Arbor: Association for Computational Linguistics, pp. 183–90.

Gutt, E.-A. (1991), *Translation and Relevance. Cognition and Context*. Oxford: Blackwell.

Hague, D., Melby, A. and Zheng, W. (2011), 'Surveying translation quality assessment: A specification approach', *The Interpreter and Translator Trainer*, 5 (2), 243–67.

Halliday, M. A. K. (2001), 'Towards a theory of good translation', in E. Steiner and C. Yallop (eds), *Exploring Translation and Multilingual Text Production*. Berlin: Mouton de Gruyter, pp. 307–25.

Hamerly, J., Paquin, T. and Walton, S. (1999), 'Freeing the source: The story of Mozilla', in C. DiBona, S. Ockman and M. Stone (eds), *Open Sources: Voices from the Open Source Revolution*. Sebastopol, CA: O'Reilly, pp. 91–5.

Hatim, B. and Mason, I. (1990), *Discourse and the Translator*. London: Longman.

Hirst, P. and Thompson, G. (1996/2000), *Globalization in Question: The International Economy and the Possibilities of Governance* (2nd edn). Cambridge: Polity Press.

Holmes, J. S. (1972/2000), 'The name and nature of translation studies', in L. Venuti (ed.), *The Translation Studies Reader*. London/New York: Routledge, pp. 180–92.

Hönig, H. G. (1998), 'Positions, power and practice: Functionalist approaches and translation quality assessment', in C. Schäffner (ed.), *Translation and Quality*. Clevedon: Multilingual, pp. 6–31.

House, J. (1997), *Translation Quality Assessment: A Model Revisited*. Tübingen: Gunter Narr.

— (1998/2001), 'Quality of translation', in M. Baker and K. Malmkjaer (eds), *Routledge Encyclopedia of Translation Studies*. London/New York: Routledge, pp. 197–200.

Howe, J. (2008), *Crowdsourcing: Why the Power of the Crowd Is Driving the Future of Business*. New York: Random House.

Hoyle, D. (2009), *ISO 9000 Quality Systems Handbook*. Oxford: Butterworth-Heinemann.

Humphrey, L., Somers, A., Bradley, J. and Gilpin, G. (2011), *The Little Book of Transcreation*. London: Mother Tongue.

International Organization for Standardization (ISO) (2005), *ISO International Standard 9000: Quality Management Systems – Fundamentals and Vocabulary*. Geneva: ISO, reference number: ISO 9000:2005(E).

Juris, J. S. (2005), 'The new digital media and activist networking within anti-corporate globalization movements', *The Annals of the American Academy of Political and Social Science*, 597, 189–208.

Kaji, H. (1999), 'Controlled languages for machine translation: State of the art', *Proceedings of MT Summit VII: MT in the Great Translation Era*, 13–17 September 1999, Kent Ridge Digital Labs, Singapore, 37–9.

Kelly, D. (2005), *A Handbook for Translation Trainers: A Guide to Reflective Practice*. Manchester: St Jerome.

Kelly, N. (2009), 'Myths about crowdsourced translation', *Multilingual*, December 2009, 62–3.

Kelly, N. and Stewart, R. G. (2010), *The Top 35 Language Service Providers*. Common Sense Advisory. [online] www.commonsenseadvisory.com/Research/CSA_Users/100528_QT_Top_35/tabid/2000/Default.aspx.

Kingscott, G. (1996a), 'Providing quality and value', in R. Owens (ed.), *The Translator's Handbook*. London: Routledge, pp. 137–46.

— (1996b), 'The impact of technology and the implications for teaching', in C. Dollerup and V. Appel (eds) *Teaching Translation and Interpreting 3*. Amsterdam/Philadelphia: John Benjamins, pp. 295–300.

— (1999), 'The evaluation of translation quality', *Journal of MPI*, International Meeting on Interpreting and Translation, School of Languages, Macau Polytechnic Institute, 6–7 May 1999, 197–202.

Koehn, P. (2005), 'Europarl: A parallel corpus for statistical machine translation', *Proceedings of MT Summit X*, Phuket, Thailand, 79–86.

— (2010), 'Enabling monolingual translators: Post-editing vs.options', *Proceedings of Human Language Technologies: The 2010 Annual Conference of the North American Chapter of the Association for Computational Linguistics*. June 2–4, 2010, Los Angeles, California, 537–45.

Koo, S. L. and Kinds, H. (2000), 'A quality-assurance model for language projects', in R. C. Sprung (ed.), *Translating into Success. Cutting-Edge Strategies for Going Multilingual in a Global Age*. Amsterdam/Philadelphia: John Benjamins, pp. 147–57.

Koppel, M. and Ordan, N. (2011), 'Translationese and its dialects'. *Proceedings of ACL*. 2011, 1318–1326.

Koskinen, K. (2008), *Translating Institutions: An Ethnographic Study of EU Translation*. Manchester: St Jerome.

Künzli, A. (2007a), 'Translation revision: A study of the performance of ten professional translators revising a legal text', in Y. Gambier, M. Schlesinger and R. Stolze (eds), *Translation Studies: Doubts and Directions*. Amsterdam/Philadelphia: John Benjamins, pp. 115–26.

— (2007b), 'The ethical dimension of translation revision. An empirical study', *The Journal of Specialised Translation*, 8, 42–56.

Kussmaul, P. and Tirkkonen-Condit, S. (1995), 'Think-aloud protocol analysis in translation studies', *TTR: Traduction, Terminologie, Rédaction*, 8 (1), 177–99.

Lagoudaki, E. (2006), 'Translation memories survey 2006: Users' perceptions around TM use', *Translating and the Computer 28*. London: Aslib, n.p.

— (2009), 'Translation editing environments', *MT Summit XII – Workshop: Beyond Translation Memories: New Tools for Translators MT*, August 29, 2009. Ottawa, Canada, n.p.

Lallana, E. C. and Uy, M. N. (2003), *The Information Age*. [online] www.apdip. net/publications/iespprimers/eprimer-infoage.pdf.

Lambert, J. (1996), 'Language and translation as management problems: A new task for education', in C. Dollerup and V. Appel (eds) *Teaching Translation and Interpreting 3*. Amsterdam/Philadelphia: John Benjamins, pp. 271–93.

Lanier, J. (2010), *You Are Not a Gadget. A Manifesto*. New York: Alfred A. Knopf.

Larose, R. (1987), *Théories contemporaines de la traduction* (2nd edn). Sillery, Quebec: Presses de l'Université du Québec.

— (1994), 'Qualité et efficacité en traduction: Réponse à F. W. Sixel', *Meta*, 39 (2), 362–73.

— (1998), 'Méthodologie de l'évaluation des traductions', *Meta*, 43 (2), 163–86.

Lauscher, S. (2000), 'Translation quality assessment: Where can theory and practice meet?' *The Translator*, 6 (2), 149–68.

Leavitt, H. J. (2005), *Top Down: Why Hierarchies Are Here to Stay and How to Manage Them More Effectively*. Boston, MA: Harvard Business School Press.

Lewis, M. P. (ed.) (2009), *Ethnologue: Languages of the World* (16th edn). Dallas, Texas: SIL International.

LISA (2003), *The Localization Industry Primer* (2nd edn). [online] www.ict. griffith.edu.au/~davidt/cit3611/LISAprimer.pdf.

— (2007), *Crowdsourcing: The Crowd Wants to Help You Reach New Markets*. [online] www.lisa.org.

Lockwood, R. (2000), 'Machine translation and controlled authoring at caterpillar', in R. C. Sprung (ed.), *Translating into Success. Cutting-Edge Strategies for Going Multilingual in a Global Age*. Amsterdam/Philadelphia: John Benjamins, pp. 187–202.

Lommel, A. and Ray, R. (2007), *Taking software to the World: Results of the LISA Global Software Survey* (2nd edn). [online] www.lisa.org.

Lönnroth, K.-J. (2005), Address at the FIT 17th World Congress in Tampere, Finland, 4 August 2005: 'How to ensure total quality in a changing translation market – a European approach'.

Makoushina, J. (2007), 'Translation quality assurance tools: Current state and future approaches', *Translating and the Computer 29*. London: Aslib, n.p.

McAlester, G. (2000), 'The evaluation of translation into a foreign language', in C. Schäffner and B. Adab (eds), *Developing Translation Competence*. Amsterdam/Philadelphia: John Benjamins, pp. 229–42.

Mitamura, H. (1999), 'Controlled language for multilingual machine translation', *Proceedings of MT Summit VII: MT in the Great Translation Era*, 13–17 September 1999, Kent Ridge Digital Labs, Singapore, 46–52.

Mossop, B. (2001), *Revising and Editing for Translators*. Manchester: St Jerome.

— (2007), 'Empirical studies of revision: What we know and need to know', *The Journal of Specialised Translation*, 8, July 2007, 5–20.

Munday, J. (ed.) (2007), *Translation as Intervention*. London: Continuum and IATIS.

— (2008), *Introducing Translation Studies: Theories and Applications* (2nd edn). London/New York: Routledge.

Munro, R. (2010), 'Crowdsourced translation for emergency response in Haiti: The global collaboration of local knowledge', *AMTA Workshop on Collaborative Crowdsourcing for Translation*. Denver, Colorado, USA.

Nadvi, K. and Wältring, F. (2004), 'Making sense of global standards', in H. Schmitz (ed.), *Local Enterprises in the Global Economy: Issues of Governance and Upgrading*. Cheltenham and Massachusetts: Edward Elgar, pp. 53–94.

Newmark, P. (1981), *Approaches to Translation*. Oxford: Pergamon.

Nida, E. A. (1964), *Towards a Science of Translating*. Leiden: E. J. Brill.

Nord, C. (1991), *Text Analysis in Translation. Theory, Method, and Didactic Application of a Model for Translation-Oriented Text Analysis* (trans. C. Nord and P. Sparrow). Amsterdam: Rodopi.

Nyberg, E., Mitamura, T. and Huijsen, W.-O. (2003), 'Controlled language for authoring and translation', in H. Somers (ed.), *Computers and Translation: A Translator's Guide*. Amsterdam/Philadelphia: John Benjamins, pp. 245–81.

O'Brien, S. (1998), 'Practical experience of computer-aided translation tools in the software localisation industry', in L. Bowker, M. Cronin, D. Kenny and J. Pearson (eds), *Unity in Diversity? Current Trends in Translation Studies*. Manchester: St Jerome, pp. 115–22.

— (2002), 'Teaching post-editing: A proposal for course content', *Proceedings of the Sixth EAMT Workshop 'Teaching machine translation'*, 14–15 November 2002, UMIST, Manchester, England, 99–106.

— (2011), 'Translation quality evaluation is catching up with the times', [online] www.translationautomation.com/best-practices/translation-quality-evaluation -is-catching-up-with-the-times.html.

O'Hagan, M. (2008), 'Fan translation networks: An accidental translator training environment?' in J. Kearns (ed.), *Translator and Interpreter Training: Issues, Methods and Debates*. London/New York: Continuum, pp. 158–83.

— (ed.) (2011), *Translation as a Social Activity*. Linguistica Antverpiensia New Series – Themes in Translation Studies 10. Antwerp: University Press Antwerp.

Olohan, M. (2011), 'Translators and translation technology: The dance of agency', *Translation Studies*, 4 (3), 342–57.

Olvera Lobo, M. D., Robinson, B., Castro Prieto, R. M., Quero Gervilla, E., Muñoz Martin, R., Muñoz Raya, E., Murillo Melero, M., Senso Ruiz, J. A., Vargas Queseda, B. and Díez Lerma, J. L. (2007), 'A professional approach to translator training (PATT)', *Meta*, LII (3), 517–28.

Orlando, M. (2011), 'Evaluation of translations in the training of professional translators: At the crossroads between theoretical, professional and pedagogical practices', *The Interpreter and Translator Trainer*, 5 (2), 293–308.

Ørsted, (2001), 'Quality and efficiency: Incompatible elements in translation practice?' *Meta*, XLVI (2), 438–47.

Owens, R. (ed.) (1996), *The Translator's Handbook*. London: Aslib.

PACTE (2003), 'Building a translation competence model', in F. Alves (ed.), *Triangulating Translation: Perspectives in Process Oriented Research*, Amsterdam and Philadelphia: John Benjamins, pp. 43–66.

Pérez, C. R. (2001), 'From novelty to ubiquity: Computers and translation at the close of the Industrial Age', *Translation Journal*, 5 (1), January 2001, n.p.

Picken, C. (ed.) (1994), *Quality – Assurance, Management and Control*. ITI Conference 7 Proceedings. London: Institute of Translation and Interpreting.

Pierini, P. (2007), 'Quality in web translation: An investigation into UK and Italian tourism web sites', *The Journal of Specialised Translation*, 8, July 2007, 85–103.

Pokorn, N. (2004), 'Challenging the myth of native speaker competence in translation theory. The results of a questionnaire', in G. Hansen, K. Malmkjaer and D. Gile (eds), *Claims, Changes and Challenges in Translation Studies*. Amsterdam/Philadelphia: John Benjamins, pp. 113–24.

Prioux, R. and Rochard, M. (2007), 'Economie de la révision dans une organisation internationale: le cas de l'OCDE', *The Journal of Specialised Translation*, 8, July 2007, 21–41.

Pym, A. (1992), 'Translation error analysis and the interface with language teaching', in C. Dollerup and A. Loddegaard (eds), *The Teaching of Translation*. Amsterdam/Philadelphia: John Benjamins, pp. 279–88.

— (1993), 'Review of C. Nord', *Text Analysis in Translation. Theory, Method, and Didactic Application of a Model for Translation-Oriented Text Analysis, TTR : traduction, terminologie, rédaction*, 6 (2), 184–90.

— (2003), 'Redefining translation competence in an electronic age', *Meta*, 48 (4), 481–97.

— (2006), *Localization, Training, and the Threat of Fragmentation*. [online] www.tinet.cat/~apym/publications/publications.html.

— (2010a), *Exploring Translation Theories*. London/New York: Routledge.

— (2010b), 'On empiricism and bad philosophy in Translation Studies', revised version of paper first published in H.C. Omar et al. (eds) (2009) *The Sustainability of the Translation Field*. Kuala Lumpur: Persatuan Penterjemah Malaysia (Malaysian Translators Association), 2009, 28–39. Revised version [online] www.tinet.cat/~apym/on-line/research_methods/2009_lille.pdf.

Quah, C. K. (2006), *Translation and Technology*. Basingstoke: Palgrave Macmillan.

Rasmussen, K. W. and Schjoldager, A. (2011), 'Revising translations: A survey of revision policies in Danish translation companies', *The Journal of Specialised Translation*, 15, 87–120.

Reiss, K. (1983), 'Quality in translation oder wann ist eine Übersetzung gut?' *Babel*, 29 (4), 198–208.

— (2000), *Translation Criticism: The Potential and Limitations* (trans. E. F. Rhodes). Manchester: St Jerome.

Reiss, K. and Vermeer, H. (1984), *Grundlegung einer allgemeinen Translationstheorie*. Tübingen: Niemeyer

Resnik, P., Buzek, O., Hu, C., Kronrod, Y., Quinn, A. and Bederson, B. (2010), 'Improving translation via targeted paraphrasing', in *Proceedings of the*

2010 Conference on Empirical Methods in Natural Language Processing.
    Massachusetts: MIT, pp. 127–37.
Rinsche, A. and Portera-Zanotti, N. (2009), *Study on the Size of the Language
    Industry in the EU.* [online] European Commission Directorate-General
    for Translation, http://ec.europa.eu/dgs/translation/publications/studies/
    size_of_language_industry_en.pdf.
Ritzer, G. (ed.) (2007), *The Blackwell Companion to Globalization.* Malden,
    MA: Blackwell.
Robertson, R. and White, K. E. (2007), 'What is globalization?' in G. Ritzer (ed.),
    The Blackwell Companion to Globalization. Malden, MA: Blackwell, pp. 54–66.
Sager, J. (1993), *Language Engineering and Translation. Consequences of
    Automation.* Amsterdam/Philadelphia: John Benjamins.
Samuelsson-Brown, G. (1996), 'Working procedures, quality and quality
    assurance', in R. Owens (ed.), *The Translator's Handbook*, pp. 103–36.
Schäffner, C. (ed.) (1998a), *Translation and Quality.* Clevedon: Multilingual.
— (1998b), 'From "good" to "functionally appropriate": Assessing translation
    quality', in C. Schäffner (ed.), *Translation and Quality.* Clevedon:
    Multilingual, pp. 1–5.
Schäffner, C. and Adab, B. (eds) (2000), *Developing Translation Competence.*
    Amsterdam/Philadelphia: John Benjamins.
Shäffner, C. (ed.) (1999), *Translation and Norms.* Clevedon: Multilingual.
Sireci, S. G., Yang, Y., Harter, J. and Ehrlich, E. J. (2006), 'Evaluating guidelines
    for test adaptations: A methodological analysis of translation quality', *Journal
    of Cross-Cultural Psychology*, 37 (5), 557–67.
Somers, H. (1998/2001), 'Machine translation', in M. Baker (ed.), *Routledge
    Encyclopedia of Translation Studies*, London: Routledge, pp. 136–49.
— (2003a), 'Translation memory systems', in H. Somers (ed.), *Computers and
    Translation: A Translator's Guide.* Amsterdam/Philadelphia: John Benjamins,
    pp. 31–46.
— (2003b), 'Machine translation in the classroom', in H. Somers (ed.),
    Computers and Translation: A Translator's Guide. Amsterdam/Philadelphia:
    John Benjamins, pp. 319–40.
Souphavanh, A. and Karoonboonyanan, T. (2005), *Free/Open Source Software:
    Localization.* New Delhi: Elsevier.
Sprung, R. C. (ed.) (2000a), *Translating into Success. Cutting-edge Strategies
    for Going Multilingual in a Global Age.* Amsterdam/Philadelphia: John
    Benjamins.
— (2000b), 'Mission-critical: Translating for regulated industries', in R. C. Sprung
    (2000), *Translating into Success. Cutting-edge Strategies for Going Multilingual
    in a Global Age.* Amsterdam/Philadelphia: John Benjamins, pp. 173–86.
Steiner, E. and Yallop, C. (eds) (2001), *Exploring Translation and Multilingual
    Text Production: Beyond Content.* Berlin and New York: Mouton de
    Gruyter.
Steiner, G. (1975/1998), *After Babel. Aspects of Language and Translation* (3rd
    edn). Oxford and New York: Oxford University Press.
Sulzberger, P. (2011), *Is 'Quality' Dead? Or Can TranslatorsTwist It Creatively
    to Find Better Paying Customers?* [online] http://translationbiz.wordpress.
    com/2011/08/23/is-quality-dead-or-could-translators-twist-it-creatively-to-find
    -more-better-paying-customers/.

Surowiecki, J. (2004), *The Wisdom of Crowds: Why the Many Are Smarter Than the Few and How Collective Wisdom Shapes Business, Economies, Societies, and Nations*. New York: Doubleday.

Teixeira, C. (2011), 'Knowledge of provenance and its effects on translation performance in an integrated TM/MT environment', in B. Sharp, M. Zock, M. Carl and A. L. Jakobsen (eds), *Proceedings of the 8th international NLPSC workshop. Special theme: Human-machine interaction in translation* (Copenhagen Studies in Language 41). Frederiksberg: Samfundslitteratur, 107–18.

Torres-Hostench, O., Biau, J. R., Cid, P., Martín, A., Mesa-Lao, B., Orozco, M. and Sánchez-Gijón, P. (2010), 'TRACE: Measuring the impact of CAT tools on translated texts', in M. L. Gea-Valor, I. García-Izquierdo and M. J. Esteve (eds), *Linguistic and Translation Studies in Scientific Communication*. Bern/New York: Peter Lang, pp. 255–76.

Toury, G. (1999), 'A handful of paragraphs on "translation" and "norms"', in C. Shäffner (ed.), *Translation and Norms*. Clevedon: Multilingual Matters, pp. 10–32.

Van der Meer, J. (2006), 'Different approaches to machine translation', in *Putting Machine Translation to Work. Report on the TAUS Executive Forum held in Beijing, September 21 and 22*. N.p.: Translation Automation User Society.

— (2009), *Let a Thousand MT Systems Bloom*. [online] www.translationautomation.com/best-practices/let-a-thousand-mt-systems-bloom.html.

— (2010), *Where are Facebook, Google, IBM and Microsoft Taking Us?* [online] www.translationautomation.com/perspectives/where-are-facebook-google-ibm-and-microsoft-taking-us.html.

Venuti, L. (1995/2008), *The Translator's Invisibility: A History of Translation* (2nd edn). Abingdon/New York: Routledge.

Wilkinson, M. (2005), 'Using a specialized corpus to improve translation quality', *Translation Journal*, 9 (3), July 2005, n.p.

— (2007), 'Corpora, serendipity and advanced search techniques', *Journal of Specialised Translation*, 7, January 2007, 108–22.

Williams, J. and Chesterman, A. (2002), *The Map. A Beginner's Guide to Doing Research in Translation Studies*. Manchester: St Jerome.

Williams, M. (2004), *Translation Quality Assessment: An Argumentation-Centred Approach*. Ottawa: University of Ottawa Press.

— (2009), 'Translation quality assessment', *Mutatis Mutandis*, 8 (1), 3–23.

Wooten, A. (2011), 'Can companies obtain free professional services through crowdsourcing?' *Deseret News*, 18 February, [online] www.deseretnews.com/article/705366964/.

Yamada, M. (2011), 'The effect of translation memory databases on productivity', in A. Pym (ed.), *Translation Research Projects 3*, Tarragona: Intercultural Studies Group, pp. 63–73.

Zuckerman, E. (2008), *The Polyglot Internet*, World Economic Forum Global Agenda Council on the Future of the Internet, 30 October, [online] www.ethanzuckerman.com/blog/the-polyglot-internet/.

INDEX

Quality in Professional Translation

BLOOMSBURY ADVANCES IN TRANSLATION

Series Editor: Jeremy Munday, Centre for Translation Studies, University of Leeds, UK

Bloomsbury Advances in Translation publishes cutting-edge research in the fields of translation studies. This field has grown in importance in the modern, globalized world, with international translation between languages a daily occurrence. Research into the practices, processes and theory of translation is essential and this series aims to showcase the best in international academic and professional output.

Other Titles in the Series: